Fulbright Papers

PROCEEDINGS OF COLLOQUIA

SPONSORED BY THE
UNITED STATES-UNITED KINGDOM
EDUCATIONAL COMMISSION:
THE
FULBRIGHT COMMISSION
LONDON

Volume 4

Regenerating the cities

The Fulbright Programme of Educational Exchanges, which has been in operation since 1946, aims to promote mutual understanding between the United States of America and other nations. It now operates in more than 120 countries, with forty-three bi-national commissions involved in its administration. In the United Kingdom the Commission aims to offer qualified British and American nationals the opportunity to exchange significant knowledge and educational experience in fields of consequence to the two countries, and thereby to contribute to a deeper mutual understanding of Anglo-American relations and to broaden the means by which the two societies can further their understanding of each other's cultures. Among its activities the Commission promotes annual colloquia on topics of Anglo-American interest; the proceedings are published in this series.

1. Lexicography: an emerging international profession
ed. R. Ilson

2. Ethics and international relations
ed. Anthony Ellis

3. Orphan diseases and orphan drugs
ed. I. Herbert Scheinberg and J. M. Walshe

4. Regenerating the cities
The UK crisis and the US experience
ed. Michael Parkinson, Bernard Foley and Dennis Judd

Regenerating the cities

The UK crisis and the US experience

edited by
MICHAEL PARKINSON,
BERNARD FOLEY
and DENNIS JUDD

MANCHESTER
UNIVERSITY PRESS

IN ASSOCIATION WITH
THE FULBRIGHT COMMISSION, LONDON

COPYRIGHT © THE US – UK EDUCATIONAL COMMISSION, 1988

Published by MANCHESTER UNIVERSITY PRESS
Oxford Road, Manchester M13 9PL

in association with THE FULBRIGHT COMMISSION,
6 Porter Street, London W1M 2HR

British Library cataloguing in publication data
Regenerating the cities: the UK crisis and the US experience.
 —(The Fulbright papers; v. 4).
 1. Urban renewal—United States
 2. Parkinson, Michael II. Foley, Bernard
 III. Fulbright Commission (U.K.) IV. Series
 711'.4.0941   HT175

ISBN 0-7190-2475-7 *hardback*

Printed and bound in Great Britain by
Anchor Brendon Ltd, Tiptree, Essex

Contents

Foreword   JOHN E. FRANKLIN   vii
Preface   MERFYN JONES   ix
Acknowledgements   x

1   Urban revitalisation in America
and the UK – the politics of   MICHAEL PARKINSON
uneven development   AND DENNIS JUDD   1

2   Urban revitalisation in the US: DENNIS JUDD AND
prisoner of the federal system   DAVID BRIAN
   ROBERTSON   9

3   Social, economic and political
trends and their impact on
British cities   MICHAEL GOLDSMITH   27

4   Bristol: a study of economic
change in the UK 'Sunbelt'   MARTIN BODDY   37

5   Local state response to economic
decline: development and
diversification strategies
in Texas   JOE R. FEAGIN   55

6   Private sector urban regeneration:
the Scottish experience   ROBIN BOYLE   74

7   The uses of linked development
policies in US cities   MICHAEL PETER SMITH   93

8   Liverpool's fiscal crisis: an
anatomy of failure   MICHAEL PARKINSON   110

9   The politics of redistribution in
Chicago: is balanced growth
possible?   MICHAEL B. PRESTON   128

10   Race, politics and urban
regeneration: lessons from
Liverpool   GIDEON BEN-TOVIM   141

11   The politics of planning   NORMAN I. FAINSTEIN
      New York as a world city   AND SUSAN S. FAINSTEIN   156

      Index   178

Foreword

This volume records the proceedings of the Fulbright colloquium which was held at the University of Liverpool from Sunday 28 September to Tuesday 30 September 1986. The Fulbright Commission in London much welcomed the proposal to relate Anglo-American experiences in this important area of topical interest, and was delighted to give the Centre for Community and Educational Policy Studies at the University of Liverpool its full support in mounting the colloquium.

In meeting its aim of promoting Anglo-American cultural understanding, the Commission sponsors at least one, and generally two, colloquia each year on subjects of mutual interest and importance to the United States and Great Britain. These meetings of distinguished scholars and practitioners in specialist fields augment the Commission's traditional award of studentships, scholarships and fellowships to British and American citizens for study, teaching, research or work experience in the other's country. Over 10,000 such exchanges have been supported in this way since the Commission was established in 1948.

The colloquium at Liverpool attracted representatives from a diversity of interests in America and Britain, drawn from academe, industry and the local community. Presentations and discussions focused on the fundamental problems affecting inner cities on both sides of the Atlantic and, in contrasting and comparing experiences, participants were led to a fuller understanding of the issues involved. In this way the colloquium provided a forum for Anglo-American debate on a topic of much transatlantic importance.

The opinions expressed are, of course, personal to the contributors and do not necessarily reflect the views of the Commission. Nevertheless, the Commission believes publication of the proceedings will be welcomed by a wide audience. It hopes that this will lead to a greater awareness of the particular difficulties facing the inner cities, in both Britain and America, and stimulate further discussion on this contemporary issue, a matter of serious concern to both countries.

John E. Franklin, Executive Director
United States-United Kingdom Educational Commission
The Fulbright Commission, London

Preface

The Centre for Community and Educational Policy Studies at the University of Liverpool was delighted to be able to organise and host the Fulbright Colloquium, not only because the Centre is committed to establishing and nourishing international contacts but, more particularly, because the organising theme of the gathering seemed so pertinent to its location. Liverpool, as readers of this volume will be reminded, has attracted much attention because of the scope and nature of its urban crisis. The city which was once 'the second city of the Empire' and 'the gateway to America' is now too often perceived as a synonym for economic and social stasis as well as for political challenge. And yet Liverpool's problems are neither entirely new, nor unique. The colloquium was an exercise in the comparative study of selected British and American cities and by focusing on the latters' experience of revitalisation provided, not only instructive contrasts, but also disturbing parallels.

The colloquium was a stimulating event which produced authoritative papers and challenging intellectual insights and which succeeded, also, in instigating lively and expert discussion amongst the various participants. The reader of the present volume must be satisfied with the papers only, and will hardly be disappointed. But it is worth noting that this Fulbright Colloquium was a meeting of minds not only from opposite sides of the ocean but also from a variety of professional standpoints. The Centre for Community and Educational Policy Studies has thus seen many of its aspirations crystallised in one event: the encouragement of British-American intellectual traffic; the involvement of academics with policy makers and practitioners; the concern with tackling difficult issues of central relevance and, as in this volume, the publishing of research papers. Needless to say, none of this would have been possible without the assistance of many colleagues and the generous and informed support of the Fulbright Commission.

R. Merfyn Jones, Director
Centre for Community and Educational Policy Studies
University of Liverpool

Acknowledgements

A volume of this nature necessitates the co-operative efforts of many people and several organisations. We are indebted to the Fulbright Commission and the University of Liverpool's Research Committee for their financial help in sponsoring the colloquium, and to the Elsie Talbot Bridge Trust for financing the final preparation of the papers. Colleagues in the Centre for Community and Educational Policy Studies provided both moral and material support at crucial times. Particular thanks are due to Jeff Bryson for his organisational skills, to the various authors who produced their papers on time and to Grace Martin for the speed and excellence of her typing.

Urban revitalisation in America and the UK – the politics of uneven development

MICHAEL PARKINSON
University of Liverpool

DENNIS JUDD
University of Missouri-St. Louis

This book is the product of a conference sponsored by the Fulbright Commission, organised around the question: what can Britain learn from America in the 1980s about the problems of regenerating declining cities? The timing was appropriate. Since 1979 Britain's Conservative government has consciously imitated the American strategy of relying on private market mechanisms rather than upon public intervention to revitalise its cities and urban areas. The Conservatives' urban policy has been one component of a comprehensive strategy to regenerate Britain's ailing economy by creating an enterprise culture. A new definition of the 'public good' underpins the government's efforts to reduce Welfare State programmes; to cut public spending, taxation, and employment; to replace public services with private provision; to increase individual choice in the provision and consumption of public services, and to charge consumers the full economic price for collective services.

As in the United States, the thrust of the government's urban policies has moved away from support for social welfare towards the regeneration of urban economies through private sector investment. Private sector institutions are targeted to receive funding from the government's urban programme. Cities are required to consult the private sector when constructing their bids for urban programme money. City action teams, task forces, urban development corporations, enterprise zones, freeports, and urban development grants have been established to encourage private sector-led economic revitalisation (see Boyle, this volume).

URBAN CHANGE: MYTH AND REALITY

The practice of transferring policy solutions from one country to another is well established. And the routes across the Atlantic have not been travelled in only one direction. There has been a rhythm in the learning process which has kept time with the changing perceptions of urban problems. In the mid-1960s, for example, the British government was heavily influenced by the race riots that broke out in American cities, and by the Federal government's response to them. When Labour introduced its 'urban programme' in 1968, much of it was modelled on urban programmes adopted in the US.

However, as several American cities teetered on the edge of financial collapse in the 1970s, Britain appeared to be coping better than America with the strains of urban change. In an effort to discover the explanation, in 1975 a Congressional committee held hearings on the question, 'What Can Foreign Cities teach American Cities?'

But by the 1980s the spectre of economic decline, riots and financial crisis haunted some British cities and heads once more turned across the Atlantic. This time the intention was to examine the claim that American cities had successfully adjusted to the traumas of the 1970s and discovered new ways of restoring wealth and tranquillity to the urban landscape. Cities as diverse as Boston, Denver, Houston, New York, and San Francisco appeared as the revitalised centres of service sector-based urban economies.

The reality of urban change in both Britain and the United States, however, does not accurately reflect popular perceptions. Since the 1960s cities in the two countries have been subjected to similar pressures. The fates of individual cities and urban areas have been shaped by the global restructuring of the international economy, especially the shift from the secondary to the tertiary sector in the advanced economies, the exporting of manufacturing industries to the Third World, and the emergence of highly mobile international capital.

The importance of such changes in the international economy for cities cannot be overstated. Nevertheless, most cities are not the helpless pawns of multinational finance, industry and commerce. They are in a position to mediate and direct their own destinies. Some have coped better with change than others. One of the Fulbright colloquium's aims was to examine the variety of policy responses to structural economic transformation, and to assess the social and political consequences of national and local policies.

DIFFERENCES AND CONVERGENCE

The processes of global economic restructuring are mediated through national institutions and policies. As a result, how urban political leaders in Britain and the US can respond to economic change is rather different. For example, as Judd and Robertson's essay in this volume demonstrates, the fragmentation of power in America's federal system remains an important barrier to the redistribution of federal money towards declining cities. By contrast, the British state retains the capacity to allocate public resources to cities with social and economic problems. In fact – as Goldsmith points out – the Conservative government has increased central authority in recent years but has not used that power to reorient resources. Nevertheless, the difference in central government capacity remains important. Indeed, the recent centralisation in Britain actually enhances the government's power to implement redistributive policies.

Differences between the two countries' party systems are also important for understanding their urban policies. America lacks Britain's disciplined national party system, and as a result federal policy-making is influenced by a very large number of interest groups. In Britain, the political parties, not pressure groups, dominate national urban policy. In principle at least, this permits a coherent national policy response to urban economic change. It is also true that party control can generate conflict. For example, during the past seven years, Labour-controlled cities have attempted to pursue alternative strategies to those advocated by the Conservative government, especially in local economic development, social welfare, and housing. Indeed this antagonism between local and central government has been the most important source of conflict in recent British politics.

The ideological traditions of the national political parties also have affected city politics in the two countries. Local Labour parties in Britain at least have ensured that the urban underprivileged have been more directly represented in city politics than in America. Also the absence of a social democratic party tradition in America is one important reason why cities are so little involved in the provision of social welfare. In Britain, Labour control has meant that cities provide relatively generous levels of public housing, welfare and education. Many of these services remain outside municipal control in America. And when they are financed by city governments, they lack political support, and constitute small proportions of city budgets.

Even though it has been eroded during the past decade, this safety net of the British welfare state remains a crucial difference between British and American cities. Even the most prosperous American cities contain extremes of wealth and poverty which are exacerbated by the absence of a safety net. Education, housing, health and welfare programmes still leave out large proportions of the poor and working class. Equally important, the revitalisation of American cities has often increased not only wealth but such inequalities and segregation.

There are important differences in the financial structure and service responsibilities of the two countries' cities. British cities have wider responsibilities than their American counterparts. In one sense, the British have more limited sources of income than American cities, which can draw on sales and income as well as property taxes. However, in Britain central government, historically at least, has provided far more financial support. Limited local sources of revenue have been compensated for by generous central support. In this way, British cities avoided the fiscal stress experienced by many American cities in the 1970s.

But the position has changed fundamentally during the last decade. Since 1976 both Labour and Conservative governments have cut public spending with varying degrees of severity, including financial support for cities, and have forced them to rely increasingly on their local resource base. Since the resource base itself has been deteriorating for many cities during this period, in the 1980s many now face the financial problems faced by American cities a decade earlier. This does not mean that cities are necessarily being brought to the verge of bankruptcy. But fiscal retrenchment and reductions in services and public jobs are inevitable (Parkinson, this volume). This reduces the ability of cities to provide social welfare services and exacerbates the problems associated with unemployment and poverty. And it marks an important policy shift toward the 'Americanisation' of urban policy in Britain.

The fragmentation of power at the federal level is replicated in metropolitan areas in America. Authority to govern urban areas is typically divided among a large number of municipal governments and special districts, which fragments political power and encourages segregation along class, income and racial lines. This fragmentation and segregation has become even more pronounced in the 1980s. In Britain, by contrast, the continuous national reorganisation of the structure of urban government has meant that cities have retained a greater capacity to respond to urban problems.

However, the abolition of metropolitan wide government by the Conservatives in 1985 has edged Britain in the direction of the American pattern because it reduces the redistributive and strategic planning capacity of urban governments. This development underlines the fact that there are important institutional differences between Britain and America that affect individual cities. In the past, institutional arrangements have probably given Britain an advantage in coping with urban decline. But as several of the essays in this volume indicate, recent political decisions mean that the paths of urban change in Britain and America may be converging.

ECONOMIC REGENERATION AND UNEVEN DEVELOPMENT

How well established is the economic regeneration of American cities? Are there lessons that can be learned for the recovery of British cities? An important one is that there are costs as well as benefits. Most big American cities have experienced a renaissance since the mid 1970s. But prosperity has not been evenly shared. High-tech, service sector-based economies provide highly paid jobs for those with professional and management degrees – and minimum wage jobs for an army of unskilled workers. The consequence is that revitalisation brings with it social, economic, and spatial segregation. The obvious policy implication is that those groups locked out of the economic mainstream will not be drawn in by economic growth, unless it is channelled and targeted much more effectively than it has been in the past. This also applies to Britain (see Martin Boddy, this volume).

The special problems of reducing the economic discrimination faced by blacks are elaborated by Preston and Ben-Tovim in this volume. When cities are controlled by white politicians who are unsympathetic to black demands, the task is enormous, as the Liverpool case powerfully demonstrates. But even sympathetic black administrations face difficulties in implementing strategies that promote economic growth and simultaneously protect the interest of racial minorities. Chicago's economic development policy attempts to do this through linked development programmes (see Preston in this volume). But the political support for these policies has proved difficult to achieve. As Michael Smith's essay points out, such linked development typically benefits developers more often than other groups.

The growth of upper echelon service sector jobs has pulled into the cities groups that demand housing commensurate with their status. Gentrification of older neighbourhoods has provided some of the housing stock for the new residents. Public money often underwrites this process, since urban development funds are used to improve the security and environment in areas designed to attract the new professionals. Rents and property prices are forced up and low income residents are displaced into other parts of the city, a process described by the Fainsteins' study of New York City in this volume. The effect has been to create oases of highly desirable high-income property isolated in the midst of low-income, run-down neighbourhoods. Where the process happens very rapidly, such development can impose enormous pressures upon housing markets throughout the city making an adequate supply of low and moderate income property a major problem.

Similar effects may be observed where high rise corporate office blocks and upmarket downtown shopping malls are built (Fainstein and Fainstein, this volume). These large-scale developments provide an excellent environment for the white collar professionals and affluent shoppers who use them, but the benefits are not shared by low income groups in surrounding neighbourhoods. Thus, urban revitalisation often reinforces inequality between different income and neighbourhood groups that share space within cities.

It is wrong to assume that economic revitalisation can or will benefit all groups in the urban environment. The logic of the market dictates that some will benefit and others must pay the price of economic 'success'. Private sector policy models assume that there will be competition between groups, neighbourhoods, cities and regions to capture scarce resources and inevitably mean there must be losers in the competition.

The competition to attract such scarce capital increases the public cost of failure. Every region and city is forced to offer incentives in the form of subsidies, tax breaks, and public assumption of development costs. The competition guarantees that losers are paying more to fail, and the winners also pay more for the success (private investment) they might have enjoyed anyway. Even when investment seems to follow subsidies, it is often difficult for city governments to recover the public costs originally incurred.

Important questions remain about the long-term social value of such publicly subsidised growth. The price of economic success in one location has to be paid by failing communities elsewhere. But there is no guarantee that 'success' will last. The experience of Houston dramatically underlines the point that today's economic successes can become tomorrow's failures (see Feagin, this volume). The rapid rise and fall of the Texas oil and agriculture-based economy and its impact upon the economic, fiscal and social health of Houston demonstrates the real costs of rapid growth for developing and declining regions, as existing capital investment is abandoned in one place to be recreated in another.

The cost of growth is not a fashionable issue in either Britain or the

US. In both countries, the private sector has managed to portray public demands from local communities as an illegitimate restriction on the economic freedom of the individual firm and has complained about the 'unreasonable' burden of local property taxes. Local communities have been accused of depressing business activity and investment through excessive taxation – despite evidence that local taxes, especially when offset against national taxes, constitute a minute proportion of business costs and exert relatively little influence on private sector investment decisions.

The political climate is uppermost in the debate over local leveraging policies. Cities are anxious to project a pro-business image. The failure to do so seems reckless: if businesses flee or the local economy stagnates, local politicians are blamed for failing to create a better business environment. This fear of losing investment underlies government policies to restrict city spending, which has exacerbated the financial problems faced by declining cities (see Parkinson this volume).

The free-market model assumes that public sector spending limits private sector activity. Public spending and borrowing allegedly crowd out private investment. In many respects, this assumption is suspect. Public sector spending often stimulates private activity. The point is made by Martin Boddy that the economic prosperity of Bristol during the past two decades is in large measure accounted for by sustained levels of public investment, especially defence-related expenditure. The experience of the United States equally underscores this point. Many currently 'successful' American cities received large amounts of public funding for a long time before they turned their fortunes around. In the case of the Sunbelt, Feagin has argued that the subsidies have been important for at least thirty years. Simple distinctions between public and private sector spending are often misleading. These forms of expenditure and investment interact in complex ways.

Urban revitalisation in the US occurred mainly because private sector institutions have responded to publicly-sponsored attempts to create a 'healthy business climate.' This fact underlies the Conservative government's new urban policies. But as the articles on American cities in this volume show, the regeneration of urban economies in the US has produced costs as well as many obvious benefits. Low levels of public spending by local governments have resulted in severe infrastructure problems – overcrowded highways, poor public transport, suburban sprawl, inadequate water and sewer systems, pot holed streets. Labour markets characterised by a vast gulf between high-status, affluent, white collar workers, and low-wage service workers are the rule. Cuts in national spending on urban and welfare programmes have aggravated social problems in many cities.

The US may lead the way in regenerating mature cities, but it has yet to learn how to share the new wealth it is creating. Britain has much to learn from its failures as well as its many successes, as readers of this volume will discover.

2

Urban revitalisation in the US: prisoner of the federal system

DENNIS JUDD
DAVID BRIAN ROBERTSON
University of Missouri-St. Louis

America's federal structure has, historically, contributed to the devitalisation of central cities. It continues to limit the options for revitalising them. The complex intergovernmental system in the United States reinforces economic and racial segregation, creates urban government incapacity, and guarantees the uneven performance of federal urban programmes. Contemporary efforts to renew neighbourhoods, local economies, and the social fabric of American cities cannot be understood apart from the complex and evolving relationships among federal, state, and local governments.

LOCAL URBAN POLICIES

At the local level, American federalism has fostered three conditions that constrain urban revitalisation: metropolitan fragmentation, exclusionary policies, and local control of education.

Metropolitan Fragmentation: Metropolitan-wide governmental authorities are almost unknown in the United States, forcing local governments to pursue urban revitalisation efforts in an intensely competitive interjurisdictional environment. Fiscally strapped central cities, battered by the steady erosion of population and economic resources, desperately use the tools permitted by superior governments to retain and attract business. These tools include tax abatements, tax increment financing, industrial revenue bonds, Urban Development Action Grants (UDAGs), and other inducements to lure business and middle class residents. At the same time, many suburban governments offer similar incentives. Businesses and affluent residents thus find themselves in a kind of governmental 'free-trade zone' in which they can shop around for the best combination of public subsidies.

Interjurisdictional competition limits local government options. The fear that a neighbouring municipality would offer a better package of incentives to a grocery store chain induced the St. Louis suburb of Webster Groves to offer the chain a tax abatement in 1985. In the same year, the city of St. Louis and St. Louis County (geographically separate but contiguous jurisdictions) began a virtual war over the St. Louis Cardinals football team after its owner threatened to move to another region. County officials began to assemble land and investors for a domed sports stadium in a sparsely populated parcel far from the central city, where the team had played for a quarter of a century. A few months later, the mayor of the city of St. Louis produced his own plan for a domed stadium downtown. The battle for the team raged on through 1986, though neither jurisdiction could easily afford so expensive a business subsidy, especially for a facility widely viewed as economically dubious in any location.

Metropolitan fragmentation reduces the fiscal capacity of jurisdictions least able to afford the subsidies necessary to attract businesses and forces their officials to downgrade services that do not promote economic redevelopment. In contrast, suburbs fortunate enough to attract shopping malls and industrial parks can increase service levels while reducing tax levies. Their ample fiscal surpluses permit them to resist the deterioration that plagues central city neighbourhoods.

This fact renders meaningless the pluralist portrait of cities as political arenas in which groups compete with one another for relative influence, and in which any group, in principle, can gain a political victory in a given arena at least part of the time. Paul Peterson's argument (1981) that 'When development policies are considered, attempts to ascertain the power of one or another individual or group are probably pointless, if not misleading', is a self-fulfilling prophecy. When wealthy institutions and individuals do not get their way, they choose exit rather than voice: they leave for a political arena (another jurisdiction) in which they always will win, rather than make trade-offs (Peterson P., 1981, p.147; Miller, 1981). Any group fighting for policies that allocate services from the privileged sectors of the community to disadvantaged neighbourhoods or residents always confronts the threat that those of privilege would rather leave than bargain, much like a game of marbles in which the loser scoops up all the marbles and runs away. Even to ask for concessions from business or affluent residents (through higher taxes, for example), runs the risk that the jurisdiction – in this case, the central city – will be deprived of the few economic resources it still retains. The 'pluralistic' politics of trade-offs and group bargaining gives way to the politics of manifest desperation imposed by the Darwinian struggle for economic survival.

If redistributionist policies are 'suicidal,' as Peterson claims, it is important to recognise that the limits on such policies are entirely artificial, imposed by the political context within which the American city is embedded. The fact that metropolitan Chicago 'enjoys' over 1,200 separate governmental units is not inevitable; but it is politically convenient for powerful political interests. Metropolitan fragmentation reflects the power of business and the affluent to win jurisdictional arrangements that can and do benefit them (Miller, 1981).

Exclusionary policies. Independent general purpose governments multiplied because the incorporation of small, economically homogenous suburbs permitted their residents to exclude 'less desirable' citizens of other classes, ethnic groups or races (Danielson, 1976). Through zoning and other land use controls, these small municipalities excluded poorer residents by, for example, requiring relatively large (and expensive) lot sizes or by excluding multiple unit dwellings.

Once established, many suburbs become islands of privilege that frustrate any attempts to redistribute resources within metropolitan areas. Suburbs cordon off much of the valuable property from the metropolitan region, placing a large proportion of the crucial property tax base beyond the reach of the central city. Thus wealthy jurisdictions can raise sufficient revenues even with low tax rates, while other jurisdictions may levy high rates and still exact only a modest revenue yield. A 1973 study of school districts in Texas, for example, found that the wealthiest districts had $100,000 of taxable property per student but the poorest districts had less than $10,000 per student (Bedichek and Tannahill, 1982, p. 361). To the extent that the poor are segregated within central cities, affluent suburbanites minimise their share of the financial burden for welfare, public hospitals, remedial school programmes and other costly services geared to the impoverished. To the extent that central cities bear most of the burden for the civic, cultural, and entertainment amenities suburbanites enjoy, suburbanites also avoid paying the full costs of the urban amenities they value.

The suburbs, in short, benefit from a parasitic relationship with the central city: 'Suburbanites are suburbanites precisely because they desire to be near enough to the city to enjoy its benefits, but not near enough to have to shoulder its burdens' (Goldston, 1970, p. 22). A redistributionist politics prevails in all American urban areas, but it is redistribution in favour of privilege and wealth.

In those cases when fragmentation works against the interests of wealth and property, special districts are created. Though the advantages of small suburbs for the middle class are clear, the cost of providing many services on a scale so small would counterbalance many of the benefits of suburban isolation. The remedy is the 'special district,' which provides a single service or a few services on a scale large enough to be affordable, but which is as limited in scope as possible, or so invisible that it is not subject to popular control. Such districts have proliferated in American metropolitan areas, keeping pace with suburbanisation: 8,299 existed in 1942, 14,405 in 1957, 25,962 in 1977 (Anton, 1984). Often these reflect the collective action of several suburbs to provide services (fire protection, street lighting, water, libraries, or sewage disposal) that are usually considered municipal services (Jackson, 1985, p. 153; Elder and Kiser, 1984, p. 274). By relying on such services, the suburbs retain their exclusivity while reducing its financial cost.

Indianapolis, Indiana exemplifies special district politics. The state legislature in 1969 approved the consolidation of the city and county government (in 'Uni-Gov'). While celebrated as a move toward metropolitan government, Uni-Gov excluded fire, police, and sewer services, poor relief and schools. No less than forty-four taxing jurisdictions remained a decade after 'consolidation.' By 1978, central city businessmen sought to expand responsibility for the increasingly costly poor relief and sewer systems (the latter under a federal order to build a sewage treatment plant) to reduce their tax burden. A federal court in 1976 ruled that by 'expressly eliminating the schools from consideration under Uni-Gov, the [Indiana state legislature] . . . inhibited the desegregation within the Indianapolis public schools'. The most significant consolidation was the merger of the city and county councils, which reduced black voting strength by expanding the white constituency of the metropolitan area's primary decision-making body (Troustine, 1978, pp.1-3).

Local control of education. The local control of education is the most powerful means by which Americans use spatial segregation to perpetuate social class and racial relationships. In the United States, education always has been vested with an enormous cultural and political burden. Universal public education is the primary institution that symbolically satisfies the liberal definition of equality as equal opportunity. It fulfils this symbolic function well, even while it is organised to perpetuate existing class relationships. Autonomous school districts have served as the front-line defence protecting white, middle-class suburban communities from encroachment, and have insured that the homogeneity of individual suburbs will be reflected in – and perpetuated by – their schools (Orfield, 1978).

Metropolitan systems of school finance and governance constitute an urban policy of overwhelming importance, so much so that all other urban policies operate within its effects. Research on 'white flight' from the central city revealed that educational quality was a primary motivation for the move to the suburbs; once they arrived, suburbanites viewed the public school as their most important community institution (Marans and Rodgers, 1975; Wood, 1958). As the consequence the proportion of poor and minority students in central city schools steadily rose. These events explain why 41% of suburbanites polled in 1971 rated their schools as 'very good,' compared to 21% of respondents in cities larger than 100,000 (Marans and Rodgers, 1985, p. 320).

The fact that inner-city schools are racially segregated and underfinanced has slowed neighbourhood revitalisation in American cities. It also helps to account for the nature of the revitalisation that has occurred: all studies show that neighbourhood renovation involves a disproportionate share of young, childless, relatively affluent young professionals (Laska and Spain, 1980; Tobin and Judd, 1982).

Many states have attempted to reduce inequality among school districts by employing equalisation formulae for distributing state aid to school districts. None of these efforts result in equalisation, principally because no states specify a maximum spending level for districts; equalisation funds constitute approximately one third, on the average, of state aid; and the formulae are only mildly redistributive. With affluent and growing suburban constituencies in charge, state legislatures are not especially motivated to make the allocation of educational funds more equitable.

The overall impact of inequalities in schooling is staggering. Schoolchildren are sorted into schools of vastly different quality – and different school subcultures – based on the property values of their local communities. They subsequently are segregated into various institutions of higher education according to the quality and reputation of their public schools (if they attended public school). Thus schooling becomes a process of maintaining societal inequalities which have previously been sorted out on the metropolitan landscape.

STATES: THE CENTRE OF GRAVITY
IN AMERICAN URBAN GOVERNANCE

Americans take federalism for granted, seldom aware of the role states play in their lives. States were and are the primary source of criminal, family, banking,insurance, occupational, and land use law in the United States. The Constitution's Tenth Amendment clearly made states the focal point of American governance by reserving to the states those public powers not specifically granted to the national government.

In an 1868 court decision, Iowa Judge John Dillon formalised the established legal view that local governments are the 'creatures' of the states and have only those powers that states permit them to exercise. States significantly limit local capacity to raise, spend, and redistribute money. States delegate only increments of self-government to cities, rarely surrendering full control over urban affairs. The constitutions of ten states grant no discretionary authority to local governments. Almost all states limit cities' options for choosing political structure, personnel practices, and financial operations. Most states constrain local governments' ability to raise and spend money. Forty-six states limit local government debt and thirty-nine states limit local tax rates. Most states mandate a balanced operating budget. Three states still require local governments to submit their budgets for approval by a state body. Most states are willing to permit local governments to levy regressive property and sales taxes, but only eleven states permit localities to levy income taxes and 87% of the local governments that levy income taxes are in Pennsylvania (Zimmerman, 1983, pp. 6, 52-6, 62-4).

The states are inherently conservative regarding public spending and services, and thus cannot be expected to initiate particularly innovative policies of any kind. Since American states exist within a continent-wide 'free trade zone' in which business can abandon any jurisdiction for another, American state policies tend to promote an appealing 'business climate' with low taxes and limited governmental regulation. Locked in a competitive struggle for economic growth, state legislatures try to prevent their tax rates from exceeding those of neighbouring states (Wasylenko, 1981). Interstate competition discourages states from becoming policy innovators. Those states that do adopt innovative policies tend to be the most prosperous (Walker, 1969, pp. 880-99), a fact that permits wide variation in policy effort across states.

States historically have been distrustful of cities. State policy-makers' anti-urban attitudes undoubtedly derive from a culture in which the small farm epitomised individual independence and wholesomeness while the city symbolised corruption, vice, and masses of foreigners. But twentieth century cities' problems in the states have been structural. Enjoying wide latitude to draw legislative districts, states allocated a disproportionate share of representation to rural areas, which provided a decisive majority for rural interests in the state legislatures (Dixon,

1968). Since slums, smoke pollution, urban transport, housing, and the lack of open space scarcely concerned these legislators, states passively permitted urban problems to mount. Most states expanded their role only in response to the economic crisis of the 1930s, and then usually only in response to prodding by the New Deal and the lure of grants from Washington.

When the federal courts finally moved against legislative mal-apportionment, the action came so late that it strengthened the suburbs instead. Only in the 1960s did federal courts begin to order equal apportionment of legislative districts. In Georgia, one of the most malapportioned legislatures in the early 1960s, the number of members from the state's metropolitan areas increased by a factor of ten in the lower chamber and by a factor of twenty in the state senate. While this shift in apportionment aided *metropolitan* representation, it came as the expansion of suburban populations accelerated, particularly in Northern and Midwestern areas where central cities were already in decline. Thus suburban and rural representatives are increasingly powerful in state legislatures (Patterson, 1983). Suburban legislators frequently ally with their rural colleagues to vote against measures that would benefit central city constituents or limit suburban autonomy.

Even if the states were more willing to help revitalise the cities, their ability to do so is constrained in three ways. First, the political capacity of state government varies widely. California (which encompasses four of the nation's twenty largest cities) has a well developed administrative structure and a full-time, professionalised legislature. Texas (with three of the twenty largest cities) governs its citizens with an antiquated political system heavily dependent on a legislature that meets for 140 days every other year. Second, state fiscal capacity varies widely. Compared to industrialised and wealthy California, relatively poor New Mexico can generate much less revenue even with a tax burden higher than the national average. Third, interstate competition creates a 'drag' on state policy innovation and expansion. Many southern states have lured Northern manufacturers with low tax rates, minimal services, and little concern for the side effects of industrial production (such as pollution) in urban areas. Political leaders even in the most progressive states are keen to provide a friendly business climate.

The logic of American federalism skews state urban policy toward the tolerance of fragmentation and a heavy reliance on the private sector. By making incorporation easier than annexation (except in parts of the Southwest), states have facilitated suburbanisation. While annexation fuelled the rapid growth of American central cities in the early nineteenth century, state legislatures eased state chartering requirements for villages. As city annexation activity increased after the Civil War, unincorporated communities seized on these lax statutes to charter themselves and prevent their own annexation by the encroaching city. When New York City annexed parts of Westchester County in the 1870s and 1890s, subdivisions near the path of city expansion incorporated to preserve their independence. Across the most urbanised states, the 'rules of the game' were similarly biased toward suburbanisation. Some states add to the central cities' problems by requiring that they provide services to newly incorporated communities at central city rates (Jackson, 1985, pp. 151-2). In 1970, only one state, Wisconsin, had a state planning agency with powers to control local annexations and incorporations (Hagman, 1971, p. 34).

American states generally grant cities only the most passive and least intrusive tools of land use planning, in contrast to Sweden, France, and the Netherlands. Land banking is virtually unknown in the United States (Heidenheimer, Heclo and Adams, 1983, pp. 248-51). Instead, American communities rely on zoning to regulate the use of land. Because cities traditionally have no inherent powers under US law, state legislatures had to delegate that power through statute law (Hagman, 1971, pp. 80-2). The US Supreme Court upheld this power in a landmark 1926 decision (*Village of Euclid* v. *Ambler Realty Co.*). Observing that 'A nuisance may be merely a right thing in the wrong place, like a pig in a parlour instead of the barnyard', the Court ruled that apartments in homogeneous single-family zones, while unobjectionable in other circumstances 'come very near to being nuisances' (Babcock, 1966, p. 4). Zoning laws ever since have reacted to rather than directed urban growth.

Rather than extend public controls over the use of land and the private sector, state urban revitalisation policies seek to attract business with packages that minimise overt public costs and maximise business discretion. Though Congress did not enact 'enterprise zone' legislation when requested by President Reagan, twenty-four states had enacted such programmes by mid-1984 to permit targeted tax, finance, and regulatory incentives to business. Many states also permitted local agencies to issue industrial development bonds. At least twenty states developed programmes to stimulate entrepreneurship by underwriting venture capital, although a minority of the programmes targeted high unemployment areas. In contrast, only three states had taken the more active route of providing state-financed grants for urban development (Marks, 1984, pp. 1513-16).

The balance of power in state legislatures makes it unlikely that states will redistribute public resources from wealthy to needy jurisdictions. Indeed, the 'new federalism' enhances states' opportunity to reallocate funds and responsibility to suburban and exurban jurisdictions. One of the Reagan administration's 'block grant' programmes, the Job Training Partnership Act, granted wide discretion to the states to administer employment and training programmes. While policy experts in Congress had expected a reduction in the number of jurisdictions responsible for such effort (there had been about 430 in the 1970s), states increased the number of administrative units by designating rapidly growing counties (for example, St. Charles county outside St. Louis) as eligible, or by splitting formerly unified areas (for example, Cook County and the City of Chicago) into new 'service delivery areas' (Anonymous, 1983, p. 1412).

In 1981, the United States Conference of Mayors expressed grave doubts about President Reagan's plans to give the states more control over social policies vital to large cities. Commenting on the Reagan Administration's 'New Federalism', the Conference noted that 'The history of city/state relations has too often been one of neglect of city needs by the state' (*New York Times*, 21 June, 1981). A former Atlanta mayor commented that of the fifty states, only California, Massachusetts, Michigan and Minnesota had not 'shown either neglect or downright hostility' towards cities (*New York Times*, 1981).

NATIONAL URBAN POLICIES

After World War II, the various political groups in the Democratic coalition forged by the New Deal began to construct a national urban policy. Under the leadership of Kennedy and Johnson in the 1960s, the federal role vastly expanded. Policy rhetoric focused on central city slums as incubators of poverty, juvenile delinquency, crime, racial segregation, inadequate educational opportunities, joblessness, and dilapidated housing. Democratic administrations made special efforts to 'target' spending geographically, holding out the promise that societal inequalities might be reduced.

But the national government's structure prevents any effective, long-term redistribution of resources to needy areas. Social programmes invariably emerge from Congress as distributive programmes that deliver benefits to a large number and variety of congressional districts. Neither Senators nor Representatives are rewarded for subordinating state to national concerns. State electorates send Senators to Washington as their ambassadors; Representatives depend on constituencies contained entirely within a state, and look to others in their state delegation for voting cues on social policy. Enormous bipartisan majorities are usually necessary for winning agreement on domestic legislation. Social programmes are crafted to distribute benefits widely across many kinds of jurisdictions in recognition of political reality.

Republican and Democratic differences on social policy after World War II narrowed to a series of skirmishes over the distribution of grants and the conditions attached to them. Each time one of the parties regained control of the White House, as in 1961, 1969, 1977, and 1981, its president steered the grants system in a new direction. Under Democratic presidents, the national government tried to direct grants to the cities and to the poor. Republicans attempted to spread grants more broadly, benefiting suburban and rural areas and Sunbelt states.

Whatever the domestic priorities of a president, Congress has a difficult time resisting the impulse to give a little bit to everyone. For example, in the 1960s Congress subverted the Johnson Administration's objectives of targeting urban programmes to needy areas. The original architects of the War on Poverty conceived of a programme that would establish its effectiveness in a few large cities before expanding to encompass the entire nation. Instead, the Office of Economic Opportunity funded 650 community action programmes nationwide within its first year of operation, and two years later 1,100 programmes had received grants. The 'Demonstration Cities' proposal of 1966 (later known as Model Cities) would have funded projects in 60 to 70 cities, providing model programmes other urban areas could emulate. By 1970 150 cities had received funds through the programme, including 55 cities smaller than 100,000 (Ripley, 1972, pp. 124-55).

Most social policy initiatives take the form of 'grants-in-aid' to subnational governments. Such grants seldom redistribute resources to needy areas, but they often compound administrative complexity and frustrate national control over social policy. The grants strategy has been bipartisan. Both Republican and Democratic administrations after World War II expanded the intergovernmental grants system and made it easier for recipients to secure grants by lowering or eliminating requirements that recipients match federal funds with state and local sources.

The grant-in-aid strategy enhanced the position of states in domestic policy. Measured by revenues and personnel (two key indicators of government capacity), the governmental capacity of the states grew more rapidly than the national government from the 1950s to the mid 1980s.

While governmental revenue at all levels has increased more than tenfold since Harry Truman took office in 1949, Washington's share of that revenue has dropped during each presidential term except for the Carter administration. The federal share of revenue dropped most precipitously during Republican presidencies. The revenue share of local governments stayed relatively constant after 1960. State government revenues increased as a share of all revenues during each presidency and now constitute a quarter of all government receipts (Advisory Commission on Intergovernmental Relations, 1985, pp. 46-7). The federal government's share of government employees dropped from 33% in 1949 to 18% in 1981, while the state share increased from just under 17% to 23.5% in the same period (ACIR, 1985).

Even these numbers overstate federal control of social policy. The grants system reduces the national government to a sort of social policy 'bank' that disburses cheques to state and local governments. One study in the late 1970s concluded that 'considerably less than one tenth of the federal budget is allotted to domestic activities that the federal government performs itself' (Mosher, 1980, pp. 541-8).

The grants strategy made policy innovation (much less redistribution) improbable by incorporating a host of subnational and extragovernmental participants in each stage of the policy process. A small 1970 federal programme designed to encourage the development of well-planned, economically and racially integrated 'new towns' failed dismally when local governments, private developers, and other mandated partners largely ignored Washington's overtures (Mazmanian and Sabatier, 1983, pp. 48-9, 279). One of the most widely cited studies of policy failure followed from US Economic Development Administration grants to the economically depressed city of Oakland, California. The EDA directed millions of dollars in grants to Oakland for port, airport, and other employment-stimulating facilities. After years of effort, the grants resulted in only a handful of permanent jobs for minorities (Pressman and Wildavsky, 1973). Most of the funds were expanded to benefit local officials and businesses. Federal administrators were nearly irrelevant to programme implementation.

Block grants, created to reform the hopelessly complex project grant system, brought their own administrative headaches. By 1969, the US Department of Labour administered job training programmes through a system of no less than 10,000 individual contracts. The Comprehensive Employment and Training Act of 1973 (CETA) was designed to simplify the system by giving money and wide discretion to state and local governments. Given responsibility but little control over CETA, national administrators found to their dismay that the federal government attracted the backlash against the inevitable abuse and fraud that occurred in some jurisdictions. When Washington tried to reassert control, grant recipients complained of 'red tape'. One result was 'an overwhelming sense of futility and impotence on the part of all concerned' (Williams in Goodsell, 1984, p. 71). Another result was the loss of support and eventual termination of CETA, the major Federal effort to provide jobs for the urban poor (and a major payroll subsidy for big cities).

CETA was only one example of a general pattern. According to Thomas Anton (1984), 'vaguely defined programme goals, increased reliance on block grants rather than categorical grants, and federal reluctance to closely monitor federal fund use have all combined to give state and local governments considerable freedom in determining their uses of federal dollars.' The grants strategy saddled the national government with a set of policy tools that 'continually place Federal officials in the uncomfortable position of being held responsible for programmes they do not really control' (Salamon, 1980, pp. 255-75).

The grants strategy drained the energy of national policy-makers and stripped legitimacy from national programmes. Rather than acting as forceful advocates of national standards and quality services for the most disadvantaged, federal agencies had to bargain with state grant recipients, much like 'a rich merchant haggling on equal terms with a sly, bargain-hunting consumer' (Ingram, 1977, pp. 499-526). Bargaining made social policy seem 'political' in the worst sense of the term. The historical role of the states in domestic governance perhaps made the grants strategy inevitable. But the complexities of the grant-in-aid system created a gap between promise and performance that fuelled public cynicism about all government efforts by the late 1970s (Lowi, 1979, p. 169).

Though the public took the promise of redistribution seriously (and segments came to resent it), Congress permitted little geographical redistribution in grants programmes. Typically, grant programmes are distributed on the basis of population, with a guaranteed minimum for each state and a maximum that prevents excessive resources going to large or needy jurisdictions. Only one seventh of federal grant formulas explicitly include criteria that emphasise aid to needy areas. In the mid-1970s, the wealthiest states actually received the most grants per capita (Douglas, 1981). Furthermore, targeted grants are modest when compared to other federal subsidies. For example, when tax expenditures are taken into account, individuals in upper income brackets receive most of the benefit from federal housing policies. While the federal budget included

$11 billion for low-income housing assistance in 1984, the homeowner tax deduction cost the federal treasury about $35 billion in that year (National League of Cities, 1985, p. 653).

Block grants reduce even the mild targeting features of urban assistance. Community Development Block Grants (CDBG), which replaced several redevelopment initiatives in 1974, increased local discretion to spend federal money on urban revitalisation. But CDBGs are less 'targeted' than the programmes they replaced. Between 1975 and 1979, the number of low and moderate income census tracts receiving CDBG funds increased by 30%, and the number of wealthier tracts receiving funds increased by 50% (Henig, 1985, pp. 184-5). The cornerstone of Ronald Reagan's 'New Federalism' is an increased reliance on such block grants.

POLITICS AND URBAN POLICY IN THE 1980s

The Reagan administration has accentuated the features of local, state, and national policy that work against urban revitalisation. In the Reagan White House, 'urban revitalisation' means the application of supply side economics to metropolitan areas. In this view, the federal government should do less to regulate behaviour and redistribute resources, all in the interest of removing roadblocks to economic growth. Urban policy is built on the assumption that free enterprise will provide a bounty of jobs, incomes, and neighbourhood renewal.

The corollary of this approach is that social goals and national standards must be sacrificed to ensure that business has maximum latitude to invest and profit. Any policies designed to redistribute resources to less viable areas or to less fortunate individuals violate the fundamental premise of supply-side theory, which holds that excessive taxation of the wealthy undercuts productivity and reduces investment capital. As dedicated budget-cutter Senator Phil Gramm (R, Texas) put the case in 1985 hearings on urban policy,

> . . . if our objective is to control spending what we've got to do is change the scope of the Federal Government. We have got to reduce functions that were set in place in another time, under other economic circumstances. While [Secretary of Housing and Urban Development Samuel Pierce] referred very fondly to programmes he administers, the choice is between sustaining a recovery, which in terms of housing and urban development through low interest rates and jobs, is going to have more impact, favourably, on those things than the very programmes we've got to control to sustain the recovery (US Senate, Subcommittee on Housing and Urban Affairs, 1985, p. 863).

Abandoning urban policy made political sense for the Republicans. Party leaders have long sought to capitalise on white suburbanites' disaffection from Democratic civil rights and anti-poverty policies. Reagan took advantage of this sentiment in 1980 and 1984. Jimmy Carter and Walter Mondale carried the vote of large cities by substantial margins, while Reagan won slightly more than a third of the big city vote in each election. But Reagan carried the suburban and small city vote by a margin of 53% to 37% in 1980, and 57% to 42% in 1984. Since only 12% of the 1984 vote was cast in large cities, while 55% was cast in the suburbs and the small cities, the Republican advantage was devastatingly effective (Pomper, 1985, pp.68-9). To illustrate, Mondale carried 65% of 173,000 votes in the city of St. Louis in 1984, while Reagan carried 64% of 308,000 votes in suburban St. Louis County (State of Missouri, 1986, pp.1250-76). Coupled with the anti-tax core of Reagan support (used car dealers, real estate firms, and other small businesses), the administration had strong incentives to abandon forms of urban revitalisation that required federal activism or intrusions on suburban autonomy.

Consistent with its ideology and its political base, the Reagan administration has sought to withdraw from urban policy and restore state control over the remaining urban programmes. In the administration's view, federal urban programmes improperly finance

> activities that logically and traditionally have been the responsibilities of State and local governments. . . Individuals, firms, and State and local governments, properly unfettered, will make better decisions than the Federal government acting for them . . . it is State governments that are in the best position for encourage metropolitan-wide solutions to problems that spill over political boundaries. . . and to tackle the economic, financial, and social problems that affect the well-being of the State as it competes with others to attract and retain residents and businesses (US Department of Housing and Urban Development, 1982, pp. 54-7).

The administration intends to devolve the 'maximum feasible responsibility for urban matters to the states and through them to their local governments'. Cities are instructed to improve their ability to compete in this Darwinian struggle for survival in which 'state and local governments will find it is in their interests to concentrate on increasing their attractiveness to potential investors, residents, and visitors' (U.S. Department of Housing and Urban Development, 1982). Rather than fund urban revitalisation, HUD (1986) how promotes glossy pamphlets extolling urban 'entrepreneurship'.

In 1981, the administration slashed grants-in-aid programmes, and put others under the control of state governments. Its budget initiatives terminated CETA and reduced Medicaid funds and cut the federal share of grants for urban mass transportation and waste water treatment. The 1982 budget consolidated 76 targeted grants (including some community development aid) into 9 block grants and reduced funding by 20%, leaving states the option of ending programmes or financing them out of state revenues (Peterson G. E., 1984, pp. 229-33). In 1985, the administration sought to go further, changing the formula for housing and community development aid in favour of rural and suburban areas.

A survey of 400 mayors of cities larger than 30,000 in size showed that city leaders' experience with four years of supply-side urban policy taught them to expect little from the states. Eighty-five per cent of the cities expected no additional funds from the states to compensate for federal budget cuts, and 94% expected no state help to compensate for the loss of General Revenue Sharing (U.S Senate Subcommittee on Housing and Urban Development, 1985) In many cases, the state governments imposed as much 'red tape' on city governments as had the federal government.

President Reagan's ill-fated enterprise zone proposal illuminates the administration's premises as well as its disinterest in the cities. In March 1982, Ronald Reagan announced an Urban Jobs and Enterprise Zone bill that would permit designated areas a corporate tax reduction of 75% or more, entirely relieve forms of the capital gains tax, provide more tax credits for employees, and reduce environmental and work regulations. It would encourage the privatisation of municipal services. The President justified the proposal as one that 'will identify and remove government barriers to entrepreneurs who can create jobs and economic growth. It will spark the latent talents and abilities already in existence in our nation's most depressed areas.' But the White House put little effort into winning the bill's approval. It died quietly in Congress, a symbol of the administration's lack of concern about revitalising cities.

USING URBAN POLICY TO INCREASE INEQUALITY

The Reagan urban policy accelerates inequality in American metropolitan areas by forcing policy down to the state level, where interstate economic competition and suburban political power promotes spatial inequality. Subnational governments believe that there is little alternative to the strategy of improving their 'business climate'. The United States does far less than other federal governments to mitigate the effects of federalism through equalisation aid or restrictions on interstate or inter-city competition (Heidenheimer, Heclo and Adams, 1983, pp. 240-

73; ACIR, 1981) and the Reagan administration has reduced still further the national government's capacity to provide fiscal assistance to governments with special needs.

Inequality within the central cities continues to grow. In the struggle to lure business, industry, and tourists, generous business incentives are the rule. Tax abatements, tax increment financing, industrial development bonds, interest-subsidised loans, and below market land are some of the many business-oriented tools to promote downtown and commercial development. Biased in this way, the unquestionable objective of revitalisation has been to replace less profitable (and less symbolic) smaller businesses with corporate towers, hotels, and shopping malls. In the neighbourhoods, revitalisation means gentrification at the expense of poor residents. Even before Ronald Reagan's election, about 370,000 households were displaced each year by such housing conversions as officially sponsored redevelopment, gentrification, and conversion of apartments into condominiums. Central cities find irresistible any formula for revitalisation that appears to enhance 'the economic position of the community in its competition with others' (P. Peterson, 1981).

As suburbanisation in US metropolitan areas continues, the inequality between central city and suburban residents becomes more pronounced. Between 1970 and 1982, the median income of suburban families remained at 115% of the national average, but the median income of central city residents fell from 99% to 93% (US Department of Housing and Urban Development, 1984, pp. 39-40). The Reagan administration has signalled the states to slow the progress of racial and class integration by enhancing the power of states and communities which historically have pursued policies favourable to business and affluent citizens. The administration also has intervened in lawsuits in opposition to school and housing desegregation.

Urban revitalisation in the United States increases societal inequalities. American cities are no doubt being 'saved,' at the same time that homelessness, crime, drug abuse, family dissipation and poverty are increasing within them. It would be difficult to change the direction of American urban policy. It is the prisoner of an intergovernmental system that utilises public resources to protect inequality and that structures politics in such a manner as to make it extraordinarily difficult to enact policies of redistribution.

REFERENCES

Advisory Commission on Intergovernmental Relations (ACIR) (1985), *Significant Features of Fiscal Federalism, 1984,* Washington, ACIR, pp. 46-7.

ACIR (1981), *Studies in Comparative Federalism: Australia, Canada, the United States, and West Germany,* Washington, ACIR.

Anonymous (1983), *Employment and Training Reporter,* 22 June, p. 1412.

Anton, Thomas J. (1984), 'Intergovernmental Change in the United States: An Assessment of the Literature', in Miller, T. (ed.), *Public Sector Performance: A Conceptual Turning Point,* Baltimore, John Hopkins University Press, p. 37.

Babcock, Richard F.(1966), *The Zoning Game: Municipal Practices and Policies,* Madison, WI, University of Wisconsin Press, p. 4.

Bedicheck, Wendell M. and Tannahill, Neal (1982), *Public Policy in Texas,* Glenville, IL, Scott, Foresman, p. 361.

Danielson, Michael N. (1976), *The Politics of Exclusion,* New York, Columbia University Press.

Dixon, Robert G. Jr. (1968), *Democratic Representation: Reapportionment in Law and Politics,* New York, Oxford University Press.

Douglas, Arnold, R. (1981), 'The Local Roots of Domestic Policy', in Mann, Thomas E. and Ornstein, Norman J. (eds.), *The New Congress,* Washington, American Enterprise Institute.

Elder, Ann H., and Kiser, George C. (1983), *Governing American States and Communities: Constraints and Opportunities,* Glenview, IL, Scott, Foresman, p. 274.

Goldston, Robert (1970), *Suburbia: Civic Denial,* New York, Macmillan, p. 22.

Hagman, Donald G. (1971), *Urban Planning and Land Development Control Law,* St. Paul, MN, West Publishing, p. 34.

Heidenheimer, Arnold J., Heclo, Hugh and Adams, Carolyn Teich (1983), *Comparative Public Policy,* New York, St. Martin's, pp. 248-51.

Henig, Jeffrey R. (1985), *Public Policy and Federalism: Issues in State and Local Politics,* New York, St. Martin's, pp. 184-5.

Ingram, Helen (1977), 'Policy Implementation Through Bargaining: The Case of Federal Grants-In-Aid', *Public Policy* 25, Fall, pp. 499-526.

Jackson, Kenneth T. (1985), *Crabgrass Frontier: The Suburbanisation of the United States,* New York, Oxford University Press, p. 153.

Laska, Shirley Bradway and Spain, Daphne (1980), *Back to the City: Issues in Neighbourhood Renovation,* New York, Pergamon.

Lowi, Theodore (1979), *The End of Liberalism,* New York, Norton, p. 169.

Marans, Robert W. and Rodgers, Willard (1975), 'Toward an Understanding of Community Satisfaction', in Amos H. Hawley and Vincent P. Rock, *Metropolitan America in Contemporary Perspective,* New York, John Wiley, pp. 311-32.

Marks, Marilyn (1984), 'New Urban Agenda: The Focus Is On Helping Cities Help Themselves', *National Journal,* 16 (32), 11 August, pp. 1513-16.

Mazmanian, Daniel A. and Sabatier, Paul A. (1983), *Implementation and Public Policy,* Glenview, IL, Scott Foresman, pp. 49-84, 279.

Miller, Gary J. (1981), *Cities by Contract: The Politics of Municipal Incorporation,* Cambridge, Mass., The MIT Press.

Mosher, Frederick C. (1980), 'The Changing Responsibilities and Tactics of the Federal Government', *Public Administration Review,* 40, November/December, pp. 541-8.

National League of Cities (1985), 'Federal Housing Assistance: Who Gets It? Who

Needs It?', in US Senate, Subcommittee on Housing and Urban Affairs, *Hearings on Housing, Community Development, and Mass Transportation Authorisations – -1986,* Washington, Government Printing Office, p. 653.

New York Times (1981), 21 June. Orfield, Gary (1978), *Must We Bus? Segregated Schools and National Policy,* Washington, Brookings Institution.

Patterson, Samuel P. (1983), 'Legislators and Legislatures in American States', in Virginia Gray, Herbert Jacob, and Kenneth N. Vines, *Politics in the American States: A Comparative Analysis,* Boston, Little Brown, pp. 139-40.

Peterson, George E. (1984), 'Federalism and the States: An Experiment in Decentralisation', in John L. Palmer and Isabel V. Sawhill, *The Reagan Record: An Assessment of America's Changing Domestic Priorities,* Cambridge, Mass., Ballinger, pp. 229-33.

Peterson, Paul (1981), *City Limits,* Chicago, University of Chicago Press, p. 147.

Pomper, Gerald (1985), 'The Presidential Election', in Pomper (ed.), *The Election of 1984: Reports and Interpretations,* Chatham, NJ, Chatham House, pp. 68-9.

Pressman, Jeffrey and Wildavsky, Aaron (1973), *Implementation,* Berkeley, University of California Press.

Reagan, Ronald (1983), Message to the Congress Transmitting Proposed Enterprise Zone Employment and Development Legislation (7 March), *Public Papers of the Presidents of the United States: Ronald Reagan, 1983,* Book I, pp. 346-9.

Ripley, Randall B. (1972), *The Politics of Economic and Human Resource Development,* Indianapolis, Bobbs-Merrill, pp. 124-55.

Salamon, Lester (1980), 'Rethinking Public Management: Third-Party Government and the Changing Forms of Public Action', *Public Policy,* 29 (3), Summer, pp. 255-75.

State of Missouri (1986), *Official Manual, 1985-1986,* Jefferson City, State of Missouri, pp. 1250, 1276.

Tobin, Gary A. and Judd, Dennis R. (1982), 'Moving the Suburbs to the City: Neighbourhood Revitalisation and the "Amenities Bundle"', *Social Science Quarterly,* 63 (4), December, pp. 771-9.

Troustine, Philip J. (1978), 'Uni-Gov – Workable But Incomplete,' *Indianapolis Star,* 15 January , Sec. 5, pp. 1-3.

US Department of Housing and Urban Development (1982), *The President's National Urban Policy Report: 1982,* Washington, Government Printing Office, pp. 54, 57.

US Department of Housing and Urban Development (1984), *The President's National Urban Policy Report: 1984,* Washington, Government Printing Office, pp. 39-40.

US Department of Housing and Urban Development (HUD) (1986), *The Entrepreneurial American City,* Washington, Government Printing Office.

US Senate, Subcommittee on Housing and Urban Affairs (1985), *Hearings on Housing, Communicy Development, and Mass Transportation Authorisations – 1986,* Washington, Government Printing Office, p. 863.

Walker, Jack L. (1969), 'The Diffusion of Policy Innovations Among the American States', *American Political Science Review,* 63, September, pp. 880-99.

Wasylenko, Michael (1981), 'The Location of Firms: The Roles of Taxes and Fiscal Incentives', in Roy Bahl (ed.), *Urban Government Finance: Emerging Trends,* Volume 20, Urban Affairs Annual Reviews, Beverly Hills, Sage, pp. 155-90.

Williams, Walter quoted in Goodsell, Charles T. (1985), *The Case for Bureaucracy: A Public Administration Polemic,* Chatham, NJ, Chatham House, p. 71.

Wood, Robert C. (1958), *Suburbia: Its People and Politics,* Boston, Houghton Mifflin.

Zimmerman, Joseph F. (1983), *State-Local Relations: A Partnership Approach,* New York, Praeger, pp. 6, 52-6, 62-4.

3

Social, economic and political trends and their impact on British cities

MICHAEL GOLDSMITH
University of Salford

The objective of this paper is a simple one: to identify some social, economic and political trends occurring both internationally and nationally and to suggest how they are affecting British cities and the people who live in them. The review will be general rather than detailed, selective rather than comprehensive.

Two caveats to begin with: first, we must remember how limited our own timespan, sense of vision and ability to predict the future actually is. We still have a tendency to be concerned with the present or immediate future, and with a frame of reference set by the recent past. A brief look at the history of cities reminds us how quickly they change. We must not be afraid of that change – rather we have to learn how to exploit it to our maximum advantage. Second, that history should also remind us that cities, in some form or other, have existed throughout all civilisation. Cities as a phenomenon are not likely to go away, though of course individual cities may rise and fall – and rise again. We can see something of this in the papers in this volume on Bristol, Boston, Chicago, and New York. But let me suggest at the outset that the importance of cities, past and future, lies in their honeypot function, and as places of experiment and experience. Any visitor to a main railway station in continental Europe is immediately struck by the large number of international visitors who pass through it, and how attractive such cities seem to be to the young. And any visitor to Rome or Athens is immediately made aware of the importance of the history of cities. Large cities are places of social, political, economic and cultural experiment – be it in new forms of economic activity, experiments in big city political structures, or simply new forms of crime or living arrangements. Big cities – especially capital cities – will be around for a long time to come.

Industrial cities and their economic and social problems have dominated political debate in recent years. These are the centre of our discussions here. What global and national trends are impacting on cities, especially those in Britain?

GLOBAL TRENDS

Just as the so-called industrial revolution produced a change in the nature of capital, so, in the Western world, is the move towards a post-industrial society. Five trends are particularly important. First, the shift in the locus of manufacturing activity, away from Europe and North America to the Far East, Latin America and,in the long run, Africa. The shift in the terms of trade (and particularly in labour costs) has hit the older primary industries of Europe and North America very heavily as the examples of steel, coal, and textiles restructuring demonstrate. More recent is the impact on secondary manufacturing, revealed for example in the overcapacity in European car and truck production, which really requires that one major European manufacturer should disappear. The changes which have taken place in the production of electrical goods provides another example.

Second, there is the rapid growth and spread of multinational companies, more powerful than most national governments, owing a loyalty to shareholders spread worldwide, but to no particular place. They move funds, operations and people around to whatever place is most profitable in the medium term involving a 5-10 years' view. But such activity gives rise to the well-known phenomenon of the branch plant economy, highly vulnerable to changes in multinational plans. What is seen as a simple rationalisation for a multinational becomes a disaster for a locality and may be for a nation state.

Third, there is the marked shift in the nature of capital, away from the now largely unprofitable manufacturing sector into the service industries, especially such sectors as finance and insurance. Most advanced countries have experienced this change: its physical manifestation can be seen in every city centre the towering office block, rented or owned (and most probably financed) by a large multinational bank or insurance company, and the commercial-retail shopping centre, with its similarity of design and of shopping facilities.

Each of these trends brings with it two other features, the increasing interdependence of local, national and international economies on the one hand and the increasing specialisation of functions – Smith's division of labour – on the other. They relate to the fourth trend: changes in the levels of unemployment now found in most Western countries, and in the nature and type of work – now frequently part-time, less skilled, and involving higher levels of female participation in the labour market. All Western countries are currently experiencing higher levels of unemployment than for most of the post-war period. At the same time most of the jobs being lost are in areas employing semi or unskilled male labour, whilst new jobs in the service or high tech sectors generally want female labour. In other sectors skilled jobs are being lost, as new technology makes it impact. The title 'de-skilling' is perhaps most appropriate for this latter trend. But we still have to see the full impact of new technology, especially in the service sector. For example, the wider use of plastic credit cards, and cashierless tills in walls will all lead to lower employment in banking and other service sectors.

The fifth and last trend is the increasing importance of the public sector in most Western countries – as a proportion of GNP and as an employer of labour (Rose, 1985). In some countries public-sector activity approaches and even exceeds 50% of all activity: the cost of maintaining – let alone expanding still further – this level of activity has been a major concern in all Western countries in recent years, giving rise to what O'Connor (1973) called the fiscal crisis of the state. And whilst we frequently concern ourselves about the collapse of private sector activity for the health of national economies, we sometimes forget to ask about the economic consequences of a collapse in the level of public sector activity. For example, many British local authorities are major employers in their localities: cutbacks in local authority services inevitably result in some job losses over and above any other effects they might have.

IS SMALL SO BEAUTIFUL, IS BIG SO UGLY?

Turning to some of the social and demographic trends apparent in many Western cities, one is forced to begin by raising again this question asked by Ken Newton without, I hope, being drawn on the economists' old chestnut about the optimum city size (Newton, 1982). A number of features can be noted briefly.

First, there is the continuing decline in the population size of large cities, and the fact that small/medium-size cities are continuing to grow. In Europe – and perhaps in North America – a population of around 250,000 is suggested as one in which people appear to be most comfortable and most happy. Large cities, particularly the inner areas, have lost population for most of this century, but it is important to remember the impact of land use planning systems on this pattern of growth. In many countries, there has been an emphasis on reducing the density of inner area populations, and in the separation of work and residential areas, a trend only reversed in the last decade.

Second, people have continued to move into the suburbs and into rural areas – a kind of back to Ruritania. This is a trend perhaps most marked in the United States. But it is mirrored in Europe, although not on the same scale of movement from Frost belt to Sun belt (and back again?) which characterised America in the late seventies and early eighties. To a large extent this process of 'counter-urbanisation' has been a kind of middle-class Yuppie migration, but it adds to the problems of the older parts of our cities.

This change is reflected in a third feature, namely the population imbalance to be found in many parts of cities, where the elderly, the very young, the incompetent, the ethnic minority/guest worker increasingly find themselves trapped in the poorer, physically run down parts of the city. This trend is also reflected in the increasing abandonment of parts of the city not yet so marked in parts of Britain and Europe as it is in cities such as Philadelphia and New York, but especially a feature of older cities. Other important trends include the increasing number of single person households and of single-parent families, as well as the changing pattern of interpersonal relationships – AIDS notwithstanding.

Fourth, there is increasing social segregation in cities, which partly follows from some of these earlier changes. An important element of this – at least in European cities – concerns housing quality and housing tenure, where an important distinction is between poor quality public housing and better quality private housing. This distinction is particularly marked in those countries with large public housing sectors – Britain, France and Scandinavia all provide examples.

Finally there is the increasing importance of the informal/black economy and of alternative life cultures for those left in the city. Whilst there is some evidence (Pahl, 1985) which suggests that the black economy is strongest where the formal economy is also strongest, the alternative culture may be important for ethnic minorities and other disadvantaged groups as they seek to survive the harshness of inner-city life.

Yet despite all these trends which pose problems for big cities, the latter remain vibrant centres of different forms of activity. Nobody is seriously suggesting that London should close down, or Paris or Rome, let alone New York or Houston. Anybody familiar with the work of nineteenth-century urban historians could point to similar trends and features in that century (Wohl, 1983). Those cities adapted to the needs of the twentieth century: no doubt their modern counterparts will do likewise. All of these features can be found in many Western European cities: they are not unknown to North America they are also found in some Eastern bloc countries. Some of them are particularly severe in Britain but before I turn to Britain in specific terms, I want to highlight two political trends which are important for a discussion of cities.

POLITICAL TRENDS

In recent years, most Western governments have had to try and cope with the changes which have just been described. There are two trends which are clearly apparent in what such governments have attempted to do. First, there has been a general shift to the right politically in most Western countries during the eighties. France was an early exception in 1981, but joined the rest with the result of the 1986 elections and the return of the Chirac government. Even the relatively long lasting social democratic regimes in Scandinavia have come under pressure: the Schlouter government in Denmark is an example where a conservative regime has taken over from the social democrats. An important consequence of this trend is for such governments to mistrust previous centre or radical solutions to problems, and for current opposition parties equally to mistrust the new right wing suggestions. Nevertheless, the shift to the right is marked by the neo-liberal rallying call to roll back the state, free market forces and trust market-led solutions. As a result there has been a redefining of the political agenda of cities. Statist solutions and services are out of fashion. Liberating the market (with all its consequences especially for inner cities) is the new trend. Cutting back city hall – in an attempt to reduce the scope of government actions – becomes the means by which welfare state services and expenditures can be restricted, if not actually reduced.

The second trend which is apparent is that most countries – and here Britain is the exception – have seen decentralisation as the means by which solutions to the problems can be most easily achieved. Moves towards decentralisation have taken place throughout both northern and southern Europe. Norway, Sweden, Denmark, as well as France, Spain and Italy have all undergone the process in the last ten to fifteen years. As the American contributors to this collection also show, Reagan's policies have been very much concerned with reviving the states at the expense of federal involvement in the cities. However, this trend poses two problems. In the first place there is the important question whether genuine decentralisation of power has in fact taken place. This involves an understanding of just what functions and powers have been decentralised, the way they have been decentralised and with what effects. For example, if decentralisation simply means that American states have fewer resources to meet increasing functional responsibilities, then in effect the American citizen may be worse off than before especially if little has been done to reduce the demand that services be provided to some minimum (but possibly high) legally enforceable standard. (A similar issue faces the so-called 'free commune' experiments in Denmark and Sweden, whereby a number of localities have been freed from the duty of providing particular services to levels set by the central government, but at the same time have lost central resources previously provided to help finance local services). The second problem posed by these attempts at decentralisation involves an assessment of whether these attempts are only a cover for the centre's offloading onto the periphery – or sub-national levels of government – problems which the centre is itself unable or unwilling to solve.

Despite these problems, however, both a shift to the right and a move towards decentralist solutions for the welfare and economic development problems facing cities is apparent in many Western countries. But how is Britain affected by the trends? And what are the likely consequences for its cities?

BRITAIN

Britain has experienced most of the trends. Its inner city areas remain places of poverty, poor environmental conditions and high unemployment, with a declining industrial base. To a greater or lesser extent, these same areas have seen an increase in service industry and associated female employment, most having similar central area shopping centres offering very similar ranges of goods and services. But there are three features in particular which demonstrate how British inner cities – and perhaps Britain generally – differ from other countries. These features mean that the possibilities for economic development, redistribution and change may be more limited in Britain than elsewhere.

First, there is the particular nature of British capital. This has moved very rapidly from a locally or regionally based manufacturing form – predominant in the late nineteenth and early twentieth century – into its current multinational, service finance based form today. Along with Tokyo and New York, London is one of the great finance centres of the world. And there is an increasing concentration of finance capital and headquarters activities within the London region at the expense of the rest of the country, a process likely to be fuelled even more by the recent 'big bang' in the London Stock Market. But both multinationals and financial institutions are notoriously footloose, owing loyalties only to their worldwide institutional shareholders. As such they have no real spatial base, and their flexibility means that they can move their operations and resources around quickly as market trends determine.

One result is that the United Kingdom has little privately based regional or local capital. Furthermore, it has very little venture or high risk capital when compared with its competitors, since British financial institutions are generally conservative in their risk taking. Indeed, British finance capital's current distaste for manufacturing investment, when linked with the marked failure by government to use North Sea oil revenue for little more than unemployment benefit, is one of the reasons why the British economy has not fully shared in the limited recovery currently taking place in Europe.

Second, this lack of investment, linked to the government's reversal of previous post World War II regional policies designed to minimise differences in the country, has exacerbated the differences between north and south, and between east and west. For example, part of the problems faced by Liverpool, as Parkinson (1985) clearly shows, derives from the fact that it is in the wrong place at the wrong time. Overall regional differences – economic, social and political – currently produce a more divided country than at any time since 1945 a feature emphasised by the concentration of government electoral support within the more prosperous 'golden triangle' in the South and South East. The latter, always more attractive to industry and other economic activities because of its proximity to London, continues to grow as the main high tech region (see Martin Boddy's contribution in this volume) and the centre for finance capital. These trends are further fuelled by the proximity of the region to Europe – Britain's largest market – and by the continuing development of the region's airports and the proposed Channel tunnel.'

Third, rather than using decentralist solutions to problems, Britain has become even more centralised so that perhaps it is now the most centralised country outside eastern Europe (Newton and Goldsmith, 1983). This trend has consequences for cities outside the London-based core of the country and for those who manage them and live in them. These consequences and reinforced by the sense of 'cultural disdain with which the core regards the rest of the country' (Bulpitt, 1983; Greenwood, 1981). These who live and work as part of the London-based elite establishment regard the rest of the country not only a provincial but also as incompetent and untrustworthy. This view is reinforced by the recent history of central – local relations in Britain, in which a right wing government has sought to bypass elected local governments in its efforts to roll back the state. As these efforts have proved increasingly unsuccessful, so the government's proposals have become increasingly draconian.

The government's centralisation strategy has been a multi-dimensional one. The barest summary will suffice here. In the area of finance, it has moved from the introduction of expenditure targets for individual local authorities, with sanctions for overspending, through the introduction of local tax capping with limits placed on the level of local taxes which selected (mainly Labour controlled) local governments may levy, to the abolition in 1986 of area wide metropolitan government in Britain. The strategy has also involved the removal of functions from local government, their compulsory privatisation and a marked increase in legal forms of control over local authorities. Examples include the recent deregulation of public transport; the sale of (public) housing at generous discounts – some 750,000 houses since 1980 – and the introduction of the Audit Commission charged with introducing 'value for money' in local government.

All this has been accompanied by a growth in special purpose bodies with responsibilities, particularly in inner city areas; an increase in specific conditional grants, and a reduction in the level of financial support overall for local authorities. The latter have few options other than to introduce heavy local tax increases in an attempt to maintain local services, as well as indulging in some of the finer arts of creative accountancy (Parkinson, 1986). Currently the centre proposes to reform the local tax system, despite the almost total opposition to the proposed community charge and the national business rate. All these central efforts have met with considerable opposition, not only from other political parties and from local government, but from within the ranks of the Conservative party in Parliament as well. The increasingly strict controls are themselves largely the result of a partisan political war between centre and locality as much as a result of an ideological one between left and right.

The consequence of this is well demonstrated by Parkinson's contribution on Liverpool. The city is a particularly severe victim of the central strategy, as a result of which the city is not only run by its own Labour-controlled council, but also by many non-elected bodies dealing with the city's problems on little more than a symbolic basis and with symbolic funding. Because of the recent history, Liverpool finds itself cut off effectively from the political and administrative core. Not even the national Labour party wishes to deal with its local variant in Liverpool, and has removed from membership the Militant tendency members in Liverpool.

Other parts of the country have not been so badly affected by these trends, and until 1985 at least much of English local government was under the control of local Conservatives, many of whom were not disposed generally towards what the central government planned to do. However, the 1985 local election which resulted in a large number of hung councils – particularly amongst the more rural shire counties – were perhaps a sign of the electorate's dissatisfaction with the continuing battle between centre and locality.

SIGNS OF HOPE?

The picture painted is a somewhat pessimistic one. Many British cities reveal all the signs of decline and decay common to most European and some North American countries. Britain's form of capital is largely unsympathetic to industrial and manufacturing activity and the level of high risk venture and local capital is low. Its government, far from being concerned with improving welfare state services in the face of continuing high levels of unemployment, remains committed to a policy of rolling back the state and bypassing local government. But there are some signs of hope. First, some of the economic development agency strategies, such as the Scottish Development Agency, appear to be working (see Boyle, below), though it remains to be seen how real and long term the improvement actually is. Similarly, some of the local economic initiatives undertaken by local governments do seem to be able to attract private investment alongside public, and to create jobs at a lower cost per job than many central initiatives. Third, current manpower initiatives are more generally concerned with improving labour skills than simply keeping youth off the streets: lack of appropriate skills amongst the workforce is a cry frequently made by British industrialists, even if they are unable to say precisely what skills they want their labour to possess. Fourth, there remains the great unexplained paradox that, even with four million unemployed and after ten years of cutbacks in local government activities, there is still no revolution on the streets of Britain – miners' and printers' strikes and inner-city riots notwithstanding. Fifth, there is the fact the the South remains vibrant and expanding, a process which will be further encouraged with the building of the Channel tunnel and the third London airport. And last, most of our cities continue to attract commercial development and service industry, even if not all cities benefit equally from this growth. All these signs give some cause for optimism, and if we can learn from past mistakes, from present successes and others' experiences, and not be afraid to experiment, then there is a chance that adaptation to the post industrial society may be less difficult in Britain than it currently appears.

LESSONS TO BE LEARNT

The first lesson is simply that local government reform and change did not simply drop off the political agenda with abolition, even if the return of area wide metropolitan government is unlikely. Two scenarios seem possible: a continuation of present policies designed to bypass local government and reduce its already diminished status much further, a policy which seems likely, if the present Conservative administration retains office. Alternatively, there is the possible introduction of some form of elected regional government in England – together with further devolution of powers to Scotland and Wales, a policy supported by the Alliance and Labour parties.

This would presuppose considerable devolution of powers from the centre and the possible abolition of another tier of local government – possibly the shire counties. And both of these vested interests would be formidable opponents of such a development (Goldsmith, 1985).

Second, some form of regional development agency is necessary in England, distinct from the regional tier of government, organised on a similar basis to the Scottish and Welsh agencies or some of the local government development bodies. These would have their own funds and would be able to co-operate with the private sector in planning and selecting suitable strategies for future regional economic development. There is much to be learned here from the experience not only of the two other national agencies and their Northern Ireland counterparts, but from that of the development corporations in Merseyside and the dock-lands, from the many local authority experiments (and from other countries, such as France). We need to learn from their mistakes as well as from their successes. But if this is the way to develop a regional venture capital fund and to attract private investment back into such deprived regions as the north west and north of England, then such a policy must be adopted.

Third, we have to experiment in forms of partnership between the private and public sectors; we have to think about new and different forms of public sector activity as well as private, and we have to learn how to make the market work for the public good as much for private gain. Some French experience may well be relevant in this context, as may that of the US in regulating private sector activity to its own benefit.

Fourth, we have to begin to overcome the problems posed by the increasing segregation and disintegration of our cities: urban sociologists world-wide have increasingly revealed the extent of social polarisation to be found in cities. Ways and means have to be found of overcoming such problems together with the resulting differences in housing standards, access to private and public services and consumption.

Last, and by no means least, we have to consider the kind of post industrial society we want and ways and means of achieving it. Instead of simply reacting to environmental changes around us, we have to think about what values we wish to retain and encourage. Within such a framework, it is likely that cities will remain with us. They are part of history, even though the industrial city has only occupied ten per cent of Christian history. We should seek to preserve what is valuable from it and not to preserve it for its own sake. As part of this exercise we shall need to think less in terms of paid work and a job for life, but more about developing the potential for individuals in the round – of providing fulfilment in a variety of ways, of training and re-training, of changing direction, and of trying all the experiences which the city has to offer. In the end we shall have to return to a consideration of humanist rather than material values, thinking about people before profits. By thinking in these terms, the UK urban space can become defensible space: otherwise it may become the battleground for a new class and race war which will make the long hot summers of American cities in the late sixties seem like Paradise.

NOTE

1 Perception of regional differences does depend very much on where one lives and works. Readers should be aware that the author is a southerner who has lived and worked in the north west of Britain for over 25 years, but with frequent excursions to the London core and elsewhere.

REFERENCES

Bulpitt, J. (1983), *Territory and Power in the United Kingdom,* Manchester, Manchester University Press.

Greenwood, R. (1981), 'Fiscal Pressure and Local Government in England and Wales', in Hood, C. and Wright, M. (eds.), *Big Government in Hard Times,* London, Allen & Unwin, pp. 77-99.

Newton, K. (1982), 'Is Small Really So Beautiful, Is Big Really So Ugly? Size, Effectiveness and Democracy in Local Government', *Political Studies,* Vol. 30, no. 2, pp. 190-206.

Newton, K. and Goldsmith, M. (1984), 'Central-Local Government Relations: The Irresistible Rise of Centralised Power', in Berrington H. (ed.), *Change in British*

Politics, London, Frank Cass, pp. 216-33.

O'Connor, J. (1973), *The Fiscal Crisis of the State,* New York, St. Martin's Press.

Pahl, R. A. (1985), *Divisions of Labour,* Oxford, Basil Blackwell.

Parkinson, M. (1985), *Liverpool on the Brink,* London, Policy Journals.

—— (1986), 'Creative Accounting and Financial Ingenuity in Local Government', *Public Money,* 5, pp. 27-32.

Rose, R. (1985), *Public Employment in Western Nations,* Cambridge, Cambridge University Press.

Wohl, A. H. (1983), *Endangered Lives: Public Health in Victorian Britain,* London, Methuen.

4

Bristol: a case study in economic change in the UK 'Sunbelt'

MARTIN BODDY
University of Bristol

A hundred and thirty miles west from London along the M4 motorway, the city of Bristol is one of the country's most successful major urban areas. It lies at one end of the 'M4 Growth Corridor', seen by some as Britain's own economic 'Sunbelt', equivalent to California's Silicon Valley or Boston's Route 128. Such parallels have fed on hopes of major high tech development along the corridor, hopes which significant investment by US companies such as Hewlett Packard in Bristol have fostered, although financial services have been much more important locally in terms of job gain.

Bristol offers in many ways a direct contrast with the experience of places like Liverpool or Newcastle which have borne the brunt of Britain's post-war decline and recently, deepening economic recession. It also invites comparison with those successful US metropolitan areas, characterised by strong growth in business and other services (Stanback and Noyelle, 1982). In terms of urban renewal as well, it parallels US-style 'gentrification' with the growth around the 'historic' city-centre docks of new private housing schemes, speciality shopping and leisure and recreational facilities.

Any simple juxtaposition of 'success' and 'failure' in terms of urban economic change inevitably, however, obscures much of the complexity of the situation. In September 1986, Bristol again hit the national headlines as violent clashes with the police erupted in the St Pauls area of the city. Yet almost in the same week, Lloyds Bank announced that it was relocating its 800 strong Head Office from London to the city, the latest in a series of such moves by financial institutions. And while government figures for the country as a whole, issued in early 1987, again stressed the north/south divide in terms of economic prosperity at the national level, Bristol itself has its own two nations – the relatively well off and securely employed on the one hand and, on the other, the unemployed

TABLE 4.1 MANUFACTURING AND SERVICE EMPLOYMENT CHANGE
BY GENDER, 1971-81, BRISTOL AND GREAT BRITAIN

	Number	Bristol %	GB %
Total	−2,084	−0.7	−2.3
Manufacturing[a]	−23,660	−22.0	−24.9
Service	21,694	13.1	15.3
Male	−15,604	−8.1	−6.0
Female	13,520	12.4	3.1
Male manufacturing	−14,962	−18.7	−23.0
Male service	1,175	1.3	15.2
Female manufacturing	−8,700	−31.9	−29.1
Female service	20,520	26.2	15.3

(a) Manufacturing, SICs III-XIX; Service, XXII-XXVII
Source: Annual Census of Employment, Department of Employment.

and those on the margins of employment, concentrated in the older inner city areas and the peripheral, public housing estates.

This chapter sets out the pattern of economic and employment change in the Bristol locality since the early 1970s. It then looks at the implications of this pattern of change for different sections of the population. Finally it draws out some of the policy implications. In doing so it draws on a much longer study of the Bristol region, written up in detail elsewhere.[1]

ECONOMIC STRUCTURE AND CHANGE

To give an initial picture of economic structure, employment in the locality totalled almost 300,000 in 1981.[2] Proportions in manufacturing and services were roughly equivalent to national figures, with male employment marginally up and female employment marginally down. Within manufacturing, the locality had a higher than average share of employment in food, drink and tobacco, particularly the third; vehicles (mainly aerospace); and paper, printing and publishing. Within services it had a higher than average share of employment in financial services, particularly insurance; professional and scientific services – mainly public sector education, medical and dental employment; transport and communications; and public utilities.

Employment overall fell by less than one per cent (2,500) over the decade to 1981. This however disguises more fundamental changes, the switch from manufacturing to service employment, and the decline in male employment offset numerically at least by expanding female employment (Table 4.1). These shifts mirror national trends, but with a particularly marked increase in female service employment locally and a slower rate of decline in male manufacturing. Much of this increase in female service employment, however, represents part-time employment.

THE PATTERN OF CHANGE

Total employment in the locality had grown rapidly through the 'long boom' of the 1950s and 1960s. Employment trends mirrored the national picture, but with Bristol in effect gaining more than its share of national growth when jobs were expanding and losing less in periods of decline. Food, drink and tobacco, and paper, printing and packaging in particular, were sustained by the prosperity of national mass consumer markets while a succession of major civil and military projects underpinned the aerospace sector. Together these sustained other elements of the economy including engineering and metal manufacture. Then as manufacturing growth slowed through the 1960s, services expanded strongly, particularly public employment in education and medicine. Unlike many localities where the post-war picture was one of accelerating decline in their traditionally basic industries, it was not really until the 1970s that major job loss and restructuring reverberated through Bristol's dominant manufacturing sectors. Bristol's longer term legacy had been in industries set to expand in the post war boom rather than for example coal, iron and steel, textiles, shipbuilding or heavy engineering.

From the early 1970s, however, manufacturing job loss did accelerate. The failure of the Concorde project hit jobs in aerospace, and declining demand for the locality's consumer- oriented industries throughout the decade was exacerbated by deepening recession from the late 1970s. Growth in public services fell away through the 1970s, compensated to some extent by the rapid expansion of private services, particularly early on. This expansion however failed to offset a sharp drop in overall employment in the early 1970s which brought a brief, localised economic crisis pushing unemployment, for a time, above the national rate (Table 4.2).

Major job losses in absolute terms over the decade to 1981 were thus concentrated in the traditionally dominant manufacturing sectors. Food, drink and tobacco, and printing, paper and publishing, moreover, both declined much faster than nationally. Together they lost over 16,000 jobs up to 1981 and several thousand more by 1987. There were significant losses also in parts of aerospace, the distributive trades and metal manufacture.

TABLE 4.2 UNEMPLOYMENT, BRISTOL AND GREAT BRITAIN
1976-86

Mid-year	Bristol %	Great Britain %	(Bristol/GB) x 100 %
1976	5.6	5.6	100
1977	6.3	6.2	102
1978	6.1	5.9	103
1979	5.5	5.6	98
1980	6.0	6.9	87
1981	9.1	10.9	84
1982	10.4	12.6	83
1983	10.1	12.3	82
1984	10.8	12.7	85
1985	11.4	13.2	86
1986	10.7	12.9	83

(a) Rates have been affected by a number of changes in the government definition of unemployment, mainly in a downward direction. The most significant was in April 1983 affecting figures after this date. Comparisons between Bristol and Great Britain are however valid in relative terms.
Source: Department of Employment Gazette.

TABLE 4.3 UNEMPLOYMENT, BRISTOL AND SELECTED LOCALITIES,
1978 AND 1986

Locality[a] %	January 1986 %	November 1978 %	Increase in rate[b] %
Reading	6.9	4.2	64
Swindon	11.0	6.9	59
BRISTOL	10.6	6.8	56
Cardiff	13.8	7.7	79
Glasgow	17.0	10.3	65
Newcastle	17.9	9.4	90
Birmingham	15.9	6.3	152
Great Britain	12.8	5.9	117

(a) Travel to Work Areas.
(b) Definitional changes mean that unemployment rates are not strictly comparable in absolute terms between 1978 and 1986. The increase in unemployment is significantly understated. Comparisons *between* localities of the increase are however more valid.
Source: Department of Employment Gazette.

TABLE 4.4 HIGH TECHNOLOGY EMPLOYMENT IN BRISTOL, 1981

	Bristol %	Great Britain %
Aerospace	7.3	0.9
Other high technology[a]	0.8	2.0
All high technology	8.1	2.9

(a) Defined in terms of Census of Employment 'minimum list headings' (SIC 1968) and including: pharmaceutical chemicals and preparations; scientific and industrial instruments and systems; radio and electronic components; broadcasting equipment; electronic computers; radio, radar and electronic capital goods.
Source: Annual Census of Employment, Department of Employment.

The picture of employment collapse in traditional manufacturing sectors countered by the expansion of service employment is familiar enough. The locality shared in the more general failure of manufacturing industry nationally to reinvest and restructure through the long boom (Gamble, 1981). Aerospace however, employing nearly 24,000 in 1971, contracted much more slowly than manufacturing as a whole over the decade, and in fact expanded towards the end of this period. This shored up an important component of manufacturing employment, maintaining a dynamic core of technologically advanced activity and employment with wider economic and employment implications for the locality as a whole. There were significant job losses in other manufacturing sectors, and severe short term crises for a number of local employers. Much of this, however, reflected corporate restructuring, reorientation of markets and 'shakeout' of employment delayed by the continuing boom of the 1960s and early 1970s, rather than outright collapse. Decline, generally, came later and was less severe than in many localities which have suffered longer term decline in basic industries or, like the West Midlands, the more recent and rapid collapse of engineering and metals-based industries (see Table 4.3). And while manufacturing employment in the locality declined overall, *output* in many sectors including aerospace, electronics and tobacco continued to expand, even after the sharp downturn of the late 1970s. This emphasises the fact that job loss is by no means synonymous with economic decline.

Despite the optimistic parallels drawn with Silicon Valley, development of technologically advanced activity including electronics-based R & D production is heavily concentrated in the long-established aerospace sector, much of which is specifically defence related. High technology growth in the sense of an influx of rapidly expanding electronics and computer companies or the mushrooming of new enterprises has been modest in overall terms (Table 4.4), and by no means exceptional in national terms (for more detailed discussion see Boddy and Lovering, 1986).

The major employment growth has in fact been in the service sector, much of it in private services. Insurance, banking and finance expanded at twice the national rate and 'miscellaneous services' also outpaced national growth. Growth in professional and scientific services, mainly public sector education, medical and dental employment, was important in absolute terms though less rapid than in the country as a whole. Employment in these three sectors together increased by over 25,000 in the decade up to 1981. Employment declined, however, across a broad band of services, mainly public services and utilities but also wholesale and retailing.

Growth in financial services, particularly insurance, reflected both relocation of head office functions from London and the increasing concentration of other functions into Bristol as a regional centre. Four UK insurance company administrative headquarters, a finance company and several departments of one of the big four banks have moved to Bristol since the early 1970s and Lloyds Bank headquarters is soon to follow. Employment in financial services grew by nearly 9,500 in the decade to 1981 reaching a total of over 22,000 – significantly up on aerospace for example – and expansion continues.

Miscellaneous services includes the 'eating, drinking, cultural and entertainment' services but also the mixed bag of 'other services' not broken down in official statistics, all of which expanded much faster than nationally. Commonly seen as 'dependent' on demand generated elsewhere in the local economy, the major growth of these activities reflects the strength of other sectors locally. The scale and character of their growth seems to reflect in particular demands generated by the growth of relatively well paid white collar, professional and technical staff concentrated for example in aerospace, finance and business services. They also reflect less tangible changes in patterns of consumption, culture and lifestyle. This supports Hall's suggestion that: 'the growth of a relatively small industrial base especially in innovative, high-technology industry and associated producer services, can create a very large income and employment multiplier effect in the form of construction, real estate, recreation and personal service industries' (Hall, 1985, p. 10).

Service growth at the locality level is, however, more than simply dependent. The positive role at the urban and regional level of 'basic' services and the business service infrastructure has increasingly been recognised (Marquand 1979, Stanback 1979). Going beyond this, a range of personal and miscellaneous services would also appear to be, in the Bristol case, an important component of the image and attractiveness of the locality both to corporate decision makers and to particular types of labour, key professional and technical strata, which these companies must attract and retain. And these same services are a factor in the growth of tourism, and business activities including conferences, exhibitions and other trade events.

THE PROCESS AT WORK

Employment locally has obviously been affected by a variety of processes at national and international scales, specific to particular sectors and companies. The decline of paper and packaging locally, for example, reflects specific, industry-wide pressures, particularly foreign competition. The tobacco sector has been affected both by falling demand in general and the specific corporate circumstances of the industry locally, including decisions to locate new production capacity and company headquarters in the city. Aerospace employment has reflected continuing corporate commitment to existing capacity in the locality, labour and expertise, together with overall market strength and the success of specific products. And insurance decentralisation to Bristol reflected in particular the relative cost of office space in central London, accessibility and the locality's attractiveness to key staff. The area's specific legacy of previous rounds of investment was also in many ways favourable. As we have seen, traditional manufacturing declined later and less severely than in many localities, while aerospace gave the area a major stake in one of the few manufacturing sectors to survive relatively well in employment terms. A number of more specific factors can be drawn out.

Access to London, Heathrow and the rest of the country including the early introduction of the High Speed Train has been important, particularly to financial services, aerospace and electronics sector. This has not only facilitated business contact and movement of goods, but also functioned to tie in the locality to London and the rest of the south east 'heartland', easing the transfer in and attraction of higher grade staff. Regional nodality, also, has reinforced Bristol's role across a range of distribution and service functions. The local labour market is both substantial in scale and diverse, including both higher grade technical and professional staff, skilled manual labour, female employment and good quality school leavers. This has been reinforced from the employers' perspective by a good industrial relations reputation.

The cost and availability of land and premises, including both central area office space and major greenfield sites, particularly on the northern fringe, have facilitated the relocation and growth of office based services, regional warehouse and retail functions and electronics related activities. Speculative overprovision of office space in the early 1970s led to the city's locational attractions being 'undervalued' in terms of office rents (Knight, Frank and Rutley, 1983). The amenability of the local planning environment has also been a factor in some instances – particularly important in the M4 growth corridor context, in which Avon County and the second tier district councils have generally been more pro-development than Wiltshire and Berkshire to the east.

The scale and attractiveness of the urban environment, housing, education, leisure and cultural facilities, access to countryside – the consumption, lifestyle and image factors – have facilitated the recruitment and retention of higher level technical, professional and managerial staff, and influenced corporate investment and location decisions. The locality has a positive social image for elite labour market groups and corporate decision makers and has avoided any of the stigma which attaches to designated regional or inner city problem areas.

In contrast to other major conurbations, Bristol has inherited little in terms of physical dereliction or image from its industrial past, with the city centre docks, virtually deserted by commercial traffic by the 1960s, providing instead the opportunity for what has been seen as showpiece renovation and redevelopment for arts, leisure and recreational uses and the revival of city centre private housing development.

WINNERS AND LOSERS

The overall picture in terms of unemployment and job loss compares favourably with cities in the Midlands and North (Table 4.3). Unemployment at the end of 1986 locally was 10.6% compared with 15.9% in Birmingham, 17.0% in Glasgow and 17.9% in Newcastle upon Tyne. This was, nevertheless, significantly up on places such as Reading or Basingstoke closer to London down the M4.

It is obvious however that the benefits of this relative prosperity are not evenly distributed through different groups in the labour market. This is emphasised by the scale and persistence of unemployment for particular groups in the labour market, the young, the old and members of minority ethnic groups. The unemployment rate for under 25 year olds in the county had reached nearly 19% by October 1984 – 25% discounting government training and community programme schemes – compared with 11% overall, and equalling the national rate. Fifty nine per cent of those out of work in the 55-59 age bracket had been so for more than a year compared with 52% nationally. And the unemployment rate locally for male workers of West Indian origin was 24% in mid-1982 compared with 12% for male workers as a whole.

This is indicative of a growing mismatch not only in terms of numbers of jobs but also the types of employment offered by those sectors expanding locally. Job loss has been concentrated on manual employment, much if it semi-skilled and unskilled and, typically, male employment. Employment growth on the other hand has been mainly in the service sector, much of it offering job opportunities to women, frequently part-time. There is a sense in which as traditional manufacturing declined and services expanded, male manual workers, particularly older workers, moved into unemployment, frequently long term. Women, on the other hand, were drawn into the rapidly expanding service sector.

Service sector growth has clearly not provided job opportunities for those losing jobs in manufacturing. In the more resilient manufacturing sectors, moreover, such as aerospace and the newer electronics companies, the qualifications, technical knowledge and experience required are major barriers, with many jobs being filled by those already employed. In the service sector the qualifications required for higher grade positions within, for example, financial services, similarly exclude the great majority of school leavers and other job seekers. Growth has created few job opportunities for, in particular, the majority of less qualified school and Youth Training Scheme leavers and for many of the semi-skilled and unskilled 'shaken out' of employment. Recruitment, generally, has emphasised skills, experience and qualifications which exclude the majority of these groups. In many major companies there has been little recruitment from the unemployed. Where vacancies have arisen they have generally been filled internally or by recruitment from those already in employment, with skills and experience. In the context of employment shrinkage, many vacancies do not, in any case, lead to new recruitment. The main exceptions have included jobs in miscellaneous services, retailing, typing and junior clerical occupations.

These processes have been reflected in increasing polarisation between core and peripheral groups in the labour market. Core groups include the relatively well paid and securely employed with relevant skills, technical knowledge or professional expertise, together with those possessing the qualifications who can successfully compete to join them. They are likely to enjoy the prospect of career or salary progression and the possibility of job mobility with little risk of unemployment, certainly for any length of time. Union structures remain important in much of manufacturing and public sector employment while other groups benefit from relatively benign management-labour relations based on the enlistment of cooperation and consent, and a non-conflictual technical and professional ethos. Employment is disproportionately white and male.

Peripheral groups include the semi-skilled and unskilled, the less well qualified school leavers and those whose employment or employment prospects are tied to routinised, deskilled work in manufacturing. It also includes parts of the expanding service sector offering relatively low paid and insecure employment, possibly part time and commonly non-unionised, and routinised office and clerical work with little prospect of career advancement, groups that have been termed 'service workers' as distinct from white collar career grades and professionals. Peripheral groups are characterised by a much greater concentration of black workers and, particularly in services, women.

Polarisation in part reflects simply the pattern of job gain and loss and its impact on different groups in the labour market. Core employment has been maintained by the resilience of certain sectors while peripheral employment has grown in particular with service sector expansion. Core labour in both manufacturing and services is however structurally linked to a dependent growth of peripheral employment, much of it female and part time, in the service sector particularly miscellaneous services. The relationship between basic and dependent activity and the operation of what have been called 'trickle down' effects are thus reflected in structured inequalities in the labour market.

There is also evidence both locally and nationally of increasing differentiation *within* particular firms and sectors, between those in occupations where skill, specialisation and technical content are increasing, and with career prospects, and those performing tasks such as routine assembly, data input and basic clerical work. This overall process of polarisation is likely to continue. In part this reflects the continuing shift from manufacturing to service employment. The latter tends overall to have a higher proportion of lower paid workers, women and members of minority ethnic groups, part time work and less secure employment. Technical change is moreover likely to increase polarisation within specific firms and sectors in both manufacturing and services. Particularly relevant to Bristol, Rajan (1984) predicts increasing differentiation within financial services between 'career' and 'non-career' clerical staff. In the UK electronics industry Soete and Dosi (1983), similarly, see job gain in high skill categories but significant losses affecting operators and to a some extent clerical and craft workers, with female employment most affected by decline. Within more dynamic sectors such as electronics, aerospace and insurance, economic recovery will moreover be characterised by 'jobless growth' in output with less than proportional employment increase. In terms of services as a whole the Bristol case parallels Stanback's suggestion from the US experience that 'we are moving towards a sharply dichotomized service work force offering, on the one hand, the skilled, responsible, and relatively well-paying jobs of certain professionals, trained technicians, or artisans, but on the other, the unskilled, undemanding, and poorly paid jobs of salespersons, service workers, or labourers' (Stanback, 1979, p. 106).

POLICY IMPLICATIONS

The wider policy implications of the Bristol case turn both on the extent to which specific policy measures are implicated in the observed patterns of change and on the extent to which these are relevant or reproducible elsewhere. In naive terms of direct and practicable policy lessons applicable more widely, the conclusions are limited. In part this is simply because Bristol is no more divorced than other localities from the working out of national and international scale processes. Nor can the complex legacy of historical processes which constitute this particular locality be in any simple sense reproduced. No specific urban or regional policy measures, central or local are heavily implicated in the particular processes of economic and employment change described earlier. The Bristol locality has never had assisted area status under central government regional policy. It has received individual grants under the government's Urban Programme but did not have the additional resources and powers afforded by designated Inner Area Programme status until criteria were broadened in 1986. In this sense it is almost unique among the country's major urban areas. There are examples of innovative and at the local scale, effective initiatives from which lessons can be drawn. Their impact in overall economic and employment terms has however been essentially irrelevant. Location, environment, quality of life, regional centrality, labour market structure and in particular the legacy of past rounds of economic activity are among the key explanatory factors – and among the least tractable in policy terms.

The importance of image, urban environment and 'milieu' and quality of life factors does emphasise the importance of policies and expenditure which bear on these. The strength of miscellaneous services and the possible importance of the personal service sector as a positive, attractive factor similarly suggests the role of measures to stimulate personal and business tourism, leisure and recreational activities. This does however have particular employment implications including the growth of relatively low paid, part time female employment. Together with the importance of financial services, Bristol's experience nevertheless emphasises the importance of developing explicit policies relating to the service sector and breaking spurious and outdated obsessions with manufacturing as the only source of 'real' jobs. Service growth locally cannot however be divorced from the specific character of the Bristol area and the 'raw material' this afforded. Finally, the importance of site and premises availability to suit specific users and the ability of the local authorities and other agencies to respond positively has been emphasised in specific instances. Again however, these are merely necessary factors, reproducible and indeed duplicated in many localities and far from sufficient to attract economic growth.

It is in fact precisely the absence of explicit central government urban and regional policy measures which characterises the area. As suggested earlier however, while the area has clearly lost out in straight financial terms from lack of Urban Programme funds and regional assistance, this does not appear to have been a major disadvantage in overall economic and employment terms. Policies to disperse offices from London and the rest of the South East in fact worked to Bristol's advantage and, with hindsight, suggest some misconception in the way these policies were applied.

In terms of specific inner city policy, Bristol's problems are clearly less severe than in many major urban areas. The absolute scale of unemployment and related adverse indicators are however masked by authority-wide averages and their multi-locational character. They display the increasing double-sided nature of 'inner-city' problems including both older inner areas of mixed housing tenure and peripheral council estates. On the latter, problems of escalating housing and environmental problems, coupled with the continuing link between the poorest housing and the worst off households relate in particular to local authorities' financial capacity. This capacity has been particularly limited in the present political and economic climate, with both capital and revenue expenditure cut back and tightly controlled by the Conservative central government.

Official Urban Programme spending has been minimal given the scale of economic, social and environmental problems it confronts. The Bristol case supports nevertheless the need for more finely focused targetting of what funds are made available. In this situation, parts of Bristol would clearly qualify for additional spending. This was in fact recognised symbolically at least, when areas designated as inner urban

TABLE 4.5 DEFENCE EQUIPMENT EXPENDITURE AND SPENDING ON
REGIONAL ASSISTANCE BY REGION

Region	Defence equipment[b] 1985/86[a] £ per head	Regional assistance[c] 1984/85[a] £ per head
North	81	40
Yorks & Humberside	34	9
East Midlands	86	3
East Anglia	128	—
South East	243	—
South West	223	3
Wales	59	50
West Midlands	64	—
North West	183	16
Scotland	98	36
TOTAL	7,520 million	615 million

(a) Note difference in years, due to data availability.
(b) Spending on defence equipment per head was derived from regional percentage shares of MoD UK procurement spending, provided by the Ministry of Defence. These were used to allocate total expenditure on defence equipment, from the defence white paper, to regions.
(c) Regional assistance includes all forms of 'regional preferential assistance to industry'.
Source: Ministry of Defence, personal communication; Statement on the Defence Estimates, volume two, 1986, Cmnd. 9763-II; Regional Trends 21. 1986, Central Statistical Office.

areas for the purposes of Urban Programme legislation were redefined – symbolic in the sense that little in the way of additional resources is likely to flow from this.

Much more heavily implicated in the locality's relative prosperity is, as already intimated, the spatial impact of government defence procurement and support for aerospace (Table 4.5). Government spending on defence equipment in the South-West totalled £233 per head in 1985/86, not far short of the South East, the lead region in terms of defence equipment expenditure with £243 per head. The South West was well up on the peripheral regions including Wales with only £59 per head, the North £81, and Yorkshire and Humberside £34 – the North-West with a concentration of military aerospace, naval and nuclear industries was well up on the peripheral regions with £183 per head. A significant proportion of this expenditure is concentrated on firms specifically in the Bristol locality and, as argued in detail elsewhere (Lovering, 1985; Boddy and Lovering, 1986; Boddy 1987b), has supported a core of technologically advanced employment in the aerospace sector. Defence spending represents in effect an unofficial regional policy. As such however, it far outweighs overt regional assistance in total resources and, as

Table 4.5 demonstrates, runs largely counter to explicit regional assistance, giving most benefit to the more prosperous parts of the country. Similar conclusions have been drawn from studies of high technology, defence industries and their urban and regional impacts in the USA (Glasmeier *et al.*, 1983; Markusen, 1984; Castells 1984). This indicates the need to look closely not just at explicit urban and regional policy but at the spatial impacts of the full range of state policies and expenditures if we are to understand spatially differentiated processes of economic and employment change, and the specific role of the state in different localities.

Finally, to the extent that Bristol has 'succeeded', it has done so largely, in a sense, at the expense of other localities. This emphasises the competitive nature of the policy issues raised. In a crude sense insurance growth, for example, was achieved at the expense of London. Had it been possible to attract the companies involved to Wales or Glasgow they would obviously then have been lost to Bristol. Similarly, had aerospace projects been allocated to the companies' other sites in Derby or Lancashire rather than Bristol, or if Nottingham rather than Bristol had been selected as the tobacco company's headquarters, Bristol would have lost out. This is essentially a truism, of course, but emphasises the fact that in terms of the conscious spatial allocation of investment and employment by enterprises or by the effects of spatially directed policies, Bristol's success is relative rather than a reflection of some intrinsic growth capability. It is the other side of the coin to relative failure elsewhere.

The uneven distribution of the benefits of Bristol's economic performance and the tendency towards increasing polarisation within the locality emphasise, moreover, that economic growth and, by implication, policies directed to this end, have specific and unequal distributional impacts. Regional and urban policy and, to a large extent, local authority policies have been primarily oriented to growth rather than redistribution. The goals of such policies as far as many localities are concerned are in effect to emulate Bristol's 'success'. Without explicit concern with the distribution of 'success', to the extent that such policies succeed, they are however destined to reproduce the sort of uneven and polarised development evident in the Bristol case. And in the case of Bristol itself it is not clear, to return to the opening comments, how long the contradictions between riots and relocation appeal can be sustained.

NOTES

1 This longer study of economic and employment change, and the role of public policy in the Bristol region has been written up at length elsewhere, together with full details of information sources and the programme of research which was carried out. The study was carried out as part of the Economic and Social Research Council's 'Inner City in Context' research initiative, funded under grant number DO 3250012. Bristol was one of five localities studied in the initiative, along with Clydeside, Newcastle, the West Midlands and two areas of London. Within this framework, Bristol was explicitly selected as an example of a locality which, has proved more resilient than many in the face of deepening recession. The Bristol study as a whole is published as: *Sunbelt City? A Study of Economic Change in Britain's M4 Growth Corridor,* M. Boddy, J. Lovering and K. Basset, Oxford, Clarendon Press, 1986. An overview of the initiative as a whole is provided by *Urban Economic Adjustment: Five City Studies,* V. Hausner (ed.), Oxford, Clarendon Press, 1987, which includes a summary of the Bristol case study (Boddy, 1987a) and the other four case studies.

2 Figures and references to 'Bristol' in the text refer to the Travel to Work Area as defined by the Department of the Environment, unless otherwise noted. This coincides roughly with the area of Avon County, but excluding Bath to the east and Weston super Mare to the west.

REFERENCES

Boddy, M. J. (1987a), 'Bristol: Sunbelt City? A study of economic and labour market change', in V. Hausner (ed.), *Urban Economic Change: Five City Studies,* Clarendon Press, Oxford.

Boddy, M. J. (1987b), 'High technology industry, regional development and defence manufacturing: a case study in the UK Sunbelt', in Robson B.(ed.), *The Once and Future City,* London, Croom Helm.

Boddy, M. J. and Lovering, J. (1986), 'High technology industry in the Bristol sub-region: the aerospace/defence nexus', *Regional Studies,* 20(3), pp. 217-31.

Boddy, M. J., Lovering, J. and Bassett, K. (1986), *Sunbelt City? A Study of Economic Change in Britain's M4 Growth Corridor,* Oxford, Clarendon Press.

Castells, M. (1983), 'Towards the informational city? High technology, economic change and spatial structure: some exploratory hypotheses', *Working Paper* no. 430, University of California, Institute of Urban and Regional Development, Berkeley.

Gamble, A. (1981), *Britain in Decline: Political Strategy and the British State,* London, Macmillan.

Glasmeier, A. K., Markusen, A. and Hall, P. (1983), 'Defining high technology industries', *Working Paper* no. 407, University of California, Institute of Urban and Regional Development, Berkeley.

Goldsmith, M. (ed.) (1986), *New Research in Central/Local Relations,* London, Gower.

Hall, P. (1985), 'The geography of the fifth Kondratieff', in Hall, P. and Markusen, A. (eds.), *Silicon Landscapes,* London, Allen & Unwin, pp. 1-19.

Knight, Frank and Rutley (Chartered Surveyors) (1983), 'Office developments in the Western Corridor', London.

Lovering, J. (1985), 'Regional intervention, defence industries and the structuring of space in Britain: the case of Bristol and South Wales', *Environment and Planning D: Society and Space,* 3, pp. 85-107.

Markusen, A. (1984), 'Defense spending and the geography of high tech industries', *Working Paper* no. 423, University of California, Institute of Urban and Regional Development, Berkeley.

Marquand, J. (1979), 'The service sector and regional policy in the United Kingdom', *Research Series,* no. 29, Centre For Environmental Studies, London.

Rajan, A. (1984), *New technology and employment in insurance, banking and building societies,* Farnborough, Gower.

Soete, L. and Dosi, G. (1983), *Technology and Employment in the Electronics Industry,* London, Frances Pinter.

Stanback, T. M. (1979), *Understanding the Service Economy,* Baltimore and London, Johns Hopkins University Press.

Stanback, T. M. and Noyelle, T. J. (1982), *Cities in Transition,* Totowa, New Jersey, Allenheld & Osmun.

5

Local state response to economic decline: development and diversification strategies in Texas

JOE FEAGIN

University of Texas, Austin

Until recently, the grand idea of Texas has been that Texans are so power-ful and independent that they can consider themselves as somehow separate from the economic trials and limitations in the rest of the United States. This Texas idea is larger than life. Texas symbolises the quintessential American Dream, the place to go to work and to do well – the place to establish oneself without government interference. Texas has the best busi-ness climate. And it is alleged to be the place where a person can make his or her way in the world with little restriction on freedom.

Yet Texas is highly dependent, so dependent in fact that it is in many ways a political and economic colony steered from elsewhere. Take the infrastructure of Texas cities. Many roads, schools and public buildings have been built with major infusions of federal government money since the New Deal of the 1930s. Moreover, Texas businesses, and their workers, are heavily dependent on agricultural and energy markets whose prices are controlled in such places as Chicago, New York and Saudi Arabia (OPEC). This state's entrepreneurs and workers can be severely affected by a rise or fall in the market price of agricultural products or oil-gas products. In con-trast to the oil state image, no major oil company has its international head-quarters in Texas. Economic changes outside shape the Texas workplace and economy in the most fundamental ways, as most Texans learned during the major economic recession that suddenly hit the region in the mid-1980s.

ECONOMIC CRISIS IN THE SUNBELT: THE TEXAS AND HOUSTON CASES

Texas. Everyone knows that the prominent pillar of the Texas economy is oil. Less well known is that the oil economy is changing and is in the first stage of long-term crisiṣ. Texas has a long-run and a short-run problem. The long-term problem is that the oil reserves are gradually being depleted. In 1972-83 about 6 billion barrels of oil reserves were discovered, substantially less than the 10.6 billion barrels pumped in the same period. More immediate, however, is the sharp drop in oil prices which has occurred in the 1980s. In 1986 the contract price for benchmark West Texas oil dropped to $14-$18 a barrel, down sharply from the more than $30 secured a few years earlier. The oil industry was in a major recession, with rigs stacked up, crews laid off, and no new drilling ventures.

Falling oil prices are not the only source of Texas's economic problems. There is the overvalued US dollar. Between 1981 and 1985 the price of oil fell 32%, but the trade-weighted dollar increased by 56%. Studies by the Federal Reserve Bank of Dallas have shown that the strong dollar had a much more damaging effect on Texas manufacturing in the 1980s than did the drop in the price of oil, in part because many Texas manufacturers are outside the oil industry. However, the recent drop in the dollar should improve the situation (Dallas Federal Reserve Bank, 1985,1).

Houston. The crisis in Texas is mirrored in the economic capital of Texas, in Houston, the city often called the 'oil capital of the world'. In the 1980s the drop in the price of oil hit Houston hard. The unemployment rate grew more rapidly in the oil capital of Houston than in the nation, hitting 9.7% in 1983, up sharply from the 4% rate of the boom period. Between 1982 and 1984 the Bayou City lost 159,000 jobs. In 1983, Houston had 952 business failures with $3.8 billion in assets, a substantial increase from 1982; in 1984-86 the number of bankruptcies remained substantial. In February 1986 the jobless rate again jumped to 9.6%, not far below the peak rate in September 1983. Tonnage at the Port of Houston dropped sharply as well (Ramirez, 1986, 1E).

Fiscal crisis. The decline in the economy of the oil region of the Sunbelt brought hard times to local governments as well. The State of Texas gets about 20% of its tax income from oil and gas severance taxes, revenues which dropped by billions of dollars as oil and gas prices declined. In 1984-1986 the Texas legislature faced a series of fiscal crises, of multi-billion dollar deficits.

Major Texas cities are facing serious budget crises. In the 1986-1987 fiscal year Houston was facing a projected $70 million city government budget deficit. In mid-1986 Houston's Mayor Kathy Whitmire ordered a hiring freeze; and there was widespread discussion of the need to lay off hundreds of city employees and to cut city employee wages (Associated Press, 1986, B4).

THE QUEST FOR ECONOMIC DIVERSIFICATION:
THE STATE OF TEXAS RESPONSE

Public-private partnerships. In a capitalist society it is often in moments of economic crisis that we observe innovations in state intervention. After World War II corporate expansion in central cities led to great pressure on the federal state to assist in land clearance. Beginning in the 1950s federally funded, large-scale urban redevelopment and urban renewal programmes facilitated the development of office buildings, convention centres, and hotels. Billions of dollars were spent by local and federal governments to destroy older housing and other older buildings in central city areas. Private investment flowed into the construction of new buildings on the government cleared land. Local governments provided other substantial subsidies in the form of tax abatements, relaxation of regulations, and public capital investments in infrastructure (Fainstein *et al,* 1983; Feagin, 1984a).

By the 1970s, the massive renewal programmes had been replaced by new 'public-private partnerships.' In the face of the accelerated movement of corporations and capital investment on a global scale, numerous alliances have been forged at local levels of government between public officials and various business interests to promote new corporate investments.

The Governor's 'Division of Economic Development' (DED). Faced with the declining oil and gas economy, many business and political leaders in Texas have belatedly started seeking economic diversification. The type of new industry sought has varied. For example, in 1984 Governor Mark White participated in a national talk show with governors from other states on the subject of General Motors' new Saturn automobile division. The Saturn division's facilities are expected to employ 6,000 people, with another 14,000 jobs in related firms. Each of the governors on the talk show tried to outdo the others in promising support and subsidies for the division and its production facilities. Some promised non-union labour; all promised various types of government subsidies to construct the plant and train the workers. These local governments are in competition with one another for industry, what Goodman (1979) has called the 'public entrepreneurs.' On 6 March, 1985 Governor White wrote a letter to George Fox, the head of General Motors' real estate division. This was a cover letter for 84 separate proposals prepared by Texas towns and cities except Austin seeking the site. The governor's 4-page letter emphasises that Texas has the best business climate, the best industrial base, the best natural resources, the best education-technology base, and the best physical climate.

Mark White took office in 1983; he was the first Texas governor in recent times to pursue economic diversification as a goal for the Texas economy. He backed legislation to strengthen the Texas Economic Development Commission; he created an Interagency Council on Economic Development to coordinate the development efforts of nine existing agencies. And in 1983 he created a Division of Economic Development (DED) in his governor's office. The DED does not have a separate budget; and it has only ten employees. Its usual procedure is to work with the Texas Economic Development Commission (see below) on particular relocation and other development projects; the DED specialises in coordinating and mobilizing state agencies.

The DED worked to bring an advanced atomic energy facility to the Houston area; it played an important role in getting the Alumax company to locate a 1500-employee plant in Texarkana; it has held numerous seminars for small businesses (Richardson, 1984, 1B). Moreover, the DED played a role in getting a financial firm to locate its headquarters in Dallas, a Sea World entertainment facility to locate in San Antonio, and a Navy homeport facility to choose Corpus Christi. Early intervention by the DED convinced Kelly-Springfield Tire Co. to change its decision to close its East Texas plant and to put $250 million into a major expansion project. In October 1985 Mark White and DED assistants travelled to Japan in an unsuccessful attempt to get Toyota to locate a plant in Texas; the trip was also used to encourage Japanese investment in plants in Texas cities (DED, 1986, pp. 2-10).

Faced with the declining oil economy, many business and political leaders have gone for what is called the 'high-tech' solution. In this view what Texas needs is another Silicon Valley. The business elites in cities such as Austin, Houston, Dallas and San Antonio are aggressively seeking out high technology firms, many of which are headquartered in cities far from Texas. Thus, Mark White and his assistants played a central role in getting the advanced computer research laboratory, called Microelectronics and Computer Technology Corporation (MCC), to the Austin area. MCC brought 400 jobs to that city. Together with Texas Commerce Bank head Ben Love, Dallas computer billionaire H. Ross Perot, and other business leaders, Governor White put together a $50 million package of incentives, which included essentially free land and facilities at a University of Texas research centre, a promise to spend millions to improve the computer science department at the University of Texas, and special subsidies (e.g., low-interest home loans) for the professional employees at MCC (Richardson, 1984, 1B). With the State's help the city of Austin won the location of the elite computer think-tank MCC in competition with business elites in cities across the nation.

The Texas Economic Development Commission. The Texas Industrial Commission, a small state agency focusing on development, was created in the mid-1960s. It was renamed the Texas Economic Development Commission (TEDC) in the early 1980s and now operates in the major areas of industrial development, research and data services, and rural development. The TEDC conducts modest advertising campaigns on behalf of the state and provides information to firms seeking to locate in Texas. Between 1979 and 1982 the agency helped in 335 new plant locations or expansions. The TEDC works with local business and political leaders to assist them in dealing with corporate clients. And the TEDC works with other Texas agencies to set up job training programmes for specific industrial clients. Between 1979 and 1982 there were 142 training programmes (LBJ School of Public Affairs, 1985, pp. 66-7). Between 1971 and the mid-1980s over 300 companies used these state-financed training programmes, which involved 30,000 jobs. In addition, the finance department of TEDC administers aid programmes for business seeking to locate or to expand in Texas cities. The Industrial Revenue Bond programme reviews and approves tax-exempt revenue bonds to aid industrial and commercial firms. This tax-exempt financing is the major subsidy provided by local governments which can under this programme create special non-profit governmental authorities to issue tax-exempt bonds. The money received from bondholders is then loaned to companies at below-market interest rates. In addition, the TEDC has a programme of grants to city governments to assist them in subsidising corporate location, by industrial site preparation or by direct loans (TEDC, 1985, pp. 28-9).

A common selling point made by the DED and the TEDC is the 'good business climate' of Texas. The TEDC has published a booklet, entitled *Texas, Space to Expand* (1984), that is designed to attract high-tech companies, including space-tech firms. The first page emphasizes that Texas has the 'most favorable business climate' in the US for new and expanding companies. The booklet further reports on educational and business organisations in the state. Then it discusses the business climate, specifically mentioning labour productivity and the 'low level' of union activity. Further, Texas is emphasised as one of few states with 'right-to-work laws.' Texas has, the report notes, low taxes, low construction costs, and much room for expansion. Such an approach suggests that high-tech may be very good for outside corporations coming to locate plants in the Lone Star State, but may mean low wages and poor working conditions for rank-and-file Texans seeking work in this 'industry of the future.'

Texas leaders have only recently recognised that Texas has a serious economic crisis. As recently as 1982, the State of Texas was spending very little to recruit industry. In 1982 the State of Texas was spending 11 cents per capita in funding economic development agencies, compared to 94 cents for Louisiana, 63 cents for Oklahoma, and 68 cents for Arizona (Anonymous, 1982, 4D). The TEDC has a staff of 50 people. It has a small budget, only $2.3 million in 1984. Given the 1986-1987 budget crisis for the State of Texas, the TEDC is unlikely even to get a significant increase in its budget. In 1986 the TEDC reorganised itself into six regional business development centres (Anonymous, 1985, p. 6).

MARKETING THE CITY: THE HOUSTON ECONOMIC DEVELOPMENT COUNCIL

A New Private-Public Partnership. In 1986 there were more than 15,000 political units in the US with economic development programmes, the majority of which were at least a decade old. So the move of the Houston business elite in this direction in 1983-1984 was rather late. Late in 1983 the president of a men's clothiers, Richard Hite, established Pro-Houston, Inc., a small booster organization. Working with prominent Houstonians, Hite prepared a special handbook called 'What's Right About Houston'. Inspired in part by Hite's organisation, the Houston Chamber of Commerce set up, in the summer of 1984, the Houston Economic Development Council (HEDC), under the leadership of Kenneth Schnitzer, chairman of the board of Century Development Corporation, one of the ten largest real estate development firms in the US. Appointed as vice-chairmen on the council were top executives of the two local papers, top executives at the four largest banks, a major independent oil man and real estate developer, the local entrepreneur heading a city booster organisation called Pro-Houston, and the treasurer of the Harris County AFL-CIO. Two local politicians, the city mayor and the county executive, were also appointed to serve with the council's 50 business members. With only two exceptions, the HEDC's chair and vice-chairs are drawn from its real-estate-oriented growth coalition, which characteristically includes bankers, developers, and newspaper editors (Anonymous, 1984 pp. 9-13).

Most city growth coalitions have drawn up economic development plans and priorities before they presented them to the general public; but in the case of Houston the HEDC was created and funds were raised long before a board vision was articulated. Indeed, the first two years of the organisation were spent in articulating a plan of action and in raising millions of dollars for its efforts. The HEDC raised $6.3 million for its first two years of operation, mostly from the local business community. The HEDC was set up in a way that allows business contributions to be deducted as 'investment expenses.' The proposed budget for the second two years of operation was $6.2 million. In the fund drive for its second two-year (1987-1988) budget, energy-related firms pledged $517,000 with Texaco and Shell leading the list. Real estate and development interests pledged more, a total of $811,000 (O'Grady, 1986: 1D).

Public aid. Even though this is a private sector-generated council, city and other local governments have played a role in financing the council. Initially, the city contributed a $150,000 grant to HEDC for its first two-year budget. And in March 1986 the Houston City Council unanimously voted to match private contributions to the HEDC, up to $1.25 million annually. Mayor Kathy Whitmire marshalled her troops to try to defeat this grant; she argued that it would require new taxes. She got the black council member Ernest McGowen to sponsor a rider calling for minority business participation in the programme. But the proponents accepted the rider; and the city controller found $1.9 million in unused money in the budget which could be transferred to support the HEDC. The Greater Houston Political Action Committee, a business PAC, worked hard to get the the grant passed. Local business leaders called it the 'first true economic wedding of the public and private sectors' (Hart, 1986: 1A).

Yet the marriage has been a bit rough. In June 1986 several city council members were reported to be upset that the HEDC had not yet signed a contract with the city government. A few blamed the mayor for footdragging on the project, but at least as much footdragging came from the HEDC, some of whose leaders were fearful that a tie to government would mean closer public scrutiny of HEDC operations, some of which had been carried on in secrecy, and of HEDC expenditures (Hart, 1986: 6A). HEDC officials, including its president Donald Moyer, worried openly that if HEDC accepted $1.25 million in grants it would have to operate in a less secretive fashion. Moyer noted in April 1986 that companies considering locating in Houston often like to keep the decision-making process secret, and he expressed the hope that elected officials and journalists would respect 'the sacred character of our business transactions' (Gravois, 1986, 1A).

HEDC goals and strategies. The HEDC's broad goals are to generate a new diversity in the economic growth of Houston and to market the city more effectively to the outside world. In 1984 the HEDC pinpointed nine business categories as the most important to accent. These were, in order of importance, 1) biomedical research and development (linking NASA and the medical centre); 2) research and development laboratories; 3) instruments, particularly medical and computer equipment; 4) communications equipment; 5) chemicals, including plastics and drugs; 6) materials processing research; 7) computers and office machines; 8) engineering and architectural services; 9) distribution services. The notable omissions from the initial public relations efforts of the HEDC were oil, petrochemicals, construction, and most manufacturing areas. The ostensible reason for this was the huge loss in jobs in these areas during the 1982-1986 recession in Houston. The target areas were initially thought to have better prospects (Clark, 1985, pp. 9-10).

But soon after these target areas were publicly articulated a number of criticisms were advanced. Some critics pointed out that the top priority of biomedical research was without much precedent. Up to 1986 Houston's predominantly treatment-oriented medical centre had not spun off a major medical technological firm. Indeed, the largest med-tech firm, Intermedics, is based in the Angleton/Freeport area. It was created in 1973 by a member of the Dow Chemical family of entrepreneurs and has become a major manufacturer of pacemakers and other surgical products. While this company regards the Houston medical complex as a major customer, much of its developmental work seems to have been done in cooperation with Massachusetts and California firms and universities. For example, in developing a microcomputer pacemaker, Intermedics worked with ZyMos Corporation, a semiconductor company created by Intermedics in Sunnyvale, California, because Houston has so few computer and electronic companies (Clark, 1984, pp. 37-8).

The Center for Enterprise at Southern Methodist University did a study on Houston that suggested that the city's leaders should look to traditional manufacturing areas for diversification ideas, that is, to basic product areas such as food, printing, paper, pharmaceuticals, and cleaning products, rather than to exotic and faddish areas such as biotechnology, space technology, and computers. The latter are criticised as unrealistic targets for new economic development. In addition, a local citizen's group, the Greater Houston Tax Coalition, raised questions about HEDC goals and opposed the use of public funds to support HEDC. One leader of the group argued that such public-private partnerships were once sleazy, backroom deals, but now had been elevated to the status of civic virtue. The Coalition pressed for an emphasis on education and on reducing taxes and regulation, as well as for an emphasis on traditional strengths, rather than on biotechnology (Crown, 1986, n.p.).

Yet another ingredient in the mix of pressures leading to a reorientation of the HEDC goals is a recognition of research-oriented universities. A May 1986 issue of Houston, the local Chamber of Commerce magazine, published a unique article, 'What Can Houston Learn From Massachusetts?' The article and the attitude suggested in the title are unique, for Houston's leaders and citizenry have traditionally detested Yankees and their ideas. Yet here was an article praising a recent symposium which featured Massachusetts officials and educators lecturing to Houston business people. The basic theme of the forum was that the presence of major research universities in Boston had created the large reserve of innovative researchers and potential entrepreneurs necessary for economic health. Massachusetts officials pointed out that Houston has no major research institutions and that the University of Houston and Rice University do not get the federal and private research funding they need. Sponsored research at these latter two institutions ran $34 million in 1985, compared to MIT's $250 million. The officials argued that Houston's leaders should not go after high-tech electronics, but rather should build on traditional industrial areas, on NASA, on chemical and mechanical engineering firms, and on medical institutions (Clark, 1986, pp. 9-13).

These various pressures and developments have had an effect on HEDC goals and strategies. By mid-1986 the HEDC had come to recognise that cities with substantial high-tech industries had first-rate educational institutions and national research labs. One HEDC report noted there were no such labs in Texas. Texas ranks third in population, but tenth in overall federal government R & D expenditures. And, as the HEDC report also points out, Texas is the only state which reduced expenditures for education in 1985-1986. Thus the HEDC recently recommended that a community-wide task force be created by the Houston Chamber of Commerce to work to strengthen research and graduate training in local universities. The HEDC recommended that the Chamber of Commerce and other 'appropriate institutions' work to establish technology transfer entities or federal labs (HEDC, 1986c, p. 4). Another recommendation was that the Chamber work to increase the flow of federal government funds to Houston's medical centre and NASA facility. In all these cases, the emphasis is on state action to assist economic development.

The HEDC's new Strategic Priorities Agenda (1986c) emphasises the need to target energy, biotechnology, space enterprises, international business, and conventions/tourism. The exotic objectives of biotechnology and space have now been put into a list that includes three areas where Houston has a long history of economic success. In mid-1986 the HEDC president Donald Moyer admitted as much and argued that the HEDC should emphasise the city's role as world energy capital and as a tourist-convention centre, in spite of the current economic recession.

HEDC actions and public relations. To this point, the lion's share of the HEDC budgets has gone for communications, public relations, and marketing efforts (HEDC, 1986a, pp. 13-15). One major preoccupation of the council has been with the image of Houston. Both the local and the national media, especially the *New York Times,* have been repeatedly attacked by Houston's business leaders for portraying Houston in negative terms. Desiring to find out more about the image of the city nationally, particularly in business circles, the HEDC conducted a recent survey of national business leaders. The survey revealed that executives whose companies have had no contact with the Houston area did have a negative view of the region as a low-tech, single-industry 'cowtown'. HEDC leaders were horrified at these survey results showing Houston in a negative light as a place to do business. These opinion data have helped to place this goal as a top priority: to create positive attitudes about Houston among decision-makers, locally, nationally, and overseas (HEDC, 1986c, pp. 8-9).

In addition, New York and Chicago public relations firms have been hired to advertise the city. In 1985 the Chicago-based firm sent letters to 120 media outlets, primarily on the East Coast, protesting the negative image of the city and praising the city's virtues (Curtis and Novack, 1985, 43A). The HEDC has set up a number of other public relations programmes. One is called the Houston Marketing Network, which gets local executives to extol Houston's virtues to their business associates across the nation. Another programme is called 'Houston Beautiful', a beautification and anti-litter campaign. Yet another is 'Houston on the Move', an attempt to educate local residents about the $1 billion being spent annually through 1995 to improve traffic and transport problems in the city (Sheridan, 1986, p. 95). Yet another public relations programme is called 'Houston Proud', an effort designed to make Houstonians think more positively about the city. A special 'Houston Proud' jingle is being aired on radio and TV, and special welcoming delegations greet convention visitors at the airport (Anonymous, 1986, p. 4).

HEDC Action. In its first year the HEDC sponsored a European trade mission and worked with the state government to try to secure the GM Saturn facility and a navy homeport for the Houston-Galveston area. The private generation and corporate orientation of the HEDC do not preclude going after state-funded projects, such as military bases. Working with Galveston officials, the HEDC put together an $18 million 'incentive package' to get a proposed naval base (homeport) for a US battleship group. The naval base would mean $100 million in construction contracts, 2,400 construction jobs, and a $60 million annual payroll. Competing with sixteen other US cities the Houston group secured an amazing array of promised state subsidies, including provision of all roads and utilities needed by the Navy, an expediting of land permits for dredging, government funds to train civilians to work at the naval base and to rehabilitate local urban areas and their public infrastructures, and even to finance the base construction through a syndication of public and private investors, thus bypassing the need for a Congressional appropriation of construction funds. The HEDC interest in the project was underscored in a recent Houston magazine article, which noted that 'the homeport is also expected to lessen the housing surplus and encourage the development of defense and high-tech industries in Houston and Galveston' (Clark, 1985, pp. 12-13). It is not surprising that the HEDC, led by a real estate and banking coalition, would emphasise the housing and high-tech industrial growth implications of the Navy homeport.

The HEDC is also working to improve support for new businesses in the city. The 1986 Strategic Priorities Agenda recognises that the city has no early-stage venture capital funds, that many sectors of local business have been 'redlined' and consciously rejected by local and national banks, and that 'public sector sources of business financing are very limited' (HEDC, 1986c, p. 5).

The good business climate. A major expressed goal of the HEDC is to maintain Houston's 'good business climate' – which included anti-union ('right to work') laws, local government officials who think first of the implications of their actions for business, low taxes, balanced budgets, weak regulation, and governmental reluctance to expand social service programmes (HEDC, 1986c, pp. 11-12). Ironically, the same Strategic Priorities Agenda which plumps for this 'good business climate' moves to the problem of Houston's 'quality of life' on the very next page. There it is noted that Houston's many social costs and area weaknesses include traffic problems, flooding, water pollution, crime, air pollution, lack of parks, and sewage crises. Yet the HEDC Agenda proposes only *two* 'quality of life' initiatives, one focusing on beautification and the other on welcome-orientation services for visitors. There is no recognition that the low taxes associated with the good business climate are a *major* reason why the city has so many social costs of growth that are not being addressed. Dealing with water, pollution, crime, sewage and park problems, as well as other quality-of-life improvements will clearly require a sharp increase in local taxes (HEDC, 1986c, p. 14).

ANALYSIS AND INTERPRETATION

The Global Context of the Economic Crisis. Analysing the Sunbelt and its cities primarily against a backdrop of declining Frostbelt areas, which has been the focus of debate between convergence and uneven development theorists, is not enough. One must go beyond the regional and national context to examine the international setting of local economic crises. This is clearly a need in studying the case of Texas, as our data above show. All three economic development agencies discussed in this paper were created in 1983-1984 as a reaction to the Texas economic crisis. That economic crisis was the result of both national and global factors. It was primarily the result of two major changes in the world capitalist system, the sharp rise in the US dollar versus other currencies and the sharp increase in the price of oil. The dollar's rise resulted from a major flow of foreign capital into the US and from action by the US central government. The rise in the price of oil was primarily due to the decision by certain members of OPEC to pump large amounts of oil.

The economic crisis and the new public-private partnerships. The economic decline which hit Texas in the mid-1980s helped to generate a significant shift in and expansion of state intervention. The three economic development efforts discussed in this paper were created in 1983-1984, although the TEDC was actually an expanded and renamed agency that had existed in a truncated from since the mid-1960s. Suddenly, state intervention in the economy was expanded well beyond the enhancement of the good business climate. The state now engaged in aggressive activity – to recruit corporations from all over the world to Texas and to keep corporations already in Texas from leaving. Thus a recent brochure from the governor's DED begins with the statement that 'Texas has flourished under policies that have limited governmental interference with business', but then in the next paragraph notes that in order to sustain the local economy the State of Texas is aggressively pursuing investment in public facilities and economic development through 'public-private partnerships.' The implicit contradiction is simply ignored, as the rest of the brochure lists the ways in which Texas agencies have recently worked to assist corporate relocation and expansion. Also listed are state efforts to bring federal capital investments to the cities, including military projects.

There is now a new public-private partnership to recruit business to Texas. This relationship ranges in the degree of state direction and involvement. We might arrange the three agencies on a continuum:

State Production and Job Creation	State Financing and Coordination of Corporate Recruiting	State Financing Only
None	DED TEDC	HEDC

There are no major examples of state-directed and state-funded production programmes in Texas; there are no programmes to meet the economic crisis by creating jobs in the public sector. The DED and TEDC efforts are primarily directed at recruiting industries or preserving extant industry in Texas cities and counties. These agencies are reactive and proactive. On the reactive side, they respond to corporations seeking to locate in, or to leave, Texas cities and counties by providing information and state subsidies for infrastructure, industrial construction, and worker training. On the proactive side, both agencies engage in trade missions and some limited advertising for Texas as a place for industry. TEDC and DED efforts are funded with about $3 million annually in state funds, a very small percentage of the $18-$19 billion annual budget of the State of Texas.

Created entirely within the private business sector, the HEDC, in contrast, involves the state primarily as a financial partner. Created by the Houston Chamber of Commerce – which is a larger organisation than the US Chamber of Commerce – the HEDC is an extreme example of a *private*-public partnership, with only modest state participation. Its guiding board is drawn for the most part from business corporations; its staff constitutes a private bureaucracy located adjacent to the private offices of the Houston Chamber of Commerce in a new downtown office building. Most of its funding in the first two years came from the private sector. However, in the next two years the expectation is that funding from the city and county governments will be about half the HEDC budget. It is also noteworthy that the HEDC budget is a bit larger than that of the DED and TEDC put together. The activities of HEDC also differ to some extent from the DED and TEDC. While all three agencies get involved in corporate retention and relocation efforts, efforts involving the HEDC working in close cooperation with the state, only the

HEDC has developed a million-dollar public relations and advertising programme designed to market Houston as an excellent place to do business. The TEDC budget for advertising Texas, in contrast, is limited to $90,000. In addition, the HEDC has been much more aggressive in identifying new industries to be sought and cultivated, such as biotechnology and computer firms, than have the State of Texas agencies (Nesenholtz, 1986).

THEORIES OF THE STATE RECONSIDERED

Accumulation and legitimacy. State intervention strategies in response to economic decline and the threat of corporate location provide useful data for understanding the role of the local and regional state in a capitalistic society. We can now assess the Texas data in light of the growing body of material on the state, with particular reference to the activities of the local state. Numerous authors have noted that the state in a bourgeois-democratic society has two basic, but often contradictory goals: facilitating capital accumulation and maintaining legitimacy among the voters (O'Connor, 1973; Offe, 1975; Jessop, 1983). The state must maintain a healthy capitalistic economy by taking such actions, including expenditures, as are necessary to facilitate corporate production, expansion, and profit making. Pressure for this state action increases in an economic crisis.

Most recently, Clark and Dear (1984) have developed a suggestive analysis of state bureaucracy and function. They distinguish between the 'state apparatus', which is the total of these mechanisms and agencies through which the state operates; the 'sub-apparatus', which is the set of agencies implementing a specific state goal; and the 'para-apparatus', the auxiliary agencies separate from the state but performing state functions. Going beyond O'Connor's emphasis on expenditures, they distinguish four functions of the state apparatus: consensus, production, integration, and administration. For Clark and Dear (1984, pp. 50-2) the local state is an important sub-apparatus that deals primarily with consensus. It is viewed as important in the maintenance of legitimacy and social control, in maintaining consensus by means of parties, elections, and targeted government action.

State apparatus. All three agencies reviewed in this paper are, in the broadest sense, part of the state apparatus. The DED and the TEDC are clearly examples of what Clark and Dear call the state sub-apparatus, that part of the state which pursues specific goals. In this case, the goal is that of enhancing economic development. The HEDC, in contrast, fits loosely into the para-apparatus category, since it is a privately-created independent organisation functioning in ways similar to state-created organisations such as the DED and TEDC and substantially funded by local state tax revenues. Indeed, the HEDC suggests the need to amplify the Clark-Dear typology by splitting the para-apparatus category into two types – (1) independent agencies created and funded by the state, and (2) independent agencies created by the private sector and funded by the state. The Clark-Dear analysis may draw too heavily from nation-states and cities where the state is centralised and strong. However, in the case of these Texas and Houston examples we find a relatively weak state dominated by capital. Not only is the HEDC a creation of the private sector (i.e., the Houston Chamber of Commerce), but it also draws on state aid in its own terms – and with some reluctance. The TEDC and DED are relatively late arrivals on the Texas economic scene; they are also linked to the powerful business elite that in effect controls the local states in Texas. It is only as that business elite has come to see the dangers of an undiversified economy that the expansion of state agencies into production-recruiting matters has been permitted. The traditional view of the Texas business elite has been called 'cowboy capitalism,' the view that the good business climate and the free market do not need any state help in their basic operation. That view has changed markedly in the past four years, with the downturn in the Texas economy. Today the 'corporatist' view is growing in strength, the view that a public-private partnership is essential in working for a diversified and reinvigorated Texas economy.

Another revision is required in the Clark-Dear typology. Many European countries have strong central states with weak local states. This may be one reason analysts like Clark and Dear see local states primarily in terms of their consensus and pass-through functions. But the US state is less centrally concentrated, is more federalist than European states. In many cases, local states in the US have a considerable role to play in enhancing production. Indeed, the local state is itself divided into a variety of types, ranging from suburban and city government to county and regional governments (e.g., the State of Texas). These different levels often have different functions and responsibilities within a federalist system. In addition, it is important to note the loosely structured, even ad hoc, character of some state structures. The literature on the local state, which is admittedly thin, neglects its organisation and structure. The three agencies examined in this paper vary in their organisation structures and embeddedness in pre-existing state structures. The TEDC is the most 'bureaucratic', in the Weberian sense, of the three. It has a firm organisation chart with 50 employees. It is a separate state agency with its own budget and grounding in the older Texas Industrial Commission. It was created by legislative action. The DED, in contrast, is made up of employees set aside by the governor, within his existing executive office, to act of behalf of capital in Texas. There is no separate budget for the DED, and no legislative action created the unit. Indeed, the placement of the DED outside existing state agencies gives it power to coordinate and integrate the sometimes competitive Texas government agencies in regard to a specific project, such as recruiting the GM Saturn plant to Texas. The HEDC is well-organised, with dozens of employees and its own budget, but its structure is completely independent of all pre-existing state structures. It is a newly created private bureaucracy, but one which is well-integrated into its parent, the Houston Chamber of Commerce.

Functions of the state. Clark and Dear provide a more detailed picture of the functions of the state than does O'Connor. O'Connor provides a useful distinction between state accumulation and legitimation which Clark and Dear elaborate into four functions: production, consensus, integration, and administration. O'Connor discusses production in terms of 'social investments'. Yet this idea of production needs development beyond the expenditures governments make for industrial parks and business infrastructure requirement. Such expenditures have been commonplace in Texas cities since World War II. But there are other kinds of actions that local states can take to enhance production into their bailiwicks. As we have seen in the case of the TEDC, DED, and HEDC, these additional actions can include marketing and advertising through the geographical space of a particular state sub-apparatus or para-apparatus, educational reforms, the coordination of formerly competing state agencies, and the creation of a new high-tech vision among the business leadership in Texas. Indeed, we have seen a remarkable emphasis in all three agencies on the importance of space-related and bio-medical-related enterprises as the type of industry Texas cities need for diversification.

The consensus-building function of the three Texas agencies is, interestingly enough, seen most clearly in the HEDC. The DED and TEDC have done very little marketing of the new visions of economic diversification and of high-tech *to Texans*. It is the HEDC that has tried to build an acceptance of a positive vision of Houston and its future among Houstonians in its 'Houston Proud' and related public relations campaigns. There is clearly a desire in that city's business elite to get the backing of the citizenry for a rosier view of a bio-tech, med-tech, space-tech city.

Clark and Dear do not give much attention to the role of the local state in fostering production. Indeed, they see the local state as critical to consensus, not to production. But, as our examples clearly indicate, theoretical analysis needs to go beyond this consensus function of the local state to consider its part in facilitating exchange-value transactions. The local state is also a sub-apparatus that plays a role in production, in enhancing the 'welfare' of the local economic system. Since no individual capitalist is able to maintain the aggregate conditions for capital accumulation, the state through the sub-apparatus of the local state operates to ensure the profitability of capitalism through social capital expenditures, marketing, and coordination.

CONCLUSION

Miliband has noted that modern capitalism 'depends to an ever greater extent on the bounties and direct support of the state, and can only preserve its "private" character on the basis of public help' (Miliband, 1969, p. 72). This view is conclusively supported in our data. The growth and expansion of state agencies in Texas are a direct response to an economic crisis whose proportions are too large to be handled without new state assistance.

The form of this assistance varies, but the aggressive feeding at the public tax trough is evident. Indeed, it is the need for expanded public tax support for private enterprise that highlights the contradictory character of modern capitalism. On the one hand, there is a demand for public tax support for a troubled private enterprise economy. On the other hand, there is the emphasis on a 'good business climate' as essential to that private enterprise economy, a 'climate' which by definition means low taxes. And there is the related contradiction between the recognition (e.g., in HEDC reports) that Texas cities have 'quality of life' problems compared to northern cities and the fierce desire to maintain the good business climate. It is, of course, the higher taxes of those northern cities that give those cities the quality-of-life advantages. That is, someone must pay the higher taxes needed to improve the quality of life in Texas cities and to fund expanded economic development efforts. This need for increased taxes will be foisted off on the general citizenry, if the Texas business elite has its way. About fifty years ago a prominent political analyst noted that 'business men collectively constitute the most class-conscious group in American society. As a class they are more highly organised, more easily mobilised, have more facilities for communication, are more like-minded, and are more accustomed to stand together in defence of their privileges than any other group' (Schattschneider, 1935, p. 287). This analysis still rings true for Texas.

REFERENCES

Anonymous (1980), 'Houston: International City', *Fortune,* 14, July, pp. 35-58.

Anonymous (1982), 'Money Matters: State Lags in Development Funding', *Houston Post,* 15 November, p. 4D.

Anonymous (1984), 'City Leadership Presents Economic Development Plan', *Houston 55,* July, pp. 9-13.

Anonymous (1985), 'Public/Private Efforts to Resources', *Austin Business Journal,* 25 November – 1 December, p. 6.

Anonymous (1986), 'Houston Proud: HEDC's New PR Push', *Houston Business Journal,* 24 February, p. 4A.

Associated Press (1986), 'Cities Brace for Oil-slump Cutbacks', *Austin American-Statesman,* 22 June, p. B4.

Chase-Dunn, Christopher (1984), 'Urbanisation in the World System', in Smith, Michael Peter (ed.), *Cities in Transformation,* Beverly Hills, California, Sage, pp. 111-22.

Clark, Gordon L. and Dear, Michael J. (1984), *State Apparatus,* Boston, Allen & Unwin.

Clark, Rosanne (1984), 'Part 2. High Tech on the Horizon', *Houston 55,* May, pp. 33-8.

Clark, Rosanne (1985), 'Development Council Maps Economic Strategy', *Houston 56,* February, pp. 9-13.

Clark, Rosanne (1986), 'What Can Houston Learn from Massachusetts?', *Houston 57,* May, pp. 9-13.

Crown, Judith (1986), 'HEDC Sets Goals for Growth by Year 2000', *Houston Chronicle,* 2 April, pp. 1, 4.

Curtis, Tom and Novack, Janet (1985), 'Bad Reputation', *Dallas Times Herald, Southwest,* 24 March, pp. 43-4.

Dear, Michael J. and Clark, Gordon L. (1981), 'Dimensions of Local State Autonomy', *Environment and Planning,* 13, pp. 1277-94.

Division of Economic Development (DED) (1986), 'Economic Development', Austin, Texas Governor's Office, typewritten.

Fainstein, Susan S. *et. al.* (1983), *Restructuring the City,* New York, Longman.

Feagin, Joe R. (1984a), *The Urban Real Estate Game,* Englewood Cliffs, NJ, Prentice-Hall.

Feagin, Joe R. (1984b), 'The Role of the State in Urban Development: The Case of Houston, Texas', *Environment and Planning D: Society and Space 2,* pp. 447-60.

Feagin, Joe R. (1985), 'The Social Costs of Houston's Growth', *International Journal of Urban and Regional Research 9,* June, pp. 164-84.

Federal Reserve Bank of Dallas (1985), 'Texas Manufacturing Affected More by Dollar Than by Oil Prices', *DallasFed,* September, pp. 1-4.

Goodman, Robert (1979), *The Last Entrepreneurs,* New York, Simon & Schuster.

Gravois, John (1986), 'HEDC Weighs Strings Attached to Tax Dollars', *Houston Post,* 14 April, p. 1A.

Hart, Joe (1986), 'Council Wins Fight to Fund HEDC', *Houston Business Journal,* 24 March, p. 1A.

Hill, Richard Child (1984), 'Urban Political Economy', in Smith, Michael Peter (ed.), *Cities in Transformation,* Beverly Hills, Sage, pp. 123-38.

Hobratschk, Marty (1986), 'Officials Expect Texas Bank Failures', *Daily Texan,* 26 June, p. 9.

Houston Economic Development Council (HEDC), (1985), 'Houston Works for Space Commercialisation', Houston, HEDC, pamphlet.

Houston Economic Development Council (HEDC) (1986a), *Fund Campaign Report,* Houston, HEDC, typewritten.

Houston Economic Development Council (HEDC) (1986b), 'An Overview of the Houston Economy', *Houston Works for Business Report,* January, pp. 1-3.

Houston Economic Development Council (HEDC) (1986c), 'Strategic Priorities Agenda', Houston, HEDC, typewritten.

Jessop, Bob (1983), *Theories of the State,* New York, New York University Press.

Lauria, Mickey (1986), 'Toward a Specification of the Local State: State Intervention Strategies in Response to a Manufacturing Plant Closure', *Antipode,* 18, pp. 39-65.

Lyndon B. Johnson (LBJ) School of Public Affairs (1985), *Policy Research Report: The Effects of State Government on Economic Development in Texas Cities,* Austin, University of Texas, Report No. 63.

Miliband, Ralph (1969), *The State in Capitalist Society,* London, Weidenfeld & Nicolson.

Nesenholtz, David (1986), DED Director of Finance, interview by phone, 2 July.

O'Connor, James (1973), *The Fiscal Crisis of the State,* New York, St. Martin's Press.

Offe, Claus (1975), 'Theses on the Theory of the State', *New German Critique,* No. 6, Fall, pp. 137-47.

O'Grady, Eileen (1986), 'Nearly $1 Million Pledged to HEDC', *Houston Post,* 5 May, p. 1D.

Ramirez, Gladys (1986), 'Houston Travels Slow Road to Recovery', *Houston Post,* 29 December, p. 1E.

Richardson, Tim (1984), 'State Leaders Target Economic Development', *Houston Business Journal,* 6 August, p. 1B.

Sassen-Koob, Saskia (1984), 'The New Labour Demand in Global Cities', in Smith, Michael Peter (ed.), *Cities in Transformation,* Beverly Hills, Sage, pp. 139-72.

Schattschneider, E. E. (1935), *Politics, Pressures, and the Tariff,* New York, Prentice-Hall.

Sheridan, Mike (1986), 'Houston: A Plan for Diversification', *Spirit,* 1 April , pp. 81-99.

Smith, Michael Peter (1987), *The Political Economy of Urban Problems,* New York, St. Martin's Press.

Soja, Edward, Morales, Rebeca, and Goetz Wolff (in press), 'Urban Spatial Structuring and Spatial Change in Los Angeles', *Economic Geography.*

Sweeney, Paul (1985), 'Widgets for Wages', *Third Coast,* 4, pp. 56-66.

Texas Economic Development Commission (TEDC) (1984), *Texas: Space to Expand,* Austin, TEDC.

Texas Economic Development Commission (TEDC) (1985), *Doing business in Texas,* Austin, TEDC and Price Waterhouse, printed report.

Wallerstein, Immanuel (1979), *The Capitalist World-Economy,* Cambridge, Cambridge University Press.

6

Private sector urban regeneration: the Scottish experience

ROBIN BOYLE
University of Strathclyde

This essay describes a contradiction in contemporary British urban policy. To be more precise, it examines a series of issues raised by the attempt to promote and develop private instruments as the solution for urban problems. Private sector-led urban regeneration stands in sharp contrast to the recent tradition of British urban policy where many of the mechanisms and resources for urban change have been found in the public domain. The implications of this attempt to reorientate policy are explored by examining the development of urban regeneration policy in Scotland, particularly in the city of Glasgow.

After a brief review of the evolution of urban policy in Scotland, the essay focuses on the activities of the Scottish Development Agency – a public body that has skilfully adapted these public traditions to accommodate the emerging ethos of a government committed to constraining public expenditure and promoting the benefits of privatism. The impact of this in Scotland, illustrated by a case study of contemporary developments in Glasgow, is used to address the following questions:

1. To what extent does current urban policy in Scotland represent a significant realignment between the public and the private sector in determining the objectives, direction and scope of urban regeneration?

2. Are the symbols of privatism important and in examining recent changes can we distinguish between political symbolism and substantive policy shift?

3. How has the state engineered this shift and which agencies of government – working with private sector interests – have taken the lead in reorientation policy? Is it possible to identify a coherent strategy that drives changes in policy?

4. What are the long-term implications of a 'strategy' that seeks to alter responsibility for addressing and searching for solutions to Scotland's urban problems? What does it mean for urban Scotland? What are

the implications for other aspects of domestic policy? Who benefits and who ultimately loses?

THE DEVELOPMENT OF URBAN POLICY IN SCOTLAND

Urban Scotland presents a fascinating case study of policy realignment by a government ideologically and politically committed to pursuing private solutions for public problems. For the problems of Scotland's cities created a legacy of policy that ran in the opposite direction: using public solutions for problems created by the private sector. This was by no means a post-Second World War phenomenon. As early as 1865, the major towns and cities in Scotland could demonstrate municipal concern and action across a wide range of social, physical and economic problems. An interesting quote used by Smout (1986) provides colourful evidence of this trend:

> [In Glasgow a citizen] may live in a municipal house; he may walk along the municipal street, or ride on the municipal tramcar and watch the municipal dust cart collecting the refuse which is to be used to fertilise the municipal farm. He may then turn into the municipal market, buy a steak from an animal killed in the municipal slaughterhouse, and cook it by the municipal gas stove. For his recreation he can choose amongst municipal libraries, municipal art galleries and municipal music in the municipal parks. Should he fall ill, he can ring his doctor up on the municipal telephone, or he may be taken to the municipal hospital in the municipal ambulance by a municipal policeman. Should he be so unfortunate to get on fire, he will be put out by a municipal fireman, using municipal water; after which he will, perhaps, forego the enjoyment of a municipal bath, though he may find it necessary to get a new suit in the municipal market. . . , (p. 45, quoting from R.E.C. Lond, 1903).

Moreover, extensive use of legislation in the 1930s and 40s by energetic City and Burgh authorities laid the foundation for the development of a 'public' city, and in particular the creation of a post-war housing market that was to be dominated by the public sector. For example, in 1984 some 67% of households in Glasgow (population 720,000) lived in dwellings owned and let by public landlords. Indeed, Scotland as a whole has a higher proportion of households living in the public sector than certain East European countries.

In addition, the spatial concentrations of economic and social problems – the result of Scotland's industrial decline – mixed with an intermittent clamour for 'Home-Rule', produced a range of political responses that gave Scotland a degree of State planning of its industrial and urban structure that was not repeated in England and Wales (Keating and Midwinter, 1983). Even in the mid-1970s, when throughout the rest of the UK the public sector was found wanting in a number of crucial areas of urban policy, Scotland had a powerful public bureaucracy that was given remarkable free rein to address the country's economic and increasingly urban problems.

With the exception of the Urban Development Corporations, England and Wales has seen only limited use of public agencies as a response to urban problems. In Scotland, the recent history of urban policy and more particularly urban innovation is inseparable from the activities of just such an organisation: the Scottish Development Agency (SDA).[1] It is this *public* agency, in the vanguard of policy development, that looks to the *private* sector to take a pivotal role in urban regeneration. For not only has the SDA sought to reduce the traditional role of (local) government in urban regeneration, but it has developed various instruments that are aimed at enticing the private sector to assume greater responsibility for urban change. But before discussing this aspect of policy it is useful to briefly review the evolution of the SDA's role in Scottish urban policy.

The SDA was originally conceived as the flagship of traditional state intervention in a troubled economy. Created by the Labour government in 1975, the SDA was based on some 35 years' experience of active central government involvement in the Scottish economy: encouraging the relocation of industry from England and overseas, the establishment of a public sector housing agency, the building of five New Towns, and countless attempts to deal with the physical, social and economic problems of the larger cities, notably Glasgow. Some have also argued that, in part, the SDA was a political response to the ascendancy of the separatist Scottish Nationalist Party (Keating and Midwinter, 1983). Whatever the reasons, the SDA was given the broad and challenging remit of reviving the Scottish economy and coordinating industrial strategy with environmental improvement. The Agency was presented with the necessary powers through absorbing the functions of existing agencies: industrial estates, assistance for small firms, clearance of derelict land. With these powers the SDA developed the capacity, if not always the inclination, for direct intervention at the level of the firm. In the early years it was not, however, envisaged that the Agency would – beyond its environmental powers – take an active role in what is now described as urban policy (Keating and Boyle, 1986: pp. 21, 85-114).

Hence, instead of generating a wholly new approach to urban policy, the Agency built on a well established Scottish tradition of area intervention and developed a range of strategies that impacted directly on local, mainly urban, economies. Nonetheless, over a relatively short period, the SDA shaped a highly sophisticated style of urban regeneration, focusing on a combination of economic, physical and environmental renewal (Boyle and Wannop, 1982). The activities of the SDA in area intervention (summarised in Table 6.1) effectively evolved through four main stages.

TABLE 6.1: AREA PROJECTS INITIATED AND/OR
CO-ORDINATED BY THE SDA

Name	Project type	Duration	Budget (SDA) (£m)
GEAR	Urban Renewal	1976-1987	470.5 (78)
Clydebank	Task Force	1980–	69.9 (25)
Glengarnock	Task Force	1978-1984	22.5 (19)
Leith	Integrated Project	1981-1986	54.7 (12)
Blackness	Integrated Project	1981-1984	8.1 (6)
Motherwell	Integrated Project	1982-1987	179.7 (37)
Dundee	Integrated Project	1982-1987	86.0 (18)
Port Dundas	Integrated Project*	1983-1986	1.9 (.9)
Coatbridge	Integrated Project	1983-1988	28.0 (10)
Govan	Integrated Project**	1986-1991	14.1 (5)
ASSET	Self Help Project	—	(3)
Kilmarnock	Self Help Project	1983-1986	1.5 (.5)
Wigtown	Self Help Project	1983-1986	1.0 (.6)
Denny/B'bridge	Self Help Project	1983-1986	3.5 (3)
Fraserburgh	Self Help Project	1983-1986	1.0 (.3)
Arbroath	Self Help Project	1984-1987	2.3 (.8)
Highland/Perth	Private Initiative	n/a	n/a
Inverclyde	Private Initiative	1985-1990	c60.0 (5)
Glasgow Action	Private Initiative	n/a	n/a
Edinburgh	Future Initiative ?		
Aberdeen	Future Initiative ?		

* Local authority-led : Glasgow District Council.
** Local authority-led : Strathclyde Regional Council.
n/a: Data not available.
Source: This table is constructed from various reports published by the SDA including the Annual Reports: 1984, 1985 and 1986. Further details on each Project are presented in Keating and Boyle, 1986, pp. 94-7 and 112-13.

STAGE 1: TRADITIONAL COMPREHENSIVE URBAN RENEWAL (1976-78)

With considerable reluctance, the SDA was directed by the Secretary of State for Scotland to take control of a major urban renewal programme in the east-end of Glasgow – what became known as the Glasgow Eastern Area Renewal (GEAR). This programme, begun in 1976 and scheduled for completion in 1987, has seen the SDA coordinate public expenditure in the order of £200 million, including some £78 million of its own resources, and generate an equivalent amount of private investment (Leclerc and Draffan, 1984; Nairn, 1983). Despite the extensive publicity circulated by the SDA, GEAR should not be perceived as the beginning of a new style of urban regeneration but perhaps embodies the conclusion of a traditional, comprehensive, approach to urban renewal. Nonetheless, GEAR is significant in that it afforded the SDA an opportunity to gradually orientate what was effectively welfare policy in the direction of urban economic policy, backed up by considerable public investment. Building on the experience of managing the GEAR project, the SDA began laying the foundations for a different approach to urban problems in Scotland.

STAGE 2: DEVELOPING THE CAPACITY FOR
SUCCESSFUL ECONOMIC INTERVENTION (1978-1980)

Towards the end of the 1970s and once again under strong pressure from the Scottish Office, the SDA was asked to take on the role of the 'fire brigade', coming to the aid of specific communities faced with the economic and social implications of major plant closure. The development of Scottish Office/SDA Task Forces in Glengarnock (a steel closure area) and in Clydebank (following the closure of the Singer Sewing Machine factory) proved to be the forerunners of a particular style of Agency intervention in the Scottish space economy (Gulliver, 1984). In both areas, the SDA established major programmes of economic and environmental regeneration, targeting their activities on industrial premises, small-firm assistance and extensive, and very expensive, land engineering. Both Task Forces were effectively controlled by the SDA with little formal involvement by local government or the private sector. But the objectives and the activities of both Task Forces were predominantly aimed at stimulating private industry, particularly stabilising if not actually increasing local employment. This second phase in the evolution of urban economic policy is also significant in that during the early 1980s the SDA developed the capacity to become selective in terms of the problems that it was prepared to tackle. Reflecting government attitudes, the SDA did not directly intervene, in an economic or welfare role, when the Scottish vehicle manufacturing industry – at Linwood and Bathgate – collapsed.

STAGE 3: AREA PROJECTS FOR ECONOMIC DEVELOPMENT (1981-1984)

With growing confidence during this period, the SDA sought to extend its capacity for undertaking economic intervention by developing and expanding its own urban policy framework. Using different criteria, based on the identification of growth potential, it selected a number of locations that were afforded the status of what became known as 'Area Projects', (see Table 6.1). Despite the initial reluctance of the SDA to address itself to urban problems, as events have shown, area policy came to occupy a pivotal position in the SDA, with some 60% of all expenditure being directed to identifiable Area Projects. Much of this expenditure was consumed by major land engineering projects with a very much smaller proportion being spent on aid to industry, reflecting the change in Agency policy introduced in 1979 (Boyle and Wannop, 1982).

The significance of Area Projects extends beyond the activities of the SDA. Using non-binding agreements between the SDA, the respective local authorities, other public agencies, such as the MSC or Health Boards, and representatives of local companies, these initiatives are based upon 'Project Agreements' that loosely determine the objectives, the timing and the funding of each project. Normally, the SDA coordinates the activities of the different partners but it does not remove nor alter the legal responsibilities of the other participants. Moreover, political control still rests with the respective levels of accountable government.

STAGE 4: PUBLIC-PRIVATE-PARTNERSHIP (1985—)

Since 1984, the SDA has attempted to shift its financial and administrative involvement in urban policy. Table 6.1 shows how there has been a noticeable change towards support for the 'self help' model where the local community, public and private, is expected to develop, motivate and organise local economic development programmes. The SDA also chose to support the emerging Enterprise Trust[2] movement, selecting a number of trusts – in smaller towns such as Fraserburgh and Arbroath – as the vehicle for implementing economic policies. At this time the Agency also introduced Local Enterprise Grants for Urban Projects (LEG-UP) – a Scottish equivalent of the English Urban Development Grant – that was initially targeted at leveraging private investment for new projects in areas of high unemployment. As with the experience of UDAG in the US, early ambitions for the programme have given way to commercial constraints, with substantial public investment in office, retail and residential development, often located in city and town centre locations, with fairly limited employment benefits (Boyle, 1985a).

Two of the latest projects – in Inverclyde and in Glasgow's city centre – moved away from the Project Agreement model entirely, introducing more flexible management and elevating, in theory at least, the role of the private sector. The aim was to increase the 'business' component in each initiative and replace increasingly scarce public funds with private investment. The evolution of policy in the mid-1980s also witnessed the selection of urban initiatives in a number of cities and selected communities that did not figure in the calculus of economic dislocation or social deprivation. The choice of Glasgow city centre, the embryonic proposals for central Edinburgh, even tentative ideas for Aberdeen – oil 'capital' of Scotland – had much more to do with commercial objectives of the business community than with the original aims of urban policy. On the one hand this new policy focus may be interpreted as removing unnecessary public involvement in local economic development. But on the other, it might be little more than a convenient justification for disengagement by the SDA from problem economies.

GLASGOW: A SUITABLE CASE FOR TREATMENT

The most striking example of this new approach is the SDA's support of Glasgow Action, a 'public-private' partnership based in the commercial core of the city. This initiative represents a radical departure from the substance and style of the earlier projects, since it focuses on the opportunities for business development in the service sector. Glasgow Action – formed around a group of prominent city businessmen – was one of the products of a major study of development potential in the city centre, funded by the SDA and conducted by consultants, McKinsey and Company. They recommended that public action should seek to strengthen Glasgow's role as a major service sector and that such a strategy should be led by a private organisation,[3] (McKinsey, 1984; McKinsey 1985; and SDA, 1986). Although two leading local politicians became board members of Glasgow Action, leadership control and direction is firmly located in the private sector, pursuing objectives that reflect the needs and aspirations of the business community in the city.

Both McKinsey and the SDA had been attracted by the US model of a partnership between private enterprise and public authority, where local business committees promote plans for city development. Such organisations became very popular in the 1950s, with numerous cities eager to underwrite private downtown development projects with Federal funds made available by Urban Renewal legislation. The model for business initiative in the guidance of urban renewal was undoubtedly the Allegheny Conference in Pittsburgh, where private industrial and financial interests in the city – not least the Mellon Bank – promoted the development of the 'Golden Triangle', attracting some 171 million dollars in public support, (Boyle and Rich, 1984; Lublove, 1969). This spectacular development became the model for similar private initiatives in Philadelphia, Baltimore, St Louis and other large US cities. A revised interpretation of business-led redevelopment efforts in the 1970s also attracted the attention of visiting officials and businessmen from Scotland. This glistening hotels, convention centres and Festival Markets in older industrial cities such as Baltimore, Boston and Detroit proved irresistible. But such commercial attractions tend to obscure the wider urban costs of determining urban regeneration on the basis of private interests (Boyle, 1985b; Judd, 1979).

Glasgow Action was born out of US public-private partnerships and was influenced in no small way by the attractive combination of private leadership and private investment in the city of Minneapolis, Minnesota. Visitors from the SDA were particularly impressed by the activities of leading companies in the city – such as Dayton-Hudson and Control Data – who supported a wider conception of corporate involvement in urban affairs as well as being highly influential in downtown commercial development. The model for Glasgow was to combine the strictly commercial goals of the downtown development committee with the somewhat more altruistic objectives promoted through the private sponsorship of community development. Perhaps most important of all, Glasgow Action came to inherit the American belief that urban regeneration depends first and foremost on creating the correct conditions for private investment. To quote from their first brochure:

> Glasgow Action is the name of a group of leading business people and politicians – and of the visionary plan they have for Glasgow's future, for the Glasgow of the 21st Century. The thinking behind the plan is that the development of a strong business and consumer service industry base will stimulate the regeneration of the city as a whole. . .; it aims to recreate Glasgow's entrepreneurial spirit (Glasgow Action, 1985).

Considering the scale of Glasgow's problems and the resulting public response, the activities of Glasgow Action and the promotion by the Council of other urban economic policies for the city present an opportunity to examine what this policy realignment means in practice. While it is much too early to review, let alone evaluate, Glasgow Action and other aspects of private sector involvement in the city's urban regeneration, four components of policy development warrant further comment. A discussion of the costs and the benefits of policy orientation in Glasgow indicates how similarly deprived cities in the U.K. may address their problems of economic transformation.

SYMBOLS OF REGENERATION

The first, and perhaps most critical feature of the approach adopted in Glasgow, was a conscious attempt to alter the perception of the city – of residents and outsiders – through careful and controlled manipulation of signals. The traditional abrasive, violent, image of Glasgow, coupled with the decades of economic decline that served to produce its harsh physical and social environment, was at the very heart of the problem (Daiches, 1977). Unless the image could be changed, especially that one projected to the outside world, any attempt to manufacture local economic, social or physical improvement would be nullified by a failure to attract visitors, companies and investment to the city. In itself, this is neither a novel nor a surprising analysis of the problem. What is different, particularly for a declining northern industrial city in late twentieth century Britain, was that this diagnosis and the resulting prescription was initially promoted, implemented and enhanced by a Labour controlled city council. And this was not just any Labour authority but one that lived with the reputation of radicalism and the memories of 'Red Clydeside' (McLean, 1983; Damer, 1980).

Well before the SDA had begun to take an interest in the city centre, the City Council launched a vigorous marketing campaign, selling a new image for the city to an unsuspecting public. The then Lord Provost (the mayor) of Glasgow had been so impressed by the success of the 'I Love New York' campaign that he convinced his authority to conceive and promote a similar venture. Combining the slogan 'Glasgow's Miles Better' with the well-known 'Mr Man' cartoon character, a series of promotions were conducted using local, regional and national media. Building on initiatives such as car-stickers, municipal merchandising and local advertising, in 1984 the council took their campaign to London, selling Glasgow on the sides of double-decker buses, taxis, on the London Underground and in the mainline railway stations. This coincided with a series of advertisements placed in the national (UK) press and, more significantly, in a number of the specialised journals targeted at the international business community.

Simply on the basis of constant demand for promotional material, the image campaign very quickly had a local impact. Reluctant city officials and sceptical local politicians were however most surprised by the relative 'success' of external promotions. Evidence that the 'signals' were being received is illustrated by a selection of newspaper and magazine headlines from 1986:

'Glasgow's Arising, on Its Own, It Says', *New York Times,* 20 January.
'The City That Refused to Die', *Time Magazine* (US), 14 April.
'Glasgow sells itself, smiles and hopes', *Financial Times*, 17 November.

In marked contrast to the more negative press attracted by the activities of other Labour controlled councils in Liverpool, Manchester and selected London Boroughs, Glasgow chose to promote a different image to the outside world. The very positive signals projected through the 'Miles Better' campaign, presented to and then accepted by the media, highlighted selective urban ingredients, carefully chosen as being palatable to the private sector. The message was not simply that the city had changed but that Glasgow could compete.

The marketing and promotional strategy adopted by the Council centred on symbols of urban economic regeneration. Despite the legacy of industrial and commercial decline, clearly illustrated in the attendant statistics of economic dislocation and social deprivation, the city could point to physical, environmental, and cultural improvements during the 1970s that taken together had changed the appearance of the city and significantly altered attitudes. This was no longer to be the negative city of the razor gang, the drunk and the corrupt machine politician but a positive, proud, forward looking community, capable of building on its fine Victorian history, the one-time 'Second City of the Empire'. Just as symbolic change had been used to promote the city through International Exhibitions in 1888, 1901, 1911 and again in 1938 (Gordon, 1985), so once more the city attempted to use figurative rather than actual change as the basis for urban promotion.

The most obvious physical changes were to be found mainly in the city centre and in the traditional owner-occupied housing areas where a programme of rehabilitation and stone-cleaning had revealed some very fine nineteenth and early twentieth-century architecture. In contrast to the clearance policies of the 1950s, demolition became the last resort for the urban planners and developers and even then was only to be used in extreme circumstances. Such change in policy, alongside the attractive financial incentives of zero land costs, falling property values and generous public subsidies, resulted in numerous new uses for old buildings: bijou housing, cafes and smart restaurants in church towers and old warehouses, a business centre in an empty carpet factory, leisure shopping in the derelict fishmarket – much of this property development concentrated on an area that became known as the Merchant City, bringing urban activity back to the inner city (Glasgow District Council (Planning), 1986a).

Environmental improvement was also used as a symbol of more significant urban change. Using the resources of the SDA and the council, numerous sites throughout the city, many that had lain vacant and derelict for years, were shaped, seeded for grass and fringed with expensive planting. Some of these were of a temporary nature; other landscaping was much more than this, with major and permanent land renewal schemes bringing managed open space back into the city centre (McDonald, 1984). Such improvement was also targeted on specific locations: along the major arterial roads, on the urban fringe of the city, by the River Clyde and close to areas that were programmed for new private housing (Glasgow District Council (Planning), 1985). Hence the symbol of environmental improvement, often merely a cosmetic response to urban decline, became instead part and parcel of the competitive strategy. Physical and environmental improvement was brought together in a number of 'flagship' developments: construction of a major office complex as the headquarters for Britoil, building of the Scottish Exhibition and Conference Centre on the disused Princes Dock, the selection of a neighbouring dock as the site for the 1988 National Garden Festival and numerous new shopping and office developments in the city centre. Not surprisingly, the SDA played a key role in promoting, financing and developing such projects and these projects figure prominently in the early activities of Glasgow Action.

It was the symbol of the cultural city that caught the national and international imagination. It is difficult to identify a municipal policy for the arts that gave rise to this phenomenon. Rather, the early 1980s was a period when a series of individual projects and events matured at the same time, producing an important critical mass of cultural activity. The opening of a new art gallery to house the eccentric but internationally renowned Burrell Collection was undoubtably the catalyst that drew the different components together. This, together with the opening of a new Royal College of Music and Drama, firm proposals to construct a new concert hall, and the rediscovery of a native artistic talent served to convince the UK government that Glasgow should be selected as the European City of Culture for 1990. Glasgow's cultural resources – home of Scottish Opera and the National Orchestra, the Citizens Theatre, the largest municipal art collection outside London – became part of the marketing literature, joining references to the city parks, access to out-door recreation and proximity to the Scottish Highlands, promoting the city for tourism, for inward investors, for business.

THE SUBSTANCE OF REGENERATION – UNEVEN DEVELOPMENT

Yet it was the substance of this urban regeneration that produced the conflict. For change in Glasgow has been selective – merchandising the city in the modern world has created different costs as well as producing mixed benefits for the place and its people. Nonetheless, the physical, environmental and cultural symbols of change do translate into tangible urban regeneration. Four very different pieces of information provide evidence of positive improvement. First, there has been a sustained period of public and private investment in land and property, particu-larly in the city centre. Much of this had the support of investment from the SDA (£13.1 million in the city between 1976 and 1984, 69% in the Glasgow Central Parliamentary Constituency) that in turn attracted con-siderable private capital. In the Merchant City, for example, between 1982 and 1985, total public subsidy of £4.4 million leveraged some £29.9 million from the private sector, admittedly mainly in the form of private house construction (Glasgow District Council (Housing), 1986).

Second, there has been a modest 'return to the city' movement, parti-cularly of young, middle-income persons and families. It is estimated that the re-use of city centre properties for housing will result in an addi-tional 2,500 people resident in the city centre, stimulating demand for local sales and services. This should not be confused with gentrification. New housing in the 1980s has not directly displaced an indigenous, working-class community although there is a strong argument that it was the success of population dispersal policy in the fifties and sixties that created the opportunities for more recent inner-city revival. Third, the tourists attracted by the cultural and retail activities in the city now con-stitute an important sector in the local service economy. In 1982, some 700,000 tourists used facilities in the city, the vast majority being short-stay visitors; in 1984 this figure had risen to 2.2 million, with a signifi-cant increase in long-stay visitors. Based on the National Garden Festi-val, the target for 1988 is set at more than 5 million visitors.

Fourth, and accepting all its limitations, one of the first pieces of sub-stantial empirical analysis of Glasgow's improvement is recorded by Cheshire *et al.* (1986). As part of a EEC funded study of urban decline and growth in Europe, a research team at Reading University found that Glasgow had improved when comparing change across a series of urban indicators in 1971, 1975, 1981 and 1984. Compared to other 'problem cities' in the UK, Glasgow 'improved strongly', this being 'particularly significant given other evidence on the nature and comparative success of policy there'. Taken as read, and in the context of the promotional material discussed above, the image being presented is one of significant urban change. It is more honest, however, to place Glasgow in its proper context. Despite the improvement demonstrated by the Reading team, in the period 1981-1984, Glasgow was ranked 97th out of 102 functional urban areas in the European data set. Only Messina, Cagliari, Belfast, Sunderland and Liverpool fall below Glasgow in a ranking of problem cities. Thus, not only is improvement selective but great care is required when interpreting the signals.

There is now an extensive literature that charts the demise of Glasgow as a world city in terms of, first, international trade and secondly as a major centre for engineering (Gordon, 1985; Gibb, 1983; and Adams, 1978). Moreover, these studies and others, notably Smout (1986), Checkland (1981) and Butt (1971) have graphically demonstrated the economic and social problems facing the city of Glasgow. Lever's recent study of economic decline of Clydeside (Glasgow's conurbation) sum-marises the very essence of the problem:

> It is not an exaggeration to say that in twenty years Glasgow has gone from being an industrial city with 60 per cent of its labour in manufactur-ing, to service centre with 60 per cent of its labour in service occupations (Lever, 1986: p. 2); moreover, the most obvious aspect of the changing employment scene has been the very substantial overall decline in oppor-tunities since 1971. Total conurbation employment stood at 789,000 jobs in 1971. By 1981, this had fallen to 687,000, an overall reduction of around 13 per cent (McGregor and Mather, 1986: p. 23).

The human cost of this economic transformation is recorded in the level of unemployment in the city. In July 1986, some 77,000 people in Glasgow were counted as unemployed – an overall rate of 21.5%. This masks much higher levels of unemployment in selected parts of the city – 8 Wards record overall unemployment levels in excess of 30%. At the level of the individual and the family, all unemployment is serious but in Glasgow it is the scale of long-term male unemployment – in some 30 of the 66 City Wards over 50% of the unemployed have been out of work for one year or more – and the difficulty of getting young people into the labour market that causes the greatest concern (Glasgow District Coun-cil (Planning), 1986b). While there is some evidence that employment opportunities in Glasgow are improving in relation to the rest of the conurbation, there are few indications that the private sector response, the symbolic change, even the city centre refurbishment, will in any way redress imbalances in the labour market. 'Glasgow's Miles Better' for some: but only for a chosen few.

The selective nature of urban economic change is most clearly demonstrated by the failure to extend the city centre improvements to the peripheral housing estates. Four large communities – Castlemilk, Pollok, Drumchapel and Easterhouse – encircle the city, with some 150,000 people living in predominantly council-owned property. All four areas were built after the Second World War as part of the city's urgent slum-clearance and rehousing programme. The early failure to provide even the most basic community facilities resulted in a chronic shortage of local services, and until the early 1980s many families travelled back into the inner city for shopping, health services and entertainment. And it didn't help that the City Fathers effectively banned all pubs and off-licences in the four 'schemes'! 'Such peripheral housing schemes were thus a parody of the traditional tenement life of Glasgow: they consisted of tenements indeed, but they were far removed from the urban context in which that mode of life had developed, and incapable of generating their own community life' (Checkland, 1981, p.68). These areas now contain the largest concentrations of poverty in the city with few local job opportunities to increase the meagre family incomes. Furthermore, the location of the estates on the edge of the city makes for difficult and expensive access to alternative sources of employment (CES, 1985).

Despite the rhetoric of local politicians and social planners, despite claims that these areas have priority for social, educational and housing programmes, it has proved difficult to bend mainstream policy and even more awkward to target economic initiatives to areas that offer so few comparative advantages (Keating and Mitchell, 1986). Yet it needs to be recognised that the policies and programmes pursued by the city, the investment patterns of the SDA and the support of the private sector has tended to favour the city centre to the detriment of these peripheral, largely residential areas: 'whereas the market approach might be a logical response in areas where there is significant economic potential, it has far less to commend it in communities suffering acute and long-term social and economic deprivation' (Moore and Booth, 1986, pp. 89-90).

Perhaps the most sobering implication of transferring responsibility for urban revitalisation on to the private sector is that the objectives of urban reconstruction will, by necessity, become commercial objectives. What is good for the business community becomes the goal of the city; 'what's good for business is good for Glasgow'. What is necessary for residential neighbourhoods may not figure at all on the agenda of corporate executives determining the shape and direction of urban investment over the long term. If the private sector can see some form of commercial benefit from direct involvement in urban governance, they will retain their interest; if not, they will withdraw, leaving a political, organisational and fiscal vacuum (Boyle and Rich, 1984).

COMMENTARY AND CONCLUSIONS

Private sector-led urban regeneration depends upon the necessary entrepreneurs being present or coming forward. One can be very sceptical of this. In the Glasgow city centre, there is a recognisable business elite – the basis of Glasgow Action – capable and motivated to help stimulate the service sector, given the necessary public support. In the towns of north Lanarkshire or other parts of Scotland's traditional industrial heartland, there is precious little evidence of a healthy native capitalism. In the Glasgow peripheral public sector housing estates such as Easterhouse and Drumchapel, devoid of an indigenous economic or commercial base, the idea is utterly fanciful. Yet it is precisely in these depressed areas, communities facing 40% male unemployment but lacking the necessary entrepreneurial infrastructure, that the SDA hopes to extend its policy of private-led urban economic regeneration (Keating and Boyle, 1986). And there is a real concern that the announcement of 'Initiatives' in areas such as these merely serves to obscure the withdrawal of state support and a reduction in traditional forms of public expenditure.

In practice therefore, what seems to be developing is a dual approach to urban policy. On the one hand, there is the business activity at the 'sharp end' of local economic policy, led by the market and responding to profit considerations. The locational implications of this increasingly dominant approach may be to move capital yet further from the deprived areas in Scotland. On the other, there are initiatives with a more 'social' purpose in places such as Easterhouse and Drumchapel, aimed at helping the casualties of economic change rather than seeking to control the pace and direction of that change itself. Both types of policy, however, are being pushed towards the very same 'bootstrap' philosophy of self-reliance and private sector leadership.

Hence, there is evidence to suggest that policy redirection, predominantly inspired by the SDA, but also supported by socialist local authorities, will result in the dilution of effective urban policy. Under the influence of central government, the Agency and elected city councils have begun to de-emphasise urban renewal as such in favour of a more limited, narrow, view of 'business development'. As so often, this has been preceded by a change of rhetoric placing the role of private initiative to the fore and talking in terms of 'opportunities' rather than 'problems'. Language, indeed, has almost become a barrier to understanding what is happening in Scottish urban policy. As new language is introduced to legitimise intervention in terms of the ideological fashions of the moment, it is not always easy to tell whether policy itself has changed and to some extent it may be true that the rhetoric of non-intervention is merely being used to cover a continuation of the old interventionist line.

But if urban policy has changed, if central government and SDA support for private sector urban regeneration is more than simply symbolic – and this certainly appears to be the case – then the implications for parts of Scottish cities may be profound. For not only is a focus on commercial criteria inappropriate for some local economies but to use a central government agency along with the private sector to implement policy may effectively remove the necessary social support that traditional policies delivered.

Finally, I offer some tentative answers to the questions posed at the beginning of this essay.

While the bulk of urban economic policy has been in the mainstream of traditional attempts to address the economic and social problems of selected communities, the recent reorientation of policy demonstrates the pursuit of very different objectives – support for the operation of the market in the most, not the least, favourable locations. In the jargon of place-marketing, it means 'picking winners for areas of opportunity'. Hence the city centre becomes the focus for policy at the expense of the decaying inner city or the peripheral estate.

Changing the objectives of urban policy and using the private sector as a vehicle for implementation essentially changes the agenda of urban policy. Issues of unemployment, social distress, or community disadvantage are effectively replaced by the priorities of the market-place – return on investment, rental yield, market capture, leverage ratios and the like. Moreover, a case is presented that the goals of business are the goals of the community and to disagree is to deny the importance of the commercial imperative and to suffer the consequences of further economic dislocation.

Adopting a private-sector strategy for addressing urban problems may be wholly inappropriate in areas that lack the necessary conditions for some form of economic regeneration. Furthermore, policy development built around private sector activity may obscure a withdrawal of any form of public support that looks beyond the most basic welfare considerations.

NOTES

1 While central government (through the Scottish Development Department and the Industry Department Scotland) is responsible for an interpretation of UK urban policy and is charged with coordinating policy that is unique to Scotland, policy implementation is effectively divided between the Scottish Office, that administers the 'Urban Programme' (£30.6 million approved expenditure in 1985/86), and the Scottish Development Agency that has responsibility for land reclamation and environmental programmes and determines the direction and allocation of spending on urban economic policy, the equivalent of inner city policy as administered by the DOE, (SDA expenditure in 1984 was estimated at £100.8 million).
2 Enterprise *trusts* are the equivalent of enterprise *agencies* operating in England and Wales. They perform very similar functions, focusing attention on encouraging the growth and stability of small firms. The organisation and development of trusts through Scottish Business in the Community is largely modelled on English experience although the active involvement (particularly in terms of financial support) by an agency of central government has no direct parallel in England. For further details see SDA, 1986; Keating and Boyle, 1986, pp. 137-57.
3 The McKinsey Studies (1984 and 1985) into the Potential of Glasgow's City Centre identified seven initiatives to strengthen the city's service industries:
Attracting HQ's to Glasgow
Developing a Software Industry
Developing Exportable Services
Building Glasgow's Tourist Industry
Developing Glasgow as a Short Course Centre
Improving the City Centre
Improving Glasgow's Image

REFERENCES

Adams, I. (1978), *The Making of Urban Scotland,* London, Croom Helm.
Barnekov, Timothy, Boyle,Robin and Rich, Daniel (forthcoming), *Towards the Private City,* London, Oxford University Press.
Boyle, Robin (ed.) (1985a), 'Leveraging Urban Development: a comparison of urban policy directions and programme impact in the United States and Britain', *Policy and Politics,* 13, 2, pp. 175-210.
Boyle, Robin (1985b), 'Waterfronts: the Urban Answer', *Planning,* 627.
Boyle, Robin and Rich, Daniel (1984), 'Urban Policy and the New Privatism in the United States and Britain', *Public Administration Bulletin,* 45, pp. 22-37.
Boyle, Robin and Wannop, Urlan A. (1982), 'Area Initiatives and the SDA: The Rise of the Urban Project', *Quarterly Economic Commentary,* 8, 1, pp. 45-57, The Fraser of Allander Institute, University of Strathclyde.
Butt, J. (1971), 'Working Class Housing in Glasgow 1851-1914', in Chapman, S.D. (ed.), *The History of Working Class Housing,* Newton Abbot, David & Charles.

Centre for Environmental Studies (1985), *Report on Peripheral Estates,* London, CES.

Checkland, S. G. (1981), *The Upas Tree: Glasgow 1875-1975 and after 1975-1980,* 2nd edition, Glasgow, Glasgow University Press.

Cheshire, Paul, Carbonaro, Gianni, and Hay, Dennis (1986), 'Problems of Urban Decline and Growth in EEC Countries: Or Measuring Degrees of Elephantness', *Urban Studies,* 23, 2, pp. 131-49.

Daiches, D. (1977), *Glasgow,* London, André Deutsch.

Damer, S. (1980), 'State, Class and Housing: Glasgow, 1885-1919', in J. Melling (ed.), *Housing, Social Policy and the State,* London.

Gibb, A. (1983), *Glasgow: The Making of a City,* London, Croom Helm.

Glasgow Action (1985), *Glasgow – the need for Action,* Glasgow, SDA.

Glasgow District Council (Housing) (1986), *Housing-Led Investment in the City Centre,* GDC.

Glasgow District Council (Planning) (1985), *District Plan 1984,* GDC.

Glasgow District Council (Planning) (1986a), *Central Area Local Plan – Draft Written Statement,* GDC.

Glasgow District Council (Planning) (1986b), *Unemployment Within Glasgow by Local Area,* July 1986, Research Memorandum, GDC.

Gordon, G. (1985), 'The City of Glasgow', in Butt, J. and Gordon, G. (eds.), *Strathclyde – Changing Horizons,* Edinburgh, Scottish Academic Press.

Gulliver, Stuart (1984), 'The Area Projects of the Scottish Development Agency', *Town Planning Review,* 55, 3, pp. 322-34.

Judd, Dennis R. (1979), *The Politics of American Cities: Private Power and Public Policy,* Boston, Mass., Little, Brown & Co.

Keating, Michael and Midwinter, A. (eds.) (1983), *Government of Scotland,* Edinburgh, Mainstream.

Keating, Michael and Boyle, Robin (1986), *Remaking Urban Scotland: Strategies for Local Economic Development,* Edinburgh, Edinburgh University Press.

Keating, Michael and Mitchell, James (1986), 'Easterhouse–An Urban Crisis', *Strathclyde Papers on Government and Politics* 47, Glasgow, University of Strathclyde.

Leclerc, Roger and Draffan, Don (1984), 'The Glasgow Eastern Renewal Project', *Town Planning Review,* 55, 3, pp. 336-51.

Lever, William and Mather, Frank (1986), 'The Changing Structure of Business and Employment in the Conurbation', in Lever, William and Moore, Chris (eds.), *The City in Transition: Policies and Agencies for the Economic Regeneration of Clydeside,* Oxford, Clarendon Press, pp. 1-21.

Lublove, R. (1969), *Twentieth-Century Pittsburgh,* New York, NY, John Wiley.

McDonald, Sheila T. (1984), 'The Scottish Development Agency and the Scottish townscape', *Town Planning Review,* 55, 3, pp. 352-67.

McGregor, Alan and Mather, Frank (1986), 'Developments in Glasgow's Labour Market', in Lever, William and Moore, Chris (eds.), *The City in Transition: Policies and Agencies for the Economic Regeneration of Clydeside,* Oxford, Clarendon Press, pp. 22-43.

McKinsey & Co. (1984), *Glasgow's Service Industries* – Current Performance: a report to the SDA, Glasgow, SDA.

McKinsey & Co. (1985), *The Potential of Glasgow City Centre,* Glasgow, SDA.

McLean, I. (1983), *The Legend of Red Clydeside,* Edinburgh, John Donald.

Moore, Chris and Booth, Simon (1986), 'From Comprehensive Regeneration to Privatisation: the Search for Effective Area Strategies', in Lever, William and Moore, Chris (eds.), *The City in Transition: Policies and Agencies for the Economic Regener-*

ation of Clydeside, Oxford, Clarendon Press, pp. 76-91; 107-19.

Nairn, Sandy (1983), 'GEAR: Comprehensive Renewal or Confidence Trick?', *Quarterly Economic Commentary,* 9, 2, The Fraser of Allander Institute, University of Strathclyde.

Scottish Development Agency (1984), *Annual Report:* The Agency in Partnership, Glasgow, SDA.

Scottish Development Agency (1986), *Annual Report:* Agency of Opportunity, Glasgow, SDA.

Smout, T. C. (1986), *A Century of the Scottish People, 1830-1950,* London, Collins.

The uses of linked development policies in US cities

MICHAEL PETER SMITH
University of California, Davis

In the larger political economic order of the United States, where the strict division of labour between state and market requires local officials to mediate between corporate control of economic functions and electoral control vested in local communities, the social construction of the local 'business climate' has become a central task of local political elites. Throughout the 1980s the national hegemony of 'Reaganomics' has materially and ideologically constrained the local political management of this task. So, too, have changing international economic relations which have accelerated the pace and scale of capital investment and dis-investment globally, leaving localities vulnerable to the threat of rapid capital flight. In this context, the local politics of urban economic development has been characterised all too commonly by a social con-struction of reality in which a 'good business climate' is defined as one in which corporate domination of productive relations is uncontested, the community adapts to economic change without resistance, and corporate influence over the policies of the local state is accepted as a benign expression of 'public-private partnership'.

Despite this general trend, a growing number of local jurisdictions in the United States have embarked upon another course. In some cities currently experiencing economic 'conversion' from an industrial to a ser-vice base, the inflationary, displacement, fiscal, and mobility inducing effects of economic restructuring have been resisted by neo-populist political coalitions (Swanstrom, 1987). The rapid development of sprawling suburbs in regions experiencing economic growth likewise has created conditions conducive to the emergence of local 'growth control' coalitions. These political developments have been associated with the rise of new types of local public policy mechanisms known as 'exactions,' 'in lieu fees,' 'impact fees,' and 'linked development' policies. Each of these is designed to make developers pay some of the costs produced by the effects of their developments.

What are these new policy mechanisms? Where have they emerged as comprehensive 'linked development' policies? How do they work? Why have 'linkage' policies occurred in some cities but not others? What have been their effects? In seeking to answer these questions the first section of this paper defines, locates, and describes the varieties of linked development policies that have emerged in a number of US cities in the current decade. The second section explains why linkage policies emerged where they did. In the third section, a brief case study of the Boston experience with linked development is used to illustrate concretely the previously advanced arguments. Once this is accomplished, the paper offers an assessment of the political consequences of the uses of linked development policies in US cities.

FROM SUBURBAN 'EXACTIONS' TO URBAN 'LINKAGE' POLICIES

Suburban municipalities facing rising costs of local public services to new subdivisions during a period of declining federal support for new infrastructure were the first jurisdictions to develop 'exaction' policies. An 'exaction' is a public policy mechanism which enables municipalities to transfer some of the financial costs associated with economic and population growth on to those who caused the growth, namely, developers and residents of new housing subdivisions (Connors and High, 1985). Initially, 'exactions' were restricted to the practice of charging suburban developers a fee in lieu of taxes for the local public services they receive. In some urban jurisdictions exactions have expanded to encompass adverse impact fees and comprehensive 'linked development' policies. Each form of exaction requires developers to make contributions in cash or in kind prior to obtaining a permit to carry forward the development of a proposed commercial or residential project.

The contributions of developers have taken many forms. The most common form in suburban areas has been a requirement that developers 'dedicate' a part of their development to public improvements within the development such as sidewalks and streets, water and sewer lines, and/or recreational spaces; sometimes suburban developers have been required to construct such 'public' improvements as a precondition for obtaining authorisation from the local state to develop their projects. When the exaction has taken the form of 'in lieu fees,' developers have been required to pay fees which are earmarked to finance specific public facilities or services generally associated with the dedication of land (e.g., infrastructure improvements, recreational or educational facilities within the geographical boundaries of the new development).

This type of in lieu fee does not address the adverse impacts that new developments often have on areas outside their boundaries. Examples of such negative spillover effects of development include: the strain on general physical capital infrastructure; school overcrowding in neighbourhoods adjacent to new residential development; pressures on housing markets caused by high-rise office construction; increased demand on public transportation facilities; increased traffic congestion; employment displacement; and the overloading of existing police and fire services by central business district (CBD) development, with corresponding service decline in urban neighbourhoods. The costs of new services to large-scale corporate developments in particular, have frequently been shown to outweigh the benefits to local communities derived from the added tax base (Smith and Keller, 1983; Hartman, 1984; Swanstrom, 1986; for evidence concerning the returns to industrial development see also Summers and Branch, 1984).

Faced with these kinds of spillover effects and unable to obtain relief from higher governmental levels in the current period of fiscal austerity, some growing US cities and suburbs have begun to assess local impact fees to cope with the fiscal demands of new growth. These fees generally have taken the form of charges imposed by local governments on developers to generate revenue for new capital projects directly necessitated by the impact of the new development (Connors and High, 1985, p. 7). In a few growing cities, 'exactions' have expanded beyond this focus upon immediate physical capital costs to encompass wider social costs that have been 'linked' to the conversion of central business districts (CBD's) to the requirements of the new service economy.

In their most fully developed form, linkage policies have tied the authorisation of large-scale commercial urban development projects to the payment by developers of compensating 'side payments' to local government trust funds to offset particular negative effects upon local communities of CDB growth. 'Linkage' has most frequently been tied to housing. Linkage fees have been defended by local government officials as a way to require developers to compensate for the adverse impact their development would have on local housing markets. It has been argued that the new jobs created in the business service sector by high-rise office development will increase the demand for housing within central cities and stimulate the conversion of rental units into condominia, thereby driving up rents and housing costs. In some relatively progressive localities, where 'neo-populist' coalitions have exercised power (e.g. Boston, Santa Monica), downtown development has been linked to other social costs and linkage has become a 'back-door' means of financing a variety of other municipal social policies (e.g. employment training, public transport) during the current period of national retrenchment in the social policy sector (see Connors and High, 1985, p. 8; Susskind, *et al.,* 1986).

THE VARIETIES OF LINKED DEVELOPMENT POLICIES

Where have linkage policies become prominent issues on the local political agenda and what do these policies look like? On the West Coast the cities of San Francisco, Santa Monica, Sacramento, and Los Angeles, California and Seattle, Washington have passed linked development ordinances. In the Northeast, the cities of Boston, Massachusetts and Jersey City and Princeton, New Jersey currently have linkage policies. The issue of linked development has been placed on the local political agenda in Chicago, Denver, Cambridge, Massachusetts and Hartford, Connecticut, but the political forces promoting linkage in these latter cities do not yet constitute a winning coalition.

San Francisco was the first city to enact a comprehensive linked development policy (Swanstrom, 1986). In San Francisco developers can develop in downtown areas only if they agree to pay for or provide community amenities or public facilities such as affordable housing, transit, parks, or child care facilities elsewhere in the city in exchange for building permission (Clark, 1987, p. 13). The core of linked development in San Francisco is its Office-Affordable Housing Production Program administered by the Department of City Planning and financed by a $5.34 per square foot office development fee charged to developers.

Prior to the passage of this policy a series of political struggles involving city government officials, developers, and community organisations had formed the basic outlines of the policy on a project by project basis. Thus, for example, in 1974, the Ramada, Holiday Inn, and Hilton Hotel chains were forced to create a $5.4 million housing fund in the low income Tenderloin district to overcome community resistance to the addition of 2,400 new hotel rooms adjacent to the district. The city justified the creation of this fund by citing the provision of the California Environmental Quality Act which mandates mitigation of the negative impacts of development (McMahon *et al.,* 1986, p. 3). The same statute has provided a legal foundation for the city's current linkage policy.

In Los Angeles, the developers of a multi-use development (MXD) project have obtained the right to develop a downtown urban renewal package in exchange for developing an Arts Trust Fund and providing facilities for a new Museum of Contemporary Art (Clark, 1987, p. 13). This difference in the substance of compensatory policies linked to downtown development in San Francisco and Los Angeles is a reflection of the different social base of opposition to development in the two California cities.

The case of Santa Monica provides the richest illustration of the variety of linkages that a robust local political process has produced. In the face of rapidly rising costs of home ownership, real estate speculation, and escalating rents triggered by these developments, the voters of Santa Monica elected a city council that imposed a moratorium on all new real estate development in 1981. The neo-populist council entered into a series of ad hoc 'development agreements' which exacted a wide variety of concessions from commercial developers. These exactions have included low income housing fees, moderate income housing construction, social service funding, preferential hiring for minorities, energy conservation measures, day care centres, and even hotel vouchers for battered women (Feagin, 1986, pp. 44-6; McMahon et al., 1986). In the face of this type of grassroots politics, it is not surprising that the formal linkage agreement enacted by the council in 1984, which tied developers' obligations to a clear formula of creating 'affordable housing' in Santa Monica, has been described by analysts as 'more lenient' than the agreements it followed (see McMahon et al., 1986, p. 38). This view is supported by the fact that there has been almost no opposition from developers to the housing fee ($2.25 per square foot for the first 15,000 square feet and $5.00 thereafter) since its enactment.

In Seattle, Washington in 1984, the city council adopted a Downtown Land Use and Transportation Plan which linked commercial development *bonuses* rather than fees to the production of affordable housing. Here, too, decreased availability of low income housing units prompted housing activists to lead a neighbourhood based coalition in favour of linked development. Under terms of a voluntary programme enacted by the city council in the face of this pressure, developers who agree to produce housing units or contribute to a fund for new moderate income housing may obtain increased floor area ratios in their office building projects. Developers also may purchase development rights for additional commercial space in exchange for preserving existing low income units. To date, approximately $6 million has been raised by five projects whose developers have sought additional floor space. The groups who originally pressed for the policy have been highly critical of its voluntary character and limited impact (McMahon et al., 1986, p. 26).

In Hartford and Chicago, grassroots activists have elected mayors sympathetic to claims that the rising housing costs and employment restructuring that these cities have experienced are attributable to the pace and scale of downtown development. In Chicago, demands that linked mitigation fees go directly to each of the city's 77 community areas on a proportional basis to be spent on local projects, subject to local voter approval, have been frustrated by the inability of the highly contentious board of aldermen (city council) to coalesce around an acceptable policy. In Hartford, community organisations opposed to a proposed voluntary bonus programme similar to Seattle's forced the City Council to create a Linkage Task Force to develop a mandatory policy (McMahon *et al.*, 1986). The task force, composed of public, business, and neighbourhood representatives recommended a linkage programme earmarking funding for both housing and employment policies; but opposition from key corporate elites has thus far blocked this exercise in 'local corporatism'.

WHY EXACTIONS IN GENERAL? WHY LINKAGE IN PARTICULAR?

It is perhaps easier to understand why exactions have emerged in a variety of local jurisdictions than why linkage policies have become a hotly contested issue in a few cities. Officials of the local state have been faced with sharp reductions in federal aid. In many states, tax limitation legislation at the state level and local taxpayer revolts have likewise constrained the revenue-raising capacity of local governments. Particularly in areas experiencing economic and population growth which require new public facilities like roads, sewers, and schools, local state officials have begun to seek innovative methods for financing these facilities (Connors and High, 1985, p. 1). State tax caps have made it difficult if not impossible for local governments to tax new commercial developments at rates high enough to generate the revenues needed to pay for the new public service demands directly occasioned by development. This has forced many municipalities to compensate partially for anticipated or actual revenue shortfalls by imposing various use charges, permit fees, and exactions on developers (Susskind *et al.*, 1986, p. 6).

These fiscal realities constitute the major contextual pressure underlying the general turn to exactions. They are also an important factor helping to explain the rise of linkage policies. Pressures on local government officials in growing municipalities in California, Massachusetts, and New Jersey to seek alternative sources of revenue following restrictions on local property taxation have been intensified by generally high public expectations for local public service provision in these states. Seven of the eight cities which have adopted comprehensive linkage policies are located in the three states. The eighth, Seattle, is the only linked development city to rely on a voluntary bonus programme rather than a mandatory fee structure.

The importance of these political and ideological factors is further underlined by the fact that the major economic contextual factor, a booming downtown office market, seems to be a necessary but insufficient condition for predicting the emergence of linkage. No political coalitions supporting linkage policies have yet emerged in large Sunbelt cities in the South which have enjoyed relatively robust downtown high rise office markets (e.g., Miami, Atlanta) in the past decade. The local politics of economic development in the more ideologically conservative South has been managed by political elites leading government-business alliances supporting 'public-private partnership' and the ideology of growth (see Smith and Judd, 1984). Hence, growth is not enough to explain the emergence of linkage.

Nor is protest enough. Where grassroots activism occurs in a context where political elites lack the resouces and organisational slack to sustain an enduring local *electoral* coalition (e.g., Cleveland under Mayor Dennis Cucinich), defeat, discouragement, and demobilisation are the likely outcomes (Swanstrom, 1985). Once this occurs, industrial restructuring and conversion of the CBD to the new requirements of a business service economy can take place without resistance (and without either gentrification or linkage), as in the case of Cleveland in the current decade (see Swanstrom, 1987).

Local politics, therefore, clearly matters. Where linkage has emerged most extensively there has been a movement of the neighbourhood organising movement into electoral politics. This has been true in San Francisco, Boston, Hartford, Santa Monica, Chicago, and Jersey City. The relations forged between local political elites (mayors and/or city council majorities) and a mass electoral base have been the decisive local element in the emergence of linkage. Where neighbourhood groups have been able to develop their political capacities in the electoral arena, they have become a powerful source of initiative in local development politics. Moving from ad hoc resistance to bureaucratic planning processes to playing a regularised role in the election of mayors and city councils has enabled them to forge alliances with political elites seeking to gain or keep power under the banner of 'neighbourhood revitalisation' (Susskind *et al.,* 1985; Swanstrom, 1987).

Although local politics matters, it does not take place in vacuum. Linkage has emerged where well organised local grassroots electoral coalitions have been combined with an economically favourable context. The demand for linkage has been a reaction to the perceived (and actual) uneven development of booming downtowns and declining neighbourhoods. It has occurred where the boom has been associated with the process of gentrification and where shortages of affordable housing threaten to produce housing displacement and conversion of declining working class and low income neighbourhoods to professional-managerial enclaves. The presence of an already established trajectory of increased capital flows into the CBDs where linkage policies have been developed has given political elites the latitude to respond to electorally focused 'pressures from below'. Unlike so many of their counterparts in declining cities, these elites have been freed from the need to preach the gospel of economic growth as urban salvation.

If Schefter (1985) is correct that local political elites are structurally constrained by a contradictory imperative to generate votes while maintaining their city's access to credit and enhancing the local economy, it may be argued that if particular locational advantages (e.g., proximity to international markets or affluent suburban consumer markets) or exogenous investment patterns (e.g., the urban and regional impacts of defence expenditures) enhance the local economic development process, than local political elites are freer to appeal to widely held community values (e.g., equity, democratic responsiveness, neighbourhood integrity) when framing economic development policies. Hence, in this context they are more likely to develop local state policies like linked development than are political elites in more economically and fiscally distressed urban centres. The latter, faced with keen competition for external economic investment, are more likely to tilt in favour of smokestack and high-rise chasing, enterprise zones, tax abatements for development, deregulation, and various other forms of what Goodman (1979) has termed 'public entrepreneurship' than to support linkage policies. The latter are more structurally constrained than the former to resolve the contradiction they experience by stressing economic growth over other policy goals.

To recapitulate, a number of underlying pressures have prompted political elites in a few US cities to develop linked development policies. These have included cuts in federal financial assistance to state and local governments; the imposition of state ceilings on local property taxation following taxpayer revolts; the activities of well organised community action groups that constitute a major electoral constituency; the presence of a robust office boom; uneven development between downtown and existing urban neighbourhoods; and a decreasing supply of affordable housing. The legacy of environmental impact assessment practices at the state level and the expansion of suburban exaction policies at the local level have been important precursors and legal supports for the reconceptualisation of private property rights embodied in the current array of linked development policies. In the last instance, however, it has been local political dynamics that have produced linkage. The experience with linked development policy-making in Boston nicely illustrates the flavour and texture of the urban politics of linked development. It is to this experience that we now turn.

THE USES OF 'LINKAGE' IN BOSTON

By 1983, Boston, Massachusetts had become the fourth most robust downtown office market in the United States (Keating, 1986). It was touted in popular periodicals as a shining success story of 'conversion' from an industrial to a service base. In the preceding decade its loss of manufacturing employment had been more than offset by a booming white collar business service sector. City planners estimated that by 1984-1985 Boston had received over $3 billion in new downtown development, a level of new investment placing it first in office construction amount the twenty largest US cities (City of Boston, 1986; Swanstrom, 1986, p. 13).

This dramatic transformation was produced by a combination of Boston's structural economic locational advantages and its political legacy. The city's own economy was always more diversified than that of many other Northeastern industrial centres, including an important regional banking and financial services component. Moreover, heavy investment in defence expenditures (accelerated under Reagan), provided a firm underpinning for its surrounding suburban high-tech industrial belt. This, in turn, sustained a relatively affluent professional consumer market which could be attracted to use the commercially 'revitalised' downtown for shopping, entertainment, and the enjoyment (albeit intermittent and vicarious) of the affluent style of urban life that successful 'conversion' was both shaping and reflecting. Boston's third major 'locational advantage' was its social base. It has been estimated that in the early 1970s, when the first signs of 'conversion' were apparent, one in five residents of Boston was connected to the many university complexes located in its metropolitan area, as teachers, researchers, staff, or students. This has provided a social base from which both the 'human capital' contributing to 'conversion' and the 'human resistance' to its negative effects have been drawn.

Politically, 'conversion' was led by Boston's long-term Mayor Kevin White (1967-1983). White had originally risen to power as a champion of the grassroots neighbourhood activism of the late 1960s. During his long incumbency, White responded to the mounting fiscal stress occasioned by industrial decline and state government mandated taxing restrictions by catering increasingly to the needs of developers willing to take advantage of Boston's favourable locational advantages. This crucial political mediation served to both usher in Boston's rubust CBD office boom and catalyse the opposition to its uneven consequences.

In his early years in office, Kevin White promoted both downtown redevelopment and social redistribution policies. While shepherding new high-rise office proposals through the city planning process, White also cultivated grassroots support by advocating rent controls, initiating neighbourhood planning procedures, and establishing 'little city halls' (Swanstrom, 1986, p. 19). Initially, White was able to manage the contradiction identified by Schefter (1985) because taxation provided by the new commercial growth gave him slack resources with which to reward a neighbourhood based electoral coalition. But by the late 1970s, White had withdrawn his earlier support for social (and political) redistribution policies. The key role of developers in financing White's election campaigns and the rising costs of servicing the new downtown developments, clearly contributed to this political shift. The principal factor consolidating this shift, however, was a tax cap restriction passed by the voters of Massachusetts in 1979 (Proposition 2 1/2). This referendum limited property taxation to 2.5% of the fair market value of all private property in local communities, both commercial and residential. Boston, which historically had taxed commercial property at higher rates than residential property (in part as a political strategy to keep the leaders of urban political machines in public office – see Mollenkopf, 1983) was especially hard hit by this restriction. Since Boston had been taxing commercial property at over twice the 2.5% ceiling, the city lost almost $150 million in property tax revenues in 1982 and 1983 alone. This forced a reduction of almost 20% in the municipal workforce, (Swanstrom, 1987, p. 25) worsened local fiscal stress, accelerated White's abandonment of social redistribution, and contributed to his ultimate demise.

As downtown boomed, city government services shrank and neighbourhood-oriented programmes were eliminated. Meanwhile, the 'gentrification' following upon downtown 'conversion' placed increasing pressures on housing costs and threatened residential stability in existing neighbourhoods. It is hardly surprising that these conditions were conducive to the resurgence of urban populism and to linked development as a policy response to Boston's housing crisis.

Consistent with his shift to a policy of growth without redistribution (and perhaps to attract a new political base), White had actually promoted residential gentrification as a 'solution' to the fiscal crisis. By early 1983, grassroots activists opposing this pattern of neighbourhood transformation had coalesced around a two-pronged electoral strategy – first successfully leading a campaign to change the local electoral form from one in which city councillors were elected at large to a district-based electoral system; then working at the district level to elect a sympathetic city council majority. This movement of grassroots activists into the electoral arena produced a relatively progressive City Council which, in turn, passed Boston's first linked development policy in March 1983.

Mayor White's initial response was to veto the policy; but sustained neighbourhood resistance forced him to appoint an Advisory Group to study the proposal and make recommendations for action. The Advisory Group, relying upon previous planning studies, issued a Report to the Mayor on 'Linkage Between Downtown Development and Neighbourhood Housing' in October 1983 (City of Boston, Advisory Group Report, 1983). The Report focused on the interrelated problems of declining housing affordability in the face of substantial downtown development and decreasing national government subsidies for low and moderate income housing (Connors and High, 1985). It recommended the kind of linkage policy that White had vetoed.

Meanwhile White had been forced to withdraw from the next mayoral election by a political scandal involving the handling of campaign contributions from developers. Following White's decision not to seek re-election, all but one of the emergent candidates for mayor ran on a pro-neighbourhood campaign and supported linkage. Backed organisationally by a cohesive coalition of tenants' groups and neighbourhood organisations, South Boston Irish populist candidate Raymond Flynn won the Boston mayorality with over 65% of the vote.

In the face of these political developments, 'linkage' had already became a city policy shortly before Mayor-elect Flynn took office. In December 1983 the City Zoning Commission passed a Boston Development Impact Plan (DIP) along the lines recommended by White's Advisory Group. By this time, the emergent policy had gained support from Boston's major developers, who had decided that it was to their advantage to 'help shape the policy' before a new mayor had a chance to develop a set of linkage rules less acceptable to them (McMahon *et al.*, 1986, p. 9).

The 1983 Boston policy focused only upon large scale construction or rehabilitation projects. Any large project was required to pay a 'Development Impact Project Exaction' of $5 for each square foot over 100,000 square feet. Payment of the exaction fee became a precondition for the city granting any conditional use permit or zoning variance or amendment to applicable projects. Fees were payable directly into a Neighbourhood Housing Trust Fund. They were due on completion of the projects in twelve annual payments (Connors and High, 1985; Keating, 1986). Alternatively, developers might agree to directly produce an amount of low-moderate income housing units equivalent to the exaction.

What has been the fate of linked development policy under the Flynn administration? Flynn had originally run on an economically neo-populist platform of redistribution of 'downtown' wealth to 'neighbourhood people'. This social construction of reality allowed him to ignore existing social class, ethnic, and racial divisions among neighbourhoods and to channel local resentment against 'downtown' business elites. Once elected, however, both Flynn's rhetoric and his policies have been more accommodative to downtown business growth. He has sought to promote 'neighbourhood revitalisation' through economic development policies which linked downtown development to some concessions from developers. And he has abandoned his earlier neo-populist rhetoric in favour of the accommodative language of social co-operation, orderly development, and rational capital planning.

Under Flynn, downtown growth has been linked to employment as well as housing goals. For example, Flynn has issued an executive order instituting a quota system requiring all major construction and rehabilitation projects to hire at least 50% Boston residents, 25% minorities, and 11% women in each building trade involved in major development projects. Likewise, when the original linkage policy was attacked as inadequate by housing and neighbourhood activists, Flynn proposed increasing the linkage fee by $1 per square foot, changing the payment schedule from 12 to 7 years, and earmarking the increase for a Job Training Trust Fund. Another employment-related linkage policy promoted by the Flynn administration has been a parcel-to-parcel 'back office' linkage programme. Under this policy the right to develop choice downtown office buildings for managerial and professional work has been tied to agreements by developers to build 'back offices' for the clerical workforce away from downtown in depressed neighbourhoods like Boston's largely black Roxbury district (City of Boston, 1986; Swanstrom, 1987, pp. 22-3).

Despite continuing popularity, Flynn's shift from neo-populism to accommodation has cost him political support at the grassroots. Although his proposed amendments to the linkage policy were adopted by the Zoning Commission in early 1986, these amendments fell considerably short of demands made by the Boston Linkage Action Coalition. The housing and neighbourhood activists supporting this coalition had demanded that the fee be doubled, that the 100,000 square foot exemption be abolished, and that the fees be paid immediately (McMahon *et al.*, 1986, p. 11). These demands stemmed from the fact that at the time of the amendments, despite Boston's multi-billion office boom, only $35 million had been committed to the housing fund, no fees had actually been collected, and no low or moderate income housing had been built. Although the Fund has currently (early 1987) increased to $52 million, first payments under the now amended policy are not scheduled to begin until April 1987.

ASSESSING 'LINKED' DEVELOPMENT

In assessing the political consequences of the uses of linked development in US cities, it is important to distinguish the policy's material outcomes from its symbolic significance. Susskind's study of the effectiveness of linkage policies in meeting their stated material objectives has found that 'effectiveness' depends upon the policy goals underlying linkage. Where, as in Boston and Hartford, public support was mobilised for 'linkage' as a way to achieve wealth redistribution from downtown to neighbourhoods, the policy has been less than successful. Not only do the required linkage payments equal but a tiny fraction of the total benefits flowing to downtown developers, the costs are not even paid by developers, but are passed along to new tenants in the form of increased fees and rents (Susskind *et al.*, 1986).

Where the policy goals have been more limited, as in the case of San Francisco's stated goal of constructing affordable housing units, linkage has shown more promise. For example, by early 1985 San Francisco had obtained commitments from developers to build 2,693 low-moderate income residential units. Yet even in such instances, when measured against either national cuts in federal support for affordable housing or official estimates of local housing need, the results have been quite modest. Federal cutbacks for social welfare policies under Reagan have been especially severe in the area of housing. Between 1981 and 1984 federal support for low and moderate income housing plummeted from $27 billion to $9.9 billion (Susskind *et al.*, 1986). Viewed in this context, even well endowed housing linkage funds constitute a 'drop in the bucket'. When Boston's linkage programme is measured against the more modest standard of providing affordable housing, the same conclusion can be drawn. The Boston Redevelopment Authority (BRA) has estimated that nearly 13,000 new housing units will be needed by 1992 to meet the increased demand created by new downtown employment and that approximately 3,000 new units of housing per year will be needed to house the low and moderate income families currently living in Boston (Swanstrom, 1986, p. 28; Susskind *et al.*, 1986). If the $35.5 million exacted by Boston by late 1985 were available all at once rather than in stages, it would still only be enough to construct 500 new units of affordable housing (*Boston Globe,* 12 November 1985; Susskind, *et al.*, 1986, p. 10).

The obvious inadequacy of linkage as a *housing* policy raises the question of opportunity costs. This question may be framed by asking the rhetorical questions 'Linked to what?' and 'Linked to whom?' To the extent that housing activists in some of the most politically dynamic US cities concentrate their efforts on expanding linkage locally, their attention is deflected from the fact that linkage is clearly a poor substitute for the promotion of national policies which guarantee affordable housing as a basic need for low and moderate income citizens. Housing provision also has tended to dominate the local political dialogue concerning linkage, thereby crowding out debate concerning other undesirable externalities (e.g. job and class restructuring, overloading basic infrastructure) which developers of the new urban service economy ought to 'mitigate' by paying adequate local taxes.

Furthermore, by focusing on the benefits flowing to developers of new large-scale commercial spaces as a justification for housing exactions, the benefits of new downtown development flowing to existing downtown commercial users and other land-based interests comprising Molotch's (1976) 'local growth machine' are overlooked. If these benefits were taken into account, then a use tax on all profitable property rather than a 'side payment' for new development would constitute a more adequate and equitable local policy.

Swanstrom (1986) has argued that it is possible for city governments with particular locational advantages to extract a 'class monopoly rent' (Harvey, 1985) from new investors in exchange for the right to develop property. Citing Boston as a case in point, Swanstrom argues that 'the strong pulling power of Boston's white collar economy opens up space for political entrepreneurs to promote policies independently of external economic pressures' (Swanstrom, 1986, p. 14). He characterises linked development as the extraction of a 'public surplus', amounting in Boston's case to an estimated $52 million over a ten-year period.

Conceived in this way, however, it becomes clear that 'linkage constitutes a particular form of taxation, a 'licence fee', if you will, whose pro-
ceeds are earmarked for specific purposes. The extraction of such fees
have proven symbolically useful to local political elites who lack adequate
financial and public policy resources to deal with the social needs of their
citizens. To the extent that its symbolic appeal is successful, this 'before
the fact' arrangement channels social discontent into a routine administrative formula; fails to take into account the long-term costs to the city
of the new service demands created by new development (e.g., police
and fire services); weakens the political support for future general tax
increases to pay for these costs; and pre-empts comprehensive 'after the
fact' adverse impact assessments. Viewed thus, a policy which seemingly
extracts a 'public surplus' from developers in exchange for political
quiescence begins to resemble a hidden form of future tax abatement –
the opposite of its intended purpose. Once developers pay a legally
required 'mitigation fee' they are in the position to use the payment as a
way to escape future taxation. If oppositional groups mobilise to demand
further impact assessments or new taxes to pay for the actual social costs
of development, developers can argue that they already have paid a
linked development impact fee. Used in this way 'linkage' could amount
to a licence to externalise the social costs of development.

Thus far, the chief real beneficiaries of linkage have been developers
themselves. Under the symbolism of 'compensation' and paying their
'fair share' of the costs of development, developers who have participated
in formal linkage policies have been freed from some of the constraints
of the political process. Their struggle with community groups has been
channelled into established bureaucratic formulae and routines. As
Susskind and his associates perceptively argue: 'Commercial developers,
desiring predictability, abhor the alternative to linkage i.e., an open-
ended bargaining situation in which project approvals are held hostage
for 'voluntary payments' set at arbitrary levels' (Susskind *et al.,* 1986, p.
12). As we have seen, open-ended bargaining stemming from community opposition to development projects on a case-by-case basis has produced a wider range of at least mildly redistributional outcomes in Santa
Monica and San Francisco, and also in Boston (see Pierce, 1983, p. 13),
than has been true in the case of linked development trust funds.

Perhaps this is the main reason why there are growing signs of a political role reversal on the question of linked development. In Santa
Monica, San Francisco, Boston, and Seattle major developers have
embraced the linked development concept. In Sacramento, it has been
the developers of the Natomas project, a multi-billion dollar mixed

development (MXD) which could increase the city's population by 20%, who have initiated various linkage and mitigation fee proposals. Community groups have sought to halt the project in court rather than fighting out the issue in terms of a political discourse based on linked development (*Sacramento Bee,* 26 November 1986). In other cities where coalitions of neighbourhood groups initially promoted linkage policies, these same coalitions have been among the policy's most persistent critics. In San Francisco, for example, neighbourhood groups have been forced to rely on citizen initiatives and lawsuits to ensure that city officials follow through in implementing linked development policies. In Boston, the city's Linkage Action Coalition launched a citywide campaign in 1985 to increase the linkage fee. When mayor Flynn responded by adding $1 to the fee, members of the Coalition argued that Flynn had stolen their thunder by promoting policy changes far less sweeping than were needed (Susskind *et al.,* 1986, p. 14).

Despite the limited material consequences of 'linkage' in addressing social needs and the immediate symbolic advantage the payment of 'mitigation' fees offer to developers, there is a deeper level of analysis which ought not to be overlooked. In the present US political economy the cultural acceptance of free-wheeling capitalism has assumed hegemonic status. The symbolism of 'public-private partnership' has elevated mundane corporate-government interplay into a sign of public interest and civic virtue (Smith, 1987). In this cultural context, the debate over 'linkage' policy at least has the potential to focus popular consciousness on the social costs of 'public-private partnership' and the profit system itself. While hardly a counter-hegemonic project, the debate over linkage, has focused on use values threatened by development. The deeper meaning underlying this debate is that cities are not only 'locations' for accumulating capital and achieving economic growth but also 'places' where people establish social ties, experience each other, and live out their everyday lives.

REFERENCES

Boston Globe (1985), 12 November.
City of Boston (1983), Advisory Group Report to the Mayor, Linkage Between Downtown and Neighbourhood Housing, Boston.
City of Boston (1986), The Flynn Administration at Mid-Term, Boston.
Clark, S. (1987), 'More autonomous policy orientations: An analytical framework', in C. Stone and H. Sanders (eds.), *The Politics of Urban Development,* Lawrence, University of Kansas Press.
Connors, D. L. and High, M. (1985), 'The expanding circle of exactions: From dedica-

tion to linkage', Boston, Choate, Holland, and Stewart, mimeo, pp. 1-29.

Feagin, J. (1986), 'Arenas of conflict: Zoning and land use reform in critical political-economic perspective', paper prepared for *Euclid* Symposium, Lincoln Institute of Land Policy Roundtable, Harvard University, Cambridge, Mass. (23-4 October), pp. 1-52.

Goodman, R. (1979), *The Last Entrepreneurs,* New York, Simon & Schuster.

Hartman, C. (1984), *The Transformation of San Francisco,* Totowa, New Jersey, Rowman & Allanheld.

Harvey, D. (1985), *The Urbanisation of Capital,* Oxford, Basil Blackwell.

Keating, D. (1986), 'Linking downtown development to broader community goals', *American Planning Association Journal,* Spring, pp. 133-41.

McMahon, G., Susskind, L., Tohn, E., Rolley, S., and Rustin, J. (1986), 'Reframing the rationale for downtown linkage programmes: New approaches to negotiated development', Program on Negotiation Working Papers Series, 86-2, July, pp. 1-77.

Mollenkopf, J. (1983), *The Contested City,* Princeton, NJ, Princeton University Press.

Molotch, H. (1976), 'The city as a growth machine: Toward a political economy of place', *American Journal of Sociology,* 82, pp. 309-32.

Pierce, N. (1983), 'A Boston development', *New Orleans Times Picayune/States Item,* 7 November, p. 13.

Sacramento Bee (1986), 26 November.

Schefter, M. (1985), *Political Crisis/Fiscal Crisis: The Collapse and Revival of New York City,* New York, Basic Books.

Smith, M.P. (1987), *City, State, and Market,* Oxford, Basil Blackwell.

Smith, M. P. and Judd, D. (1984), 'American cities: The production of ideology', in M.P. Smith (ed.), *Cities in Transformation.* Urban Affairs Annual Reviews, 26, Beverly Hills, Sage, pp 173-96.

Smith, M. P. and Keller, M. (1983), 'Managed growth and the politics of uneven development in New Orleans', in S. Fainstein, N. Fainstein, R.C. Hill, D. Judd, and M. P. Smith, *Restructuring the City,* New York and London, Longman, pp. 126-66.

Summers, G. F. and Branch, K. (1984), 'Economic Development and Community Social Change', *Annual Review of Sociology,* X, pp. 141-66.

Susskind, L., McMahon, G., Tohn, E., and Rolley, S. (1986), 'Reframing the rationale for downtown linkage policies', paper prepared for conference on 'Negotiated Development', Lincoln Institute of Land Policy, Cambridge, Mass., June, pp. 1-33.

Swanstrom, T. (1985), *The Crisis of Growth Politics,* Philadelphia, Temple University Press.

Swanstrom, T. (1986), 'Semisovereign cities: The political logic of urban development', paper prepared for the Annual Meeting of the American Political Science Association, Washington, DC (28-30 August), pp. 1-41.

Swanstrom, T. (1987), 'Urban populism, uneven development, and the space for reform', in S. Cummuns (ed.), *Corporate Elites and Urban Development,* New York, State University of New York Press.

8

Liverpool's fiscal crisis: an anatomy of failure

MICHAEL PARKINSON
University of Liverpool

For the past three years Liverpool has teetered on the brink of bankruptcy. The spectacle of a city in the throes of economic collapse, led by a Militant Labour council into a self-destructive political struggle has fascinated and appalled people. But why did it happen in this particular city, at the time it did, in the way it did, with the results it had? The answers to those questions shed light on a set of much more general issues. In the 1980s, Liverpool is at the centre of the economic, social and ideological forces shaping British cities. The city's financial crisis is symptomatic of a much deeper national economic, political and policy failure which will not be eliminated even if its budget problems are resolved.

It is a vivid demonstration of the failure of the Thatcher government's attempt to recapitalise British capitalism and to restructure the welfare state and urban economies (Tomaskovic and Miller, 1982). It confirms the argument of neo- and non-Marxists that fiscal crisis is not an automatic consequence of economic decline but is mediated by political actions, not merely those of the central state but those of local actors. More narrowly, the Liverpool story is an excellent guide to the technical processes of municipal creative accounting, which have been used by local authorities to adjust to the fiscal stresses imposed by the Thatcher government's new grant regime (Parkinson, 1986a). The city's experiences also demonstrate the failure of the central state's urban programme during the past two decades. They are an equally good guide to recent changes in the Labour party especially the emergence of specifically local forms of ideology and action (Gyford, 1985). Indeed the past three years are a perfect example of the frequently neglected political and cultural sources of local resistance to central state policies (Elliot and McCrone, 1984).

THE EVENTS

In 1983, when Labour won the first absolute majority on Liverpool city council for over a decade, the city's financial affairs stopped being a technical issue and became instead a highly charged political event. After that the Labour council used its financial problems to confront the Conservative government's strategy for the city and force the reluctant national Labour party to support its attempt to blackmail the government. In 1984 and 1985, the Labour council threatened to bankrupt the city if the government did not give Liverpool more money. In both years Labour eventually abandoned its threat after elaborate creative accounting. But it delayed setting its rate until several months into the financial year when the city was on the brink of bankruptcy. In 1986 Labour did set a rate on time but fixed its expenditure £37m higher than its income. For several months Liverpool again hovered on the brink of financial collapse, until a major financial coup in July 1986 allowed further creative accounting and the temporary postponement of the fiscal crisis for another year.

But Liverpool's campaign against the government and its national party leadership failed. In 1985 the national executive committee of the Labour Party suspended the Liverpool city party and in 1986 expelled several leading members of the Liverpool party for their membership of the proscribed Militant Tendency and for abuses of party rules during their budget campaign against the government. Meanwhile, in June 1985 48 Labour councillors were surcharged and disqualified from office by the District Auditor. The appeal process entered its last stages in 1987. After three years of Labour administration, the city's financial problems are worse than when they took office. The Labour council is politically isolated nationally and locally. But this failure has merely succeeded in diverting attention from the city's serious underlying economic and financial problems.

POLITICS, BUDGETS AND ECONOMICS 1974-83:
THE LOST DECADE

To understand the origins and nature of this failure we have to reconstruct the economic, political and financial history of the city during the past decade. The roots of the problem lie deep in that crucial period when a series of pressures pushed Liverpool towards a crisis: the collapse of its private economy as externally controlled corporations disinvested and restructured during an international recession; the election of a Conservative government with an ideological distaste for the public sector and commitment to the private sector; intense local ideological disputes and chaotic political responses to the city's economic decline; the introduction of a controversial government grant system designed to impose financial austerity on the city and finally the political radicalisation of Liverpool Labour and key municipal unions (Parkinson, 1985).

THE IMPACT OF LOCAL POLITICS

The peculiarities of Liverpool politics which are different from other English cities contributed directly to the crisis. The Labour Party has never had a grip upon Liverpool's voters. A tradition of casualism and sectarianism in the working class prevented Labour taking control in Liverpool until 1955, thirty years after many other cities had been captured. The Conservative party controlled Liverpool for virtually a century. Even after it won control in the mid-1950s, Labour had to share power with the Conservatives. But in the 1970s this pattern was shattered by a phenomenon which has never been repeated elsewhere – the emergence of a Liberal Party which controlled the city for most of a decade. But during this decade no party had an overall majority. There were constant hung councils, minority and coalition administrations and political confusion. The council was unable to develop a coherent strategy for the city as it was undergoing massive social change and economic decline.

Bitter arguments about the city's finances dominated the decade. Although Labour controlled the council for four years, it only got one budget passed in 1980. Every other year the Liberals and Conservatives imposed expenditure cuts upon minority Labour administrations. During this 'lost decade' of coalition politics the Liberal Party in its attempt to create an electoral base for itself in the most working-class city in the country, restricted council expenditure, held down the rate increases and engaged in elaborate creative accounting to raise the money to run the city. The result was that although in 1973/4 Liverpool's rate level was 45% higher than the national average, by 1978/9 it had fallen to only 1% above. And it had acquired very high levels of long-term capital debt which had been used to finance revenue expenditure. Rate rises failed to keep pace with inflation and expenditure fell behind other local authorities and even central government guidelines.

CENTRAL GOVERNMENT GRANTS

But this municipal parsimony in the search for votes during the 1970s created enormous problems for any party running the city in the 1980s when the Conservative government introduced a new grant regime. It became central to Labour's claim, which was publicly endorsed by the council's professional officers, that the grant system imposed an unreasonable burden upon the city. The grant system was introduced in 1980 in the Conservative's efforts to roll back the frontiers of the state and cut public expenditure.

The system is extremely complicated but in principle it tries to do two rather different things. It attempts to equalise the financial position of local authorities and to make sure that cities with very different financial resources can provide a similar level of service for their different populations, for a similar tax level. But at the same time, the grant system is also used to reduce cities' spending by penalising individual authorities who spend more than the government wants them to. The first is a relatively systematic, if complicated, way of allocating government money to local authorities. The second is a much more arbitrary way of reducing local expenditure which undermines the first intention of equalising the financial circumstances of different authorities. The system has changed several times, but in principle cities have systematically been asked to cut their spending in percentage terms from the levels they were at when the Conservatives took control in 1979. The government sets a target level and those authorities which spend above that figure have to pay a penalty – the government cuts the amount of grant it had originally calculated the city should get. And the penalties have become increasingly steep in recent years.

There are important technical disputes about whether the government employs appropriate measures for distributing grants to local authorities. But they are far less controversial than arguments about the way in which the government has used the target and penalty mechanism to cut local spending. Even the Audit Commission in 1984 argued that although the grant system with its needs assessment and equalisation machinery was broadly fair and consistent, it had been significantly weakened by the superimposition of expenditure targets and penalties (Audit Commission, 1984). In 1986 the target system was abandoned. However, stringent controls over central support mean that the financial circumstances of local authorities have not been improved. In Liverpool's case, the political damage had already been done.

By the mid-1980s the government was still concerned by its failure to control spending as local authorities increased rates to compensate for the loss of government grant. In 1985, the government with its rate-capping legislation assumed the power for the first time to control local spending directly by setting tax limits for local authorities. The grant system is now under constant attack, regarded by many independent observers as a complicated, irrational and arbitrary system, which has at best damaged local democracy and relations between central and local government (Jones and Stewart, 1985; Newton and Karran, 1985). Labour in Liverpool claimed it had been more adversely treated by the grant system than comparable big cities. It had three powerful points. Because of its coalition politics, Liverpool, unlike many Labour authorities, had limited its expenditure during the 1970s. Yet the government asked it to reduce its expenditure a second time in the 1980s, by giving it more stringent targets than those Labour-controlled authorities who in the 1970s had developed large base budgets on which their more generous targets rested. Labour believed its past virtue was punished while others' profligacy was rewarded.

Liverpool also had a good case about the grant system's lack of sufficient indicators of economic deprivation such as levels of income, poverty or unemployment. During the past decade, central government has increasingly defined economic decline as the central issue of urban policy. But the block grant system, a city's primary source of direct government money, does not build economic deprivation into its calculation of local need in any significant way. If this were made as central to the government's calculation of the city's grant as it is to its definition of the urban crisis, Liverpool would get more money and its financial difficulties would be more manageable (Bramley, 1984).

Finally, Liverpool had a powerful argument that the scale of its population loss – from 850,000 to 490,000 in thirty years and still continuing at 7,000 a year – made it virtually impossible to cut its expenditure as quickly as the grant system required. Despite all the sophistication of the grant system, the size of the city's population remains by far the most important determinant of how much money it gets, drowning more subtle indicators of need. When population falls so does the grant. Liverpool argued that the scale of its population loss, which remains greater than that of other declining cities, made it especially unfairly treated.

THE RADICALISATION OF LIVERPOOL LABOUR

Labour party politics during this period also contributed to the crisis. Throughout the 1970s the Liverpool Labour Party moved from its traditional right of centre position towards the far left. At the same time there was an important shift in the power of the unions within the Labour Party. As the city's traditional industries – the car factories, the docks, transportation – declined, their unions lost ground and with it some power in the Labour Party. By contrast the white and blue collar public sector unions, representing the only expanding part of the local economy, became more powerful. And their leadership was moving them to the left. These unions encouraged the Labour Party to engage in a confrontation with the Thatcher government over the loss of public sector jobs required by cuts in government aid to the city.

These trends were reinforced by the rise of the revolutionary Militant Tendency. Militant began in Liverpool and has always been important. But during the 1980s it became especially powerful, rapidly building up its membership and organisation in the city. The Tendency devised Labour's bankruptcy plan as part of its platform to recruit national support on the basis of hard left local opposition to the capitalist government. By 1981 Militant had persuaded the party that when it obtained power it should threaten to bankrupt the city. A Labour administration should set a 'deficit' budget and refuse either to increase its taxes or to cut its spending to compensate for grant cuts in an effort to blackmail the Conservative government into giving Liverpool more money. If the government did not acquiesce, the city would run out of money and schools, nurseries and old people's homes would close, housing repairs would end, the dead would not even be buried. All city employees would lose their jobs. Either way Militant calculated they would benefit. The government would concede and reveal its ...eaknesses in the face of Militant pressure. Or it would refuse and reveal the unacceptable face of capitalism. Yet this primitive argument found support from Liverpool's voters in the 1980s.

LIVERPOOL, THE GOVERNMENT AND URBAN PROGRAMMES

This mood of local chauvinism was encouraged by the city's experience of the government's urban strategy during the past twenty years. During this period, Liverpool experienced every inner-city initiative since the original Urban Programme in the late 1960s to Enterprise Zones, Urban Development Corporations, and Task Forces in the 1980s. However, the programmes did little to help the city's underlying economic problems but increased local scepticism of what it was possible to achieve in the city through 'special initiatives'.

The initiatives failed for a variety of well documented reasons (Parkinson and Wilks, 1983; Parkinson and Duffy, 1984; Parkinson and Wilks,

1985a, 1985b). Partly it was a problem of analysis and definition. Many of the earlier programmes focused on the social symptoms of Liverpool's decline but failed to identify or address its underlying structural economic decline. Partly it was a question of resources. The amounts of money involved were relatively trivial in relation either to the scale of the problem or even to the resources that go into conventional government programmes, for example housing, transportation, industry and manpower which have a major impact upon cities. Inner-city policies frequently remained divorced from those mainstream government programmes which pulled in different directions from inner-city initiatives. They rarely succeeded in getting all the government departments which had an impact upon the inner city to play a part and frequently lacked coherence. The experience convinced local officials and politicians that central government was not seriously committed to solving the city's problems.

These criticisms applied to Labour governments in the 1960s and 1970s. But they were even more applicable to the Conservative government in the 1980s. Partly it was because government money to the city had been falling since 1979, even if the money for special programmes has been sustained. But primarily it was the ideological thrust of the Conservative government's urban policy. Its efforts to wind down the public sector and replace it with private sector-led urban regeneration damaged the city's economy and shaped its political life.

FROM ECONOMIC COLLAPSE TO FINANCIAL CRISIS

Liverpool's economic problems are the key to the affair. Until the late 1970s the poor performance of the local economy did not have a major impact upon the financial health of the city because high levels of public expenditure and a relatively generous government grant system protected the local authority from the most severe effects of structural decline. But cuts in central government support since the mid-1970s under Labour but particularly under the Conservatives in the 1980s, have changed that.

The decline in the local resource base has become a much more serious problem for the city because it now has to make a larger contribution to the local authority's income to compensate for the drop in national support. When the Conservatives took power in 1979, central government was providing almost 63% of the city's net income and the rates 37%. By 1983 when Labour took control in Liverpool, the government's contribution had dropped to 44% and the rates had risen to over 55%. By the mid-1980s cuts in government financial support to the city had turned economic failure into fiscal crisis and brought Liverpool to the edge of municipal bankruptcy.

Liverpool's long-term economic decline is turning into collapse as it threatens to become the first deindustrialised city in the nation. The problem stems from the city's historic dependence upon the port. This dominated the local economy for nearly two centuries, but when it went into decline in the international economic recession that followed the World War I, it left a gap in the local economy that nothing else has filled. State policies to attract economic growth during the 1950s with regional aid for the car industry did briefly staunch the tide, but since the 1960s decline has proceeded apace.

The crucial problem of Liverpool's manufacturing economy is the pattern of ownership. Far more than in other cities, it is dominated by a small number of very large absentee employers. In the 1980s, 57% of manufacturing jobs were in plants employing over 1,000 workers. The national average is 29%. Less than 1% of the city's firms provide nearly 40% of total employment. In 1985, seven large firms controlled almost half of the manufacturing jobs in the city. Between 1981 and 1985 these seven firms shed 30% of their jobs. Many of these firms are externally controlled national or multinational corporations: in 1975 the figure was 70%. By 1985 only one of the 20 largest firms was locally controlled. These firms have national and international markets with no commitment to Liverpool. Their plants are particularly vulnerable to the loss of jobs as such firms rationalise and restructure during a recession. Production and investment in Liverpool is cut first, wiping out any marginal gains in the small firm sector and aggravating the process of disinvestment.

These changes in the economy have created a major unemployment problem. During the 1970s the city's unemployment rate quadrupled from 5% to 20%. By 1985 it was 27%, double the national average. Unemployment also lasts longer in the city. In 1979, 24% of unemployed people nationally had been out of work for over one year. In Liverpool the figure was 37%. By 1985, the national figure had risen to 39%, but in Liverpool it was 53%. The city's failure to attract high status white collar jobs in the growing service sector to compensate for the loss of manufacturing jobs has aggravated the problem. It has also increased the importance of public sector jobs. Council jobs are especially important. In 1985, the city council employed 40% of all public sector workers, constituting 15% of the city's total workforce.

Between 1973 and 1978 public employment in Liverpool increased and partially concealed the decline of the private sector. But in the second half of the decade, as governments restrained public expenditure, local authority employment in the city declined. This was a major part of the conflict between the city and the government. In this context, local authority trade unions became increasingly concerned to protect 'jobs and services' and encouraged its 'blackmail and bankruptcy' strategy. When Labour won control of the city in 1983, all these forces were pushing towards a confrontation with a Conservative government.

THE FIRST ROUND: THE 1984/5 BUDGET

Labour first tried to blackmail the government into giving Liverpool more money in 1984, producing its first 'deficit' budget. The government had set it a target of £216 million. But Labour planned to spend £269 million. In addition to this, Labour had spent beyond its 1983/4 target and ended the year with a deficit of over £34 million. When added to the 1984/5 budget the council intended to spend £269 million. At that level, the council would only get £27 million in government grant, leaving £269 million to be raised from the rates. But Labour intended to increase the rates by 9%, which would produce only £108 million. The city would inevitably run out of money before the end of the financial year and all its services would collapse.

Despite this threat of financial suicide, in the May 1984 council elections, Labour increased its council seats from 51 to 58. This popular victory dramatically changed the political picture. The national Labour leadership, who had been opposed to Liverpool's tactics, pressed the government to help the city. After two months of negotiations an agreement was reached. The government gave Liverpool some extra, but marginal funding, in return for Labour abandoning its bankruptcy plan.

But Labour had to make many concessions to the government and drop many of its spending plans. Most important the council engaged in substantial creative accounting, in particular transferring from its capital budget £13 million, which had been intended to pay for part of its house building programme, to the revenue budget to help pay the wages of workers who maintained and repaired existing housing. This 'capitalisation' of revenue spending inevitably limited Labour's major housing programme which was also its main attempt to stimulate a declining local economy. This particular device had originally been strenuously resisted by the council. However, these changes, along with some other risky creative accounting, allowed the council to cut planned spending to £223m, eliminating all government penalties.

But the council did not increase its rents or fees. It made no effort to reduce its workforce and hence its salary bills. And it only increased the rates by 17%, more than the original 9%, but far less than was necessary to get the council's finances on a sound long term basis. In other words, the 1984/5 budget was balanced by creative accounting only. The council's underlying financial problems were simply transferred into 1985/6.

ROUND TWO: THE 1985/6 BUDGET

The Labour council reopened its argument with the government almost as soon as the 1984/5 budget had been agreed, four months into the financial year. This year the politics were different for two reasons. In the first case, the Labour council had exploited the small concessions the government had offered in July and claimed a major political victory. This embarrassed and angered the Conservative government, convincing it there was no political mileage in trying to help Labour further. It decided to resist all future pleas for special treatment for the city.

The second political difference in 1985 was that Liverpool had joined with a number of other Labour controlled local authorities in a campaign to resist the government's rate-capping legislation. They adopted a strategy of refusing to set a rate until the government changed its legislation. The government did not do so however and eventually all the authorities conceded and set a rate. However, Liverpool was the last to do so. But this delay led to the Labour councillors' legal downfall. After several unsuccessful efforts to persuade Liverpool to make a rate, the District Auditor set in motion complicated and expensive legal proceedings against the councillors which lasted until 1987.

In June 1985, he argued that by delaying setting a rate the council had lost at least £106,000 and he intended to surcharge them for that amount and disqualify them from office for five years, bankrupting those councillors who could not pay. The councillors' formal reply in July essentially argued that they had delayed setting the rate because they believed the government would concede to its threat of bankruptcy as in 1984 and provide the city with extra money. The problem was that Labour's exploitation of the government's concessions in 1984 had guaranteed the city would receive no extra help in 1985. The tactic had been self-defeating. The Auditor took this view and rejected their defence. The councillors subsequently appealed against his decision. But both the High Court and Court of Appeal upheld the Auditor's view and confirmed the decision. The House of Lords heard the case in January 1987 and finally confirmed the councillors' expulsion from office.

The delay in setting the rate in 1985 led the Labour council into enormous legal difficulties. It caused equally large political problems with the national Labour Party. Throughout 1985 the Labour council once again refused to balance its books. In June, Labour presented its 1984 tactic and presented its second deficit budget. Despite its expenditure target of £222 million for 1985/6, the council planned to spend £265 million. At that level, rate support grant would fall to £29 million, leaving £241 million to be paid for from the rates, which would require a rate increase of 170%. But Labour planned to increase the rates by 9% which would produce only £125 million and leave a deficit of £117 million. The city would run out of money at some point in the autumn of 1985.

In September the council took the step that its bankruptcy tactic had always required, but which nevertheless created political turmoil. It issued redundancy notices to all its 31,000 employees. They would lose their jobs in December 1985 and be reinstated in the new financial year four months later. This tactic split the local unions. Some accepted it, but more rejected it. The district Labour Party was thrown into confusion by the move. However, the national Labour leadership, which was stunned by the tactic, was clear what it wanted. The council should balance its books, in whatever way was necessary. At the annual national party conference in October the national leadership forced the council to allow an inquiry into its finances by independent experts. The inquiry, led by Morris Stonefrost, an eminent local authority treasurer, reported in November 1985 – the first time that the council's finances had been exposed to extensive independent scrutiny, when it was within days of bankruptcy.

In many respects the report supported the council's claim that its problems arose at least partly from 'the effect of the system of grant assessments on the council's position at a time of economic and social stress in Liverpool'. Nevertheless, Stonefrost argued that the council could avoid bankruptcy. As an immediate step, the council should again use some of its capital funds to pay for revenue expenditure even though it would limit its house building programme. However, Stonefrost insisted that capitalisation on its own was not enough. The council should start to tackle its difficult financial decisions if it were to establish financial credibility and prevent the crisis returning in future years. It had to start matching income and expenditure and should cut its services, increase its fees and put its rates up by a further 15%. The problem could not be resolved 'solely by accountancy transactions which ease the problems in 1985/6 and add to the problems of 1986/7' (Stonefrost, 1985).

But this was exactly what happened in November 1985 with all the consequences Stonefrost had predicted. As political support drifted away, Labour finally abandoned its stand a few days before the city was due to go bankrupt. The council again agreed to capitalise over £23 million of revenue expenditure in two financial years. With reduced grant penalties the revenue budget was cut to £222 million, the amount that the rate levied in June would finance. But the council did not raise its rates, balanced its books by creative accounting and ignored the underlying problems.

In fact the solution adopted worsened the council's long-term problems. It raised the money to capitalise £23 million of revenue spending by making a deferred payment arrangement with a London stockbroker. Under this deal, a financial syndicate of Swiss bankers paid up to £30 million to private contractors working on the council's capital programme in 1985/6. This released an equivalent amount from existing capital resources to balance the revenue budget. But the loan has to be repaid over a five-year period. In future, the council will have to find up to £8 million a year from its capital allocation to repay the loan. This will make it difficult for the council to finance any future house building or even repair existing housing. Eventually it became clear that the financial deal had first been made in September 1985. The Labour council had allowed the city to hover on the brink of financial collapse for over three months, and threatened redundancy for all its employees, when the eventual solution had apparently been available all the time. That provoked the national leadership to suspend the Liverpool Labour Party.

THE THIRD ROUND: THE 1986/7 BUDGET

The council's second budget crisis was not resolved until the financial year was already eight months old. The council lurched from one crisis to another with virtually no long-term financial planning. This promoted the District Auditor to release a devastating attack on the Labour council which argued that its 'financial and management systems are seriously out of hand and urgent steps are needed to correct the situation'. The council was entering into commitments without knowing how they can be financed which was 'a recipe for future financial chaos'. He demanded the council produce a balanced budget for 1986/7. Instead the council presented a deficit budget for a third year running.

Since the city had spent beyond its 1985/6 target, it had been rate-capped by the government for 1986/7 at £274 million, allowing a 15% rate increase. It could spend no more and could not increase its rates further.

In 1985/6, the authority's base budget had been £262 million but had been balanced by capitalisation. In 1986/7, after allowing for inflation, it would cost £287 million to provide the same services, plus £24 million to run new services which Liverpool had inherited after the abolition of the metropolitan counties. The city needed to spend £311 million in 1986/7, but was restricted to £274 million, a gap of £37 million unless further reserves and capital receipts could be found. The city hovered on the edge of bankruptcy again for several months. However, once again at the last moment in July 1986, the council revealed it had negotiated a further deferred payment arrangement, this time with a Japanese bank. Under the deal, the banks would once again pay up to £30 million of Liverpool's capital spending in 1986/7, which would release a similar amount from its existing capital resources to help balance the revenue budget.

But once again the council made little real effort to match its income and its expenditure. The deal stored up enormous problems for any future administration. The loan has to be repaid over seven years and added to the first becomes another charge against the city's capital allocation. But it did not help the revenue problem either. The council will again have to find the resources to cover the deficit covered in 1986/7 by capitalisation. Since the government, partly in response to Liverpool's tactics, has since made deferred payments deals illegal, the city will not be able to raise money in that way. Either major tax increases or substantial cuts remain inevitable while the long-term capital debt has been dramatically increased.

Liverpool's finances remain a pack of cards which will probably come crashing down one day. The council's long term hope is that a future Labour government will provide a major increase in resources to solve the city's underlying financial problems. But that would impose an enormous strain as other authorities would also lay claim for special treatment. Secondly, the political division between the national and local Labour party has been made so great during the past three years that the prospect of special treatment for the city has probably been diminished rather than increased. The Labour council's campaign has been a political disaster. Yet the city's long-term financial and economic prospects remain bleaker than ever.

Budgets are financial statements. They are also political gestures. Liverpool remains on the edge of collapse because the Labour council refused to make the decisions necessary to balance its books. Essentially it was a political decision, devised deep within the Labour Party. The council's professional officers consistently advised against the strategy. Even the Labour group on the council did not make the policy. The theory of party democracy in Liverpool meant that the policy was determined by the district Labour Party consisting of non-elected party delegates and trade-unionists. The group simply implemented it. Within the district party, power to initiate policy was concentrated in the executive committee. Within the Labour group itself power was highly concentrated in the hands of the chairman of the finance and strategy committee. The Labour party may have endorsed the strategy. But the informal concentration of political power within the party meant that the controversial policy was made not openly but in secrecy by a narrow elite.

The centralisation and secretiveness of the Liverpool Party sharply distinguishes it from many other city Labour parties which since the 1970s have made a virtue of pluralism, participation, consultation, openness and decentralisation. It fundamentally distorted the course of Labour's campaign to get extra resources for the city. It led to a political disaster which will poison politics in the city for many years and might even affect the prospects of the election of a future Labour government.

THE FUTURE

This analysis of Liverpool's financial crisis has been an anatomy of failure. The crisis reflects a larger set of problems. It underlines many familiar but nevertheless important failings of past policies and raises equally familiar and intractable problems for the future. The overriding issue is the collapse of the city's private economy as mobile capital has fled from an immobile community in the search for greater profits beyond Merseyside. For the past decade government policies for the economy and the public sector have hastened the city's economic decline by depressing public demand in an already depressed local economy. Any attempt to rescue or regenerate the city's economy would require a quite different macro-economic strategy. There can be mo merely local solutions to Liverpool's economic problems. It requires national solutions.

The failure of special government initiatives to cope with the consequences of the economic decline of the city is equally clear. The urban programme of the past twenty years is bankrupt in intellectual terms. In resource terms it is a diversion, unable to compensate for the failure of the government's main programmes which have had a much larger, adverse impact upon the city. Cuts in the block grant, capital allocations, transport, health and social services expenditure, the priorities of industrial and regional policy have swamped the economic and organisational resources of the urban strategy.

In political terms the programme is counter-productive, merely inducing cynicism about government intentions. In institutional terms it is a fragmented package of bits and pieces from task forces to enterprise zones and development corporations, quite incapable of giving the necessary lead for the economic regeneration of the metropolitan economy. The abolition of the metropolitan county council, the only agency whose boundaries were remotely coterminous with the economic region, underlines this point. Institutional leadership for the larger region has to be found if economic regeneration is to be contemplated.

The ideological thrust of central policy to revitalise Britain through a free market and small firm strategy is equally irrelevant or damaging to Liverpool. The strategy of private sector-led recovery has not and will not work in the city. The private sector was not crowded out of Liverpool by the public sector. It left of its own accord, even while the local rate burden was relatively low. Where there has been limited private sector involvement in the city recently through the Merseyside Development Corporation, technology park or enterprise zone, it has been public sector led. The private sector, if it has invested at all, has had the risk taken out by public subsidy. If economic confidence is to be restored in the city, the public sector will have to play a lead role. The economic success of some British and American cities reinforces this argument. A variety of long-term hidden public subsidies, very often defence expenditure, have been the key to urban regeneration.

The small firm sector is hardly likely to save a city which is dominated by large employers and has less tradition of such activity than even other large cities. Even if one ignores the fact that small firms are frequently the least dynamic, most conservative part of the economy, the net contribution they can make to job creation is trivial in relation to major private sector withdrawals. Equally, the local authority can probably achieve more by directly employing people at a lower cost than trying to massage small private firms into life. Even where modest growth is possible in the local private economy, the benefits will be unequally shared. With at least 60,000 people unemployed, there are sectors of the labour market which will never be touched by a minor revival of the private sector.

Liverpool's crisis also raises questions about the cultural dimensions of failure. The secular decline of the economy, the rapid emigration of many qualified residents, the political paralysis of the 1970s and the divisions of the 1980s, the failure of so many government experiments has had an important effect upon the city's local economic and political elites. It has created a failure of confidence and an inability to mobilise existing social capital around the city's objectively powerful case. The tactical disasters of the Labour council in its budget crisis are sui generis. But the self-destructive political behaviour finds an echo in civic life in Liverpool. Economic change requires constructive political response. That has been found in some Labour-controlled cities.

But Liverpool is a house divided. Leadership rarely reaches the heights necessary to face objectively demoralising decline. The city administration itself is a demoralised and inefficient organisation, which has lacked clear political or administrative leadership for over a decade. The government is at least right in this respect, even though it is wrong to suggest that this is the primary reason for Liverpool's financial difficulties. The failure of the Liverpool business elites to respond to change at the end of the nineteenth century, in contrast for example to its near neighbour Manchester, finds a parallel in the current failure to respond. Liverpool's MPs carry little weight in parliamentary or national party politics. The absence of indigenous capital and the branch plant syndrome also drains local leadership. It is no accident that Liverpool's most powerful advocates are neither politicians nor business leaders but the city's two church leaders. This absence of effective leadership makes a difference. It means the city does not effectively lobby government or the private sector to attract its share of scare mobile capital.

This raises the question of what is necessary to break that elite culture of failure. After the Toxteth riots in 1981, the Minister for Merseyside, Michael Haseltine, sensed this subjective dimension of the city's problems and tried to break the cycle of failure with a series of prestige urban renewal projects which might begin to restore private and public sector confidence in the city and attract further investment. Whether the government's response was adequate is debatable. But the cultural dimension of failure cannot be ignored. This is not an attempt to blame the victim. There are valid objective reasons for the city's demoralisation. But institutions are not the only key to Liverpool's problems. The lack of leadership to mobilise the community against its economic problems is crucial. Many changes in policies and institutions are needed to begin the process of reconstruction. But they will still need animation.

What might those policies and institutions be? A rapid social audit indicates that too much public money on Merseyside is being wasted on the social costs of unemployment and makes no contribution to economic growth on the labour or capital side. But the declining rate of emigration from Liverpool, the low level of national investment in housing and the structural levels of unemployment nationally indicate that these costs will not fall in the foreseeable future. The real argument is about the use of that continuing expenditure.

Nevertheless, the scale of the problems should not be underestimated. The most to be expected is a way of staunching the flow while longer-term plans can be made to begin the process of structural economic and social modernisation that the city needs to cope with the decades beyond the 80s. One clear lesson from the American experience is that the policies which did lead to economic regeneration in some cities were a long time coming to fruition. The Sunbelt received major public investment for several decades before it took off on its economic flight.

What kind of institution with what kinds of powers could address the problem of the modernisation of the city? The local authority is important. Its direct contribution as a major employer to the creation of welfare and wealth in the local economy, especially through its housing programmes, cannot be underestimated. Central constraints on revenue, but especially capital, expenditure would have to be relaxed to allow the local authority to develop this role. Nevertheless there are limits to a local authority's capacity to lead urban regeneration. The experience of the past two decades is that this requires a strategic approach and a set of powers and resources that are simply beyond a bounded local authority, let alone one that is virtually bankrupt like Liverpool.

The details of a programme remain to be worked out. But there is a need for a package of measures which would: boost short term employment through public expenditure upon capital and social programmes, possibly through a community jobs initiative; upgrade the depressed physical environment, preferably involving a major project like the Mersey barrage; upgrade existing social capital with a major retraining programme designed to meet the need for future not traditional skills; assess the gaps in the labour market and the needs of the private sector and integrate the two; design a strategy for both sunrise and sunset industries and generate the investment capital to implement it.

At present, no agency has the powers to design or implement such a programme. The Merseyside Development Corporation comes nearest, but has too narrow a geographical and policy remit. The agencies in the field are reactive rather than proactive in style. This inevitably leads to a discussion of the merits of a regional economic development agency despite the questions about their effectiveness and lack of accountability. But the private market will not do it alone; the local authority cannot do it; and central government is too distant. The alternative of continued drift is ominous.

REFERENCES

Audit Commission (1984), *The Impact on Local Authorities' Economy Efficiency and Effectiveness of the Block Grant System,* HMSO, London.

Bramley, Glen (1984), 'Grant Related Expenditure and the Inner City', *Local Government Studies,* May/June, pp. 45-8.

Elliot, Brian and McCrone, Donald (1984), 'Austerity and the Politics of Resistance', in Ivan Szelenyi, *Cities in Recession,* Beverly Hills, Sage, pp. 192-216.

Gyford, John (1985), *Local Socialism,* London, Allen & Unwin.

Jones, G., and Stewart, J. (1985), *The Case for Local Government,* London, Allen & Unwin.

Newton K. and Karran T. J. (1985), *The Politics of Local Expenditure,* London, Macmillan.

Parkinson, Michael and Wilks, S. (1983), 'Managing urban decline: the case of the inner city partnerships', *Local Government Studies,* September/ October, pp. 23-39.

Parkinson, Michael and Duffy, J. (1984), 'Responding to inner city riots: the minister for Merseyside and the task Force', *Parliamentary Affairs,* 36, pp. 76-96.

Parkinson, Michael (1985), *Liverpool on the Brink,* Hermitage, Policy Journals.

Parkinson, Michael (1986a), 'Creative Accounting and Financial Ingenuity in Local Government', *Public Money,* 5, pp. 27-32.

Parkinson, Michael (1986b), 'Decision-Making by Liverpool City Council', in 'Aspects of Local Democracy', *Research,* Volume 4, The Widdicombe Inquiry into the Conduct of Local Authority Business, London, HMSO.

Parkinson, Michael (1986c), 'No Easy Options', *Public Money,* 6, pp. 7-9.

Parkinson, Michael and Wilks, S. (1985a), 'Testing Partnership to Destruction', *Regional Studies,* 19, pp. 27-32.

Parkinson, Michael and Wilks, S. (1985b), 'The Politics of Inner City Partnerships', in Goldsmith, M. (ed.), *New Research in Central-Local Relations,* Aldershot, Gower, pp. 290-307.

The Stonefrost Report (1985), circulated document, no page numbers.

Tomaskovic-Devey, Donald and Miller, S. M. (1982), 'Recapitalisation; The Basic US Urban Policy of the 1980s', in Fainstein, Norman I. and Fainstein, Susan S. (eds.), *Urban Policy under Capitalism,* Beverly Hills, Sage, pp. 23-42.

9

The politics of economic redistribution in Chicago: is balanced growth possible?

MICHAEL B. PRESTON

University of Southern California and Visiting Professor, University of Illinois-Urbana

Chicago has been called the most political city in the world. Nothing of importance happens in the city without some type of political involvement. Who sits in the skyboxes at Chicago Bears football games, to who gets public building contracts (and in some cases private ones as well), is all fair game for politicians. Although politics in Chicago has always been colourful, the city is best known for its legendary political machine, under former mayor Richard J. Daley (1955-1976). Since 1983, and the election of Harold Washington, Chicago's first black mayor, and a reformer, politics in the city has undergone some tremendous changes. But one thing has not changed – politics still takes centre stage in Chicagoans' life and culture.

Chicago is also a city of neighbourhoods which historically have been divided along racial, ethnic and class lines. The city's reputation as the most segregated in the nation has not changed in the 1980s. Indeed, the election of Harold Washington as the city's first black mayor has in some cases heightened this racial division. One is never sure whether white ethnic politicians dislike Washington so much because he is black or because he is a reformer. There is only one thing regular democratic politicians hate more than a black mayor and that is a black reform mayor. That puts Harold Washington in an unenviable position. To understand contemporary politics in Chicago is to understand the continuing significance of racial conflict and its detrimental economic and social impact.

Mayor Harold Washington has introduced the concept of balanced growth. He was unhappy, along with neighbourhood groups and others in Chicago, with the way former mayors catered to the wishes of downtown interests and neglected the neighbourhoods. Washington is not opposed to growth, but he wants to link downtown growth with neighbourhood development.

This paper examines Mayor Washington's efforts to redistribute economic development in Chicago. The central question is whether balanced growth is possible in a city where politicians have for so long catered to big developers and big business. An equally important question is whether the political and racial divisions between the mayor and his white ethnic opponents in the City Council will inhibit his efforts to achieve that balanced growth because of their fears that he will reap political gain with their constituents. Finally, is balanced growth possible in a city surrounded by suburbs on the 'make' for new business and development? These tasks are not made easier by the political infighting between the City Council and the mayor.

To answer these questions we need information on four others: 1) what role does demography play in metropolitan Chicago and what is its impact on city politics; 2) will economic development be paralysed by Chicago politics; 3) what are the key policy issues in linked development; and 4) will the future of economic development in Chicago turn on technical questions or on the issues of political and racial peace? We discuss each of these questions below.

DEMOGRAPHIC TRENDS

Chicago is the third largest city in the USA, with a population exceeding three million.[1] The metropolitan area, consisting of Chicago and its 262 collar suburbs and 1,200 governments totals 7.1 million residents and is the third largest in the nation.

The metropolitan area is growing, with its total population predicted to increase modestly over the next twenty years. For example, the Bureau of Economic Analysis of the Department of Commerce in Illinois has predicted a 7% growth of population to 7.6 million by the year 2,000.

TABLE 9.1

Race/Ethnicity	Population	% of total
White	5,210,228	73.3
Black	1,427,826	20.2
American Indian Eskimo, Aleut Asian, Pacific Islander	141,349	2.0
Other	324,221	4.5
Total	7,103,624	100.0

Source: Chicago's Assets for Business and Industry, City of Chicago, Harold Washington, Mayor, Department of Economic Development.

While the age distribution of the area is similar to that of the US as a whole, the local population is better educated and has a more active workforce. These characteristics account, in part, for the substantially higher local income levels. Nationally, 62% of the adult population participates in the labour force; in the Chicago area, participation exceeds 66%. The Chicago Metropolitan area median family income is more pronounced. The Chicago area median family income of $22,329 (1980) was 23% above that of the total United States. However, the median income for whites in Chicago is $24,535; Blacks, $14,796; Hispanics, $14,850 (Department of Economic Development, 1984; Preston, 1987b).

The census report shows the racial populations represented in Table 9.1. There are several important things to note about the Chicago Metropolitan Region. First, the suburbs are growing. The six counties, Cook, Will, DuPage, Kane, Lake and McHenry grew in population by 15.8% from 1970-1980. Second, 90.1% of this population is white, while blacks make up 6.2%. Third, Chicago's population has a large number of blacks and other minorities (see Table 9.2). While Chicago is losing jobs and people, the suburbs are gaining them at the expense of the city.

By contrast, the demographic structure of the city is quite different from that of the suburbs. The Chicago Planning Department, estimated in July 1985 that blacks made up 41.3% of the city, and whites 42.5% (Terry, 1986). The report indicated that the black population grew by only 4% in Chicago between 1980-1985, continuing a two-decade trend of declining black growth. One reason for the slow growth of the City itself is the increase in blacks moving to the suburbs. The report also indicates that Hispanics are now the fastest growing ethnic group in the city with an increase of 61,702 since 1980. Hispanics number 483,765 or 16.2% of the city population. The report also indicates that white flight has slowed in the 1980s. Between 1980 and 1984, 90,359 whites left town, compared with 601,396 who left during the 1970s (Terry, 1986).

The city's current population of 3,005,078 is down substantially since the 1960s, and the loss of white population has also meant a loss of revenue and jobs for the city. Simply put, jobs follow people.

Another consequence of this shift in population is that Chicago has lost some political influence in federal, state and county politics. Along with the cutback in federal funds, Chicago must now rely on the state and a republican governor to help make up for the loss of federal aid. For a democratic city in a republican state, that causes problems.

Another consequence of the demographic changes was the election of Harold Washington as the city's first black mayor. Washington's victory surprised and astounded white regular democrats, white ethnic voters, the media and almost everyone else in Chicago and the nation. It should not have. Black voters had given warnings since 1975 that they were unhappy with the white machine. In 1979 they voted against the machine with a vengeance and helped elect Mayor Jane Byrne whom they saw as a reformer. However, when it became obvious she was not, in the 1980 elections they defeated all of her candidates for political office. In 1983, when Harold Washington entered the race for mayor, the stage was set for black voters to reject the machine and its candidates. They did so in a way that astonished the city, the nation, and the world (Preston, 1987a). One of the key differences between Washington and past mayors was the emphasis he placed on the need to achieve balanced economic growth across all of Chicago.

TABLE 9.2
POPULATION BY RACE FOR CHICAGO, 1980

	White	Black	Other	Hispanics*	Total
No.	1,490,215	1,197,000	317,846	422,063	3,005,078
%	49.6	39.8	10.6	14.0	100.0

* Hispanic persons may be of any race. In Chicago 190,659 (45.2%) of Hispanics are white; 9,095 (2.1%) are black; 222,309 (52.7%) are of another race.
Source: 1980 Census of Population and Housing.

CHICAGO POLITICS AND ECONOMIC DEVELOPMENT: THE WASHINGTON PLAN

The election of Harold Washington introduced many changes in city government. One of the most important changes is the shift in focus on economic development. During the machine era, especially under Mayor Richard J. Daley, the emphasis was primarily on the economic growth of the downtown area. Daley welcomed and helped initiate downtown development for the machine reaped the rewards of giving out contracts and receiving contributions. Corruption was rampant and although the Mayor was not implicated, many of his top aides were. Machine politicians gave favours for votes and money, using city government for private gain. Developers were allowed to build in the downtown area with no thought given to the consequences for the neighbourhoods. It was thought that the patronage (mostly white) people received compensated for developers being given a free hand.

Corruption was glorified in Chicago. Discoveries were met largely with indifference although occasionally a few people went to jail. A typical response to impropriety was this response by Mayor Daley to his son receiving a city insurance contract in 1972:

> An angry Daley said, about his critics, 'If I can't help my sons . . . then they can kiss my ass . . . I make no apologies to anyone. There are men in this room whose fathers helped them and they went on to become fine public officials . . . If a man can't put his arms around his sons, then what kind of world are we living in?' If there was any impact on the community from these events , it was to improve the major's image as a good family man (Squires *et al.,* 1985, p.7).

Mayor Washington's attempts to reform Chicago government must be seen in the historical context of machine politicians awarding contracts to big developers and others in return for campaign contributions. Even the Washington administration has not been free of scandal in awarding contracts. However, after three years, the Washington administration has had only one major charge of corruption against it and none of the current allegations are related to downtown developers.

Mayor Washington's plan was to achieve balanced growth linking the downtown redevelopment with neighbourhood growth and development. But the concept flies in the face of the prevailing ideology in America: that growth is desirable and should be left to the private sector without government interference and the only role for government is to assist private industry in its task. In the words of Squires, Bennett, McCourts and Nyden (1985, p.14), 'the essence of the growth ideology can be stated succinctly: none of the nation's urban social problems can be resolved until greater economic growth occurs and the way to stimulate that growth is by providing financial incentives to private investors. . .'

Other legitimate concerns must simply take a back seat according to this perspective which has been advocated by government officials and private citizens throughout the nation. *Business Week* (1980), for example, argued:

> All social groups in the U.S. today must understand that their common interest in returning the country to a path of strong economic growth overrides other conflicting interests. . . In the U.S. during the past years, policy has emphasised improving the quality of life, particularly attempts to redistribute income to low income groups and minorities and to create an egalitarian society. Now it is clear that the government cannot achieve such goals no matter how admirable, without economic growth. . . Special interest groups must recognise that their own unique goals cannot be satisfied if the U.S. cannot compete in world markets. The drawing of a social contract must take precedence over the aspirations of the poor, the

minorities, and the environmentalists. Without such a consensus, all are doomed to lower levels of living, fewer rights, and increasingly dirty water.

The growth ideology is endorsed by civic groups, private individuals and politicians in Chicago. For example, James Compton, president of the Chicago Urban League, stated 'Economic activity is not simply the central preoccupation of the city, it is the reason the city exists' (Squires *et al.,* p. 17). While former independent Democratic alderman William Singer has argued, 'The future of the city of Chicago, then, depends quite simply upon its ability to grow' (Squires *et al.,* p.17). If Mayor Washington's plans for balanced growth or economic redistribution to the neighbourhoods puts pressure on business to help develop the ethnic neighbourhoods, he is likely to be opposed not just by business groups but by some civic groups as well.

Chicago's Economic Development Commission was not established until 1976. Until then, Mayor Daley did not believe it was needed. Developers would naturally gravitate to Chicago. The Commission did not issue its first report until 1981. But succeeding mayors continued to develop the Commission.

In 1984, Washington issued his formal plan. Its theme was 'Chicago Works Together'. The plan identified five major goals, providing an estimate of new job creation by each programme as well as the benefits minorities and women would receive from the Affirmative Action Plan. It remains an ambitious undertaking. The jury is still out on its overall success.

The ambitious plan's goals for the first year included:
— over 10,000 permanent jobs to be directly created or retained in the next year, which could stimulate an additional 15,000 jobs throughout the local economy;
— 12,000 persons to be trained in job skills;
— 6,000 housing units to be rehabbed or constructed;
— interim goal of 60% of total city of Chicago purchasing to local firms and 25% to minority and female-owned businesses; and
— $250 million increase in private sector purchasing from local businesses (Washington, 1984, p.1).

The mayor's plan also listed a series of innovations in contrast to his predecessors:

1. What's new is a clearly articulated set of development goals, social and economic, for the City as a whole, not just the Central Business District and large-scale public projects, approach to development emphasises the high priority given to job creation and retention and

neighbourhood development. The Mayor and the City's major development departments have agreed to the following goals:

Goal I: Increase job opportunities for Chicagoans.

Goal II: Promote balanced growth.

Goal III: Assist neighbourhoods to develop through partnerships and coordinated investment.

Goal IV: Enhance public participation in decision-making.

Goal V: Pursue a regional, state and national legislative agenda.

2. What's new is the broad-based cooperative process which produced this Plan, a process which involved a wide variety of residents, community-based organisations, labour groups, businesses, and City officials. 'Chicago Works Together' contains many of the ideas about City development generated in recent years by these diverse groups and individuals.

3. An open invitation to public scrutiny of the development process, a scrutiny which can hold the Administration accountable for meeting the clear and specific development targets outlined in this Plan. Rarely has the public been provided with such clear descriptions of many of the City's development programmes and projects.

4. What's new, finally, is the attempt made throughout this document to integrate specific programmes and projects with the goals. Both the City and the public can make judgements about development programmes in the light of a set of overarching goals.(Washington, 1984, p.1).

The mayor's plan noted that a serious effort was needed because of high unemployment, especially among blacks, in Chicago. In 1983, almost 218,000 Chicagoans, two-thirds of whom were in minority groups, were unemployed; teenage unemployment, especially among minority youth, numbered 33,000 ; Chicago suffered a net loss of 123,400 jobs between 1972 and 1981. In addition, demolition, deterioration, and arson have claimed an estimated 60,000 housing units in Chicago over the past ten years (Washington, 1984, p.2).

EVALUATION

Washington's 1984 plan listed each programme and set job creation, job development, purchasing and affirmative action targets. An evaluation of the plan in 1985-86 by the city showed the following on the four levels of performance:

EX – The impact exceeded the target performance objective.
FR – The target objective has been fully realised.
P – Part of the target objective was achieved.
O – No progress was made.

Impact	Programmes and projects assessment	
	No.	% of total
EX	11	12.8
FR	18	20.9
P	49	57.0
O	5	5.8
NA	3	3.5
Total	86	100.0

Based on the city's evaluation, they have made partial progress on more than 90% of the programmes and projects included in 'Chicago Works Together,' and exceeds its performance targets in 12.8% of them. Alternatively, no progress was made in 5.8% of city development efforts. (Department of Economic Development, 1986).

The *Chicago Sun-Times* review of the mayor's performance on his public works record concluded that it was more mixed. However, it still pointed out that neighbourhoods had gained more than under any recent mayor. The report also argued that Mayor Washington's planning department had opened the way for more building downtown. However, unlike, San Francisco and Boston, Chicago has not so far used its leverage to obtain amenities from developers. This does seem, however, to be changing as the Planning Commissioner has been asking developers to help with neighbourhood activities and developers have recently been asked to pay infrastructure costs of $70m for the City Front Centre Project. The interim judgement is that the mayor remains pro-growth but is attempting to achieve balance growth in the neighbourhoods (*Chicago Sun-Times*, 1986).

THE POLITICS OF LINKED DEVELOPMENT

The mayor also has been involved with the policy issue of linked development which was originally put by a neighbourhood group called Save Our Neighbourhood/Save Our City Coalition (SON/SOCC). Their proposals were similar to the city's Economic Development Plan of 1984. Linked development is one method for achieving such balanced growth, by funding neighbourhood revitalisation from revenue generated by economic development in the central business district.

At their first annual convention in April 1984, 1,000 delegates from most of the city's white neighbourhoods passed a resolution supporting linked development. The Chicago Urban League reported that the proposal had three elements:

1. Developers of commercial office buildings will pay a mandatory up-front contribution of $5.00 per square foot over the first 100,000 square feet of new construction or substantial rehabilitation to a city-wide linkage fund.

2. Funds collected through linkage will be distributed to all of Chicago's 77 community areas, in an amount proportionate to the population of each area.

3. Residents of each community area will determine how linkage funds are spent in their neighbourhood by voting between various local project proposals for their neighbourhood. (Chicago Urban League, 1986, p. 1)

In September 1984, the SON/SOCC invited Mayor Washington to attend, which he did, for several reasons. First, the Mayor generally supported the concept of support for the neighbourhoods. These were in fact themes that he had been advocating since his election campaign. He created an Advisory Committee, a logical follow-up action to the city's earlier Development Plan. But, Washington also advocated the idea as a way of courting the white ethnic bloc, by responding to the coalition positively and stressing the similarities in their approach to city government (Chicago Urban League, p. 2). The Mayor also provided staff support for the programme. The committee subsequently issued both majority and minority reports. The minority report was the product of the business members who strenuously disapproved of the neighbourhood members' findings, primarily on the question of revenue sources for the neighbourhood plan.

The minority report focused specifically on the proposed 'Exaction Fee on New Office Space.' The majority report wanted to impose an exaction fee on office space in excess of 50,000 square feet, with $2 payable on receipt of the building permits and $2 per square foot of occupied space payable annually for the next four years. The 'Minority Report' argued the proposal was illegal and ill-advised. The exaction taxes had been upheld by Illinois courts only if there was a 'significant and unique' relationship between the development and the problem created. In Chicago, however, the minority argued the connection would be between commercial office development of the central city area and disinvestment in housing in Chicago neighbourhoods. It also argued that the tax could raise office rents, would exacerbate the 'rent gaps' between city and suburbs, encouraging city business, especially the outer fringes, to relocate to the suburbs. The minority also objected, if less strenuously, to taxes which extended coverage of existing taxes to include land trust and insurance companies (Chicago Urban League, p. 6).

A critique of the majority report by the Chicago Urban League also found that the plan had a number of flaws:

1) lack of criteria for choosing projects for each neighbourhood;

2) lack of an administrative mechanism(s) on who would run the projects and be held accountable for fiscal control;

3) lack of specificity on who would allocate funds: the peculiar nature of Chicago politics makes this a key question;

4) lack of specificity on the overall cost: the question of another layer of bureaucracy was raised as was the possibility of a new patronage army being developed;

5) lack of rational nexus – unlike San Francisco and Boston, the Chicago report did not make a convincing linkage between downtown development and pressure on housing in the neighbourhoods: the argument was that the two other cities were smaller and land was at a premium so any development downtown strained the neighbourhoods. However, Chicago is a much larger city and it is difficult to argue that building on Michigan Avenue hurt neighbourhoods in Pill Hill;

6) lack of evidence on how linked development would hurt local business development by pushing commercial space to the suburbs;

7) lack of evidence on how $0.10/square feet/year on all businesses would hurt small businesses (Chicago Urban League, pp.9-10).

The Chicago plan differed from San Francisco and Boston in two respects. First, in San Francisco the programme is mandatory for all developments over a certain size. In Boston the law only applies to projects that require zoning relief. Second, San Francisco's law only applies to office buildings. Boston's applies to hotel, retail and institutional developments as well. The Boston programme specified that any commercial project over 100,000 square feet that is seeking zoning relief must contribute to housing. The developer can opt to pay a fee of $5.00 per square foot for every foot over 100,000 square feet. These monies are paid into a housing trust fund over a period of twelve years.

The amount and timing of the fee represented a compromise between housing advocates and developers. Developers offered an up-front fee of $2.50, housing advocates wanted $5.00. The developers responded with the $5.00 over 12 years. This may be taken as a victory for the developers, since it amounts to about $0.42 a square foot a year, an amount which can easily be passed on to tenants without serious damage to the developers' competitive position.

The San Francisco plan had a very detailed report on cost of transportation systems, housing, infrastructure costs and other related costs. In Chicago, the linked development programme never made a clear linkage between downtown development and neighbourhood costs. While there is a crisis of housing in Chicago for low income residents, it was not clear how to link this to downtown development.

Mayor Washington was caught between the opponents of the plan and those in favour of it. The Mayor, in November 1985, was about to announce his own plan which would seek a middle ground, for the creation of $10 million to support neighbourhood economic development. The funds were to come from three sources: $2.5 million from developers' repayment of low interest HDAG loans; $1 million from real estate transfer tax which normally flows to the city's corporate fund, and $7 million in voluntary contributions from downtown developers (Chicago Urban League).

However, the linked development plan was never formally announced because of the city's budget crisis which resulted in a 6% lease tax. Business interests opposed the $78 million tax on them and neighbourhood groups opposed money going to the city's operating fund. The lease tax was eventually ruled unconstitutional. Currently the Mayor is awaiting a report by a Task Force on how to fund the linked development programme.

As the Mayor waited, a new report was issued revealing a 'Super Loop' of new offices, hotels and apartment buildings. One study of the plan argues that the net effect of eight years of record construction is no less than a reversal of the economic physical decline of the central area (McCarron, 1986). But neighbourhood groups argue that this boom has already widened the gap between downtown and neighbourhoods.

Neighbourhood groups want the Mayor to still push for $5 tax from developers–for every square foot they build. The report argues that a 'link tax' might kill the boom altogether (McCarron, p. 2) because downtown tax is already relatively high and investors can take their money elsewhere. It also suggests that Chicago's 'pro-growth reputation' would suffer. In essence, the Masotti and Ludgin report believes that Chicago will continue its downtown growth because it has more space than San Francisco or Boston (McCarron, p. 2).

Given that the mayoral election is only a year away, Washington now seems likely to temper his response to any mandatory policy on business contributions. Linked development will remain a political issue in Chicago for several years.

THE IMPACT OF POLITICS ON
ECONOMIC REDISTRIBUTION IN CHICAGO

Chicago is not a distressed city. But it has serious problems of economic dislocation and uneven growth. Its history of racial intolerance, labour unrest, conflict with the suburbs, are a part of its past and present. Chicago's future may depend less on the issues of linked development and economic redistribution than on the ability of the Washington Administration and white ethnic politicians to form a coalition that reduces potential political and social conflict in the city. It does not matter how attractive Chicago is as a market or location, if political and racial peace cannot be achieved.

Chicago's suburbs are growing and will continue to grow. But their future to a large degree depends on that of the city. A declining city also eventually may lead to a declining suburban region. Whether they concede it, or not, their fate is inextricably tied to the city. One can expect the suburban cities to exploit political conflict in the city to lure business to their areas. They will be partially successful. But the city has an economic significance that is not likely to fade unless the political situation deteriorates significantly.

For all of its problems, Chicago is still a city where a number of national corporations have home offices. It is also a transportation hub and a financial centre of the Midwest. Chicago also has strong neighbourhood organisations that have been successful in negotiating reinvestment commitments from banks for their growth and survival. In 1984, a coalition of community housing groups secured a $100 million commitment for neighbourhood reinvestment from the First National Bank of Chicago (Swift and Pogge, 1984). The Harris Bank also agreed to lend $60 million to low-income neighbourhoods (*Chicago Defender,* 1984).

The Mayor is reaching for broad city support in his attempts to get 'Chicago to work together'. He remains pro-growth, but he is also cognizant that growth downtown must be accompanied by renewal or development of the neighbourhoods. But whether linked development can become his way to achieve this goal will depend on how politically feasible it is for him in an election year. As a progressive Mayor, he can ill afford to push blindly for growth at the expense of the unemployed and minority communities that are depending on him for jobs and neighbourhood revitalisation. There is some hope that he can find a middle ground between what neighbourhood groups want and what business interests will tolerate. But as ever in Chicago, politics will determine everything.

NOTES

1. Chicago was until 1980 the second largest city in the United States. Since the 1980 Census, Los Angeles has now surpassed Chicago as second largest city in the United States by a few thousand votes. However, Chicago politicians are asking for a recount because they have found out that some people were only counted once, which is contrary to Chicago tradition.

REFERENCES

Business Week (1980), special issue, 'The Reindustrialisation of America', 30 June, pp. 24-7.

Chicago Defender (1984), 'Harris Bank's loan to help low-income neighbourhoods', 23 May, p. 21.

Chicago Sun-Times – Special Supplement, (1986), 'Washington's Chicago: A Critical Examination' October-November.

Chicago Urban League (1986), 'The Policy Issue Linked Development: A Preliminary Report to the Board of Directors', 28 January, p. 1.

Department of Economic Development (1984), *Chicago's Assets for Business and Industry,* City of Chicago, p. 2.

Department of Economic Development (1986), '1984 Chicago Development Plan Accomplishment Analysis', City of Chicago.

McCarron, John (1986), 'Loop rides fast track in growth', Chicago Tribune, 21 October.

Preston, Michael B. (1987a), 'Black Politics in the Post-Daley Era', in Gove, Samuel K. and Masotti, Louis H. (eds.), *After Daley: Chicago Politics in Transition,* Champaign, University of Illinois Press, pp. 88-117.

Preston, Michael B. (1987b), 'The Election of Harold Washington: An Examination of the SES Model in the 1983 Chicago Mayoral Election', in Preston, Michael B., Henderson, Lenneal J., and Puryear, Paul (eds.), *The New Black Politics,* White Plains, New York, Longman.

Squires, Gregory D., Bennett, Larry, McCourt, Kathleen, Nyden Philip (1985), 'Chicago: The City That Works, For Less'. Paper presented at the Midwest Political Science Association, Chicago, Illinois, April, p. 7.

Swift, Larry D. and Pogge, Jean (1984), *Neighbourhood Reinvestment Partnership,* Chicago, Woodstock Institute.

Terry, Don (1986), 'City's black, white totals about even', *Chicago Sun-Times,* 24 September, p. 34.

Washington, Harold, Mayor (1984), Chicago Development Plan, City of Chicago, p. 1.

10

Race, politics and urban regeneration: lessons from Liverpool

GIDEON BEN-TOVIM

University of Liverpool

INTRODUCTION: AREAS FOR COMPARATIVE ANALYSIS

Racial politics in Liverpool have broader implications for the rest of the country, and for comparison with the United States of America.' Liverpool has a long-established black community constituting about 8% of the local population (which totals about half a million inhabitants) and spanning several generations. The largest group is the Liverpool-born Blacks of mixed Afro/White British origins. The community has been involved in the most violent of the British disturbances (the 'riots' or 'uprisings') of 1981. Since then it has been the site of attempts by the Conservative Government to introduce private sector-led urban regeneration with several new initiatives, ie a 'Minister for Merseyside', the Merseyside Task Force and the Merseyside Development Corporation. On the other hand, Liverpool has since 1983 been controlled at local political level by a far-left socialist City Council, with the Trotskyite entryist group, Militant, at its core.

Liverpool provides a good case-study of two dominant British political approaches towards issues of racial inequality in the context of urban regeneration. One approach pins hopes for revival on the involvement of the private sector, in association with improved local coordination of central government departments and resources, as well as direct investment through a non-elected development corporation. A second is to attack urban deprivation through a local council's centralist job-creation and house-building programme.

The conclusion we shall reach in this paper is that in terms of racial inequality, the approaches adopted by both the Conservative government in Whitehall and the socialist administration in Liverpool's Town hall have been nearly identical. The socio-economic inequalities that lay behind the riots of 1981² have not been diminished to any significant degree by either central or local government initiatives. Both strategies have failed because of their underlying assumption that the issue of race is simply a general form of economic deprivation, to be addressed by general economic policies. This assumption has linked both left and right, albeit in different modes, and has ensured practically zero impact on entrenched patterns of racial discrimination and disadvantage. But neither central nor local government has attempted a serious strategy of positive action in employment or the targeting of resources towards the black community. Neither at central nor at local level has there been any effort to involve the black community in the decision-making process. Indeed the black community has frequently been deliberately excluded from the relevant power structures (see Ben-Tovim *et al.*, 1986).

Developments in Liverpool generate important areas for debate about theories of race and class as much as the role of legislation in equal opportunity policies. For those who argue that American affirmative action policies have failed and a more overtly class oriented anti-capitalist programme is needed, the British experience is of some significance. No attempt has yet been made by central government or the judiciary to use affirmative action in the race relations field. The colour-blind approaches of central and local government, whether Conservative, Liberal or revolutionary Socialist, have wholly failed to narrow the gap of racial inequality in Britain (see Glazer *et al.*, 1983).

Equally interesting for comparative purposes, several British cities are at last beginning to fall under black political leadership, if not control. The leaders of the inner London boroughs of Brent, Haringey and Lambeth are black – two of them black women – whilst it is expected that there will be at least six black Labour MPs in the next Parliament. But the history of black political control of American cities may also throw light on black political strategy in Britain today. A strong Black Sections Movement has emerged within the Labour Party yet it has been actively opposed by the leadership of the Labour Party, by the Militant Tendency, and by some black activists who reject the Labour Party as a potential vehicle for black liberation.

The final area is that of central government's urban policy in general and racial inequality in particular. The general framework in Britain is ambiguous and permissive with respect to race. Although British urban policy has frequently been introduced or changed in the light of concerns over racial conflict (Edwards and Batley, 1978) there has always been official uncertainty as to whether, and to what extent, urban policy should have an explicit focus of race.

The attempt to marginalise race has always been the hallmark of British urban policy. Thus Labour politicians (Harold Wilson introducing the 1968 Urban Programme in response to Enoch Powell's racial incitements) and Conservative politicians alike (Michael Heseltine setting up the Merseyside Task Force in the wake of the 1981 riots) have adopted a common strategy of responding to the threat of racial disorder by generalising the response and providing no direct means of coming to terms with racial inequality.

Politicians have rationalised this failure of urban policy to directly address the race dimension by citing anti-discrimination legislation and the Commission for Racial Equality, as the appropriate mechanism for combating racial discrimination and disadvantage (Department of the Environment, 1977). But the weak and permissive nature of the existing legislation has made this an ineffectual means of tackling racism. The sections of the Race Relations Act that deal with overt discrimination lack adequate powers of enforcement or sanctions and have had very little impact. Those dealing with 'positive action', i.e. measures to redress the balance of racial disadvantage, are purely permissive. Employers, including local authorities, may take measures to actively attempt to recruit black personnel, to initiate preferential training and promotion schemes, and to overhaul existing practices in the field of employment. But there is no mandatory pressure for them to do so (Commission for Racial Equality, 1985).

In this discretionary climate, central government has enormous potential to introduce racial equality programmes and practices, but it has made no effort to set an example as an employer, or to use its powers of contract to press employers into fairer employment initiatives. This was as true of the Labour governments of the 1960s and '70s as of the Conservative governments of the 1980s. There are, however, exceptions at local government level. Some councils do attempt to use their powers of contract to encourage equal opportunity policies amongst local employers and also adopt their own programmes for race equality.

RACIAL INEQUALITY AND IDEOLOGICAL COLOUR-BLINDNESS, RIGHT AND LEFT

How serious is the failure of policy in Britain? A large body of national evidence points to the worsening socio-economic position of black people. Many sources have documented: the disproportionate growth of black unemployment; the failure of the black community to make inroads into white collar and professional layers of the labour market; the difficulties placed in the way of black businesses (e.g. with grants, banks, planning permission); the particularly vulnerable position of black youth who suffer chronically high rates of unemployment and, when involved in government schemes, are consistently allocated poorer training and job opportunities than their white counterparts (Brown, 1984; Newnham, 1986).

At the local level in Liverpool, for example, there has been no change over a long period in the broad occupational position of the black population in terms of employment by central or local government agencies. The reluctance of both central and local government to adopt ethnic monitoring makes it difficult to quantify precisely the position, but the evidence is that Liverpool City Council still has a less than 1% black proportion of the workforce as a whole. The figure has remained constant since the first figures were produced in 1980 (Ben-Tovim, 1983; Merseyside Community Relations Council, 1986).

What explains this extraordinary figure? It is the persistence of ideological colour-blindness, by both Conservatives and Socialists, which justifies the refusal to move beyond conventional generalist principles of resource distribution, job creation mechanisms, and recruitment and training practices. That refusal both at national and local level has been in the face of consistent pressure from race relations agencies and black organisations to develop more specific mechanisms to reduce racial inequality.

MERSEYSIDE TASK FORCE

When the Minister for Merseyside, Mr Heseltine, was developing his strategy for dealing with urban decline in Liverpool after the 1981 riots, he was urged to develop mechanisms to ensure that race and the needs of the black community were built into any local initiatives. Indeed the official brief that was adopted by the Merseyside Task Force emphasised the need to 'promote good community relations and reduce disadvantage among ethnic minority groups' (Central Office of Information, 1981).

However this pressure from local black representatives had little effect as the race brief of the Task-Force was quickly marginalised. A few 'projects' to benefit the black community were ultimately introduced. But they were secondary to the broader Merseyside-wide initiatives which were almost entirely irrelevant to the black population. The proposal by black community representatives for an ambitious, locally controlled Liverpool 8 Development Corporation was rejected. Very little incorporation of any kind of black perspective or racial dimension took place in the ensuing developments. The Task Force was set up consisting of civil servants seconded into the area and of local business representatives. No attempt was made to second to the Task Force representatives of black organisations (who might have benefited more from the subsequent fact-finding trip to the United States than the local establishment elite). No attempt was made to develop any equal opportunity strategy for contracts and employment or training initiatives for the post-Task Force developments.

A parallel racial amnesia has affected many academics, practitioners and politicians in their evaluation of the Task Force. In several hundreds of pages of detailed evidence to the House of Commons Environment Committee (1983) virtually no reference was made to race. The Committee made no attempt to seek the views and experiences of the local black community whose problems had in fact provided the catalyst for the whole enterprise.

LIVERPOOL CITY COUNCIL

A similar refusal to incorporate a black perspective in decision-making was reflected at the other end of the political spectrum by the left-wing leadership of the Liverpool City Council. There has in fact been massive conflict between the Labour leadership and the local black community since 1984 when Labour attempted to impose as Principal Race Relations Adviser for the city a man appointed on sectarian grounds to support the Militant faction rather than to promote the cause of racial equality (Liverpool Black Caucus, 1986). The appointment exemplified Labour's policy stance on race: they have opposed positive discrimination, ethnic monitoring and initiatives targeted towards the black and ethnic minority communities because they 'divide the working-class' and create a 'white back-lash'. It illustrated their refusal to allow an authentic independent black voice in the local decision-making process. Indeed the committee set up to provide legitimate black access to Council policy-making, the Race Relations Liaison Committee, was abolished by the Labour leadership in 1985 because of its critical stance towards Council policies and practices.

One result of the conflict is that Labour has maintained a number of the existing employment routines and procedures which reinforce the unequal position of the local black community. These include the use of the Council's internal trawl procedure which maintains the privileged position of predominantly white Council workers in all new appointments; the increased reliance on trade union nomination rights, with an in-built racial disadvantage; the reliance on filters and routes into the Council workforce, such as the use of 'waiting-lists'; the use of particular agencies to oversee training or apprenticeships; or the use of standard qualification criteria which again can favour the local white population.

The Liverpool experience contradicts simple structuralist explanations that the socio-economic position of black people has deteriorated exclusively because of the current Conservative government offensive against the working class and against the spending levels of Labour councils. The generality of this analysis disguises the degree of autonomy that local councils retain to distribute their economic resources and vary their own employment practices.

Thus despite the haemorrhage of resources that has genuinely afflicted the City (Parkinson, 1985), Liverpool's Labour leadership have nonetheless embarked on their own set of priorities, saving and creating certain jobs and inaugurating an ambitious house-building, leisure and environmental improvement programme. They have then shown little regard for the financial and political constraints of their position. Indeed they appear to have engaged in all the subjectivist and authoritarian distortions of the Stalinist version of socialist politics.

For the leaders of Liverpool Labour Party, Militant Tendency in alliance with a few like-minded 'fundamentalists', the vision of socialism is that of a tightly controlled centralised local state, with power exercised by the party elite, with loyalist trade union branches used as transmission belts for party policies. Independent political forces (the voluntary sector or the housing co-operative movement) are undermined. The Party machine itself is manipulated to ensure near unanimous assent to leadership decisions. Internal or external opposition is stifled or vilified. The perks of jobs, office, promotion and power are used to maintain the leadership's position. These classical instruments of control are compounded by a refusal to adopt a realistic assessment of the ultimate consequences of their actions and policies. It leads to triumphalist declarations of the inevitability of their victory over the forces of opposition; the ritual denunciation of the 'middle-class', 'careerist' or 'right-wing traitors' who are the only reason for defeats or set-backs; and a powerful workerist rhetoric that they are the true representatives of the working-class against the class enemies, the Tory government, the local Liberal opposition, and the 'right wing' of the Labour party.

Inevitably this workerist vision leaves no space for the particular oppressions and inequalities facing the black community. This

monolithic vision of class contains no gradations or internal differentiation. Advocates of black equal rights have been branded as 'divisive' and
'middle-class careerists'. This refusal to acknowledge the reality of the
racial segmentation of the local population has itself had racist effects.
The existing privileges of the white working class have been protected,
if not enhanced, by Labour's political priorities in employment and
housing. The new jobs that the Council has created in its new political
units, in the security force, in the recreation department, in housing,
have gone to politically acceptable, and overwhelmingly white appointments. Of 1,271 appointments to the Council from June 1984 to September 1985, only 42 were black (MCRC, 1986). New housing has been
concentrated in the white working-class areas of Liverpool. No
mechanism exists to prevent previous patterns of stark differential allocation of housing on racial grounds from being perpetuated (CRE, 1984).

This monolithic approach to the exercise of power has involved major
conflicts over the Race Adviser appointment and the abolition of the
Council's race relations forum. The subsequent persistent opposition by
black community organisations to the Labour leadership in Liverpool,
including an official two-year boycott of the Adviser post by all town hall
unions and nearly all local black groups, has increased Labour's vilifica-
tion of local black organisations in the city. This has led them to try to
set up 'front' organisations to divide and rule the black community ,
although with little success so far.

RACIAL INEXPLICITNESS AND MARGINALISATION: THE GOVERNMENT FRAMEWORK

Resistance and obstruction to the development of a strategy of race
equality in Liverpool has derived not simply from the abrasive colour-
blindness of the socialist leadership. It has been prolonged by a similar
reluctance of leading Liberals when in office to develop serious policies;
by the conservatism of council officials unwilling to radically overhaul
'normal' policies and practices; and by trade unions opposed to giving
up their privileges.

Such marginal responses to the problem of racial inequality have to be
seen at least partially in terms of external conditions including the pattern of government funding and current race relations legislation. The
only central money exclusively available to meet the needs of local black/
ethnic minority communities is *Section II* of the *1966 Local Government
Act,* which gives local councils 75% of the costs of employees working
with minority populations. This has been notoriously abused in many

local authorities, widely used simply to improve general teacher-pupil ratios rather than to have any explicit race focus. Local black organisations are frequently ignored in decisions over the use of this resource. Although current Home Office guidelines suggest local communities should be consulted, there is no adequate monitoring of the scheme. The Act also has a strongly culturalist flavour which encourages the view that marginal changes to meet the special needs of ethnic minorities will resolve issues of race, as opposed to mainstream changes that are really required to overhaul the racial bias embedded in normal employment practices and service provision.

Similarly, funding under the *Urban Programme/Inner City Partnership* schemes has encouraged the funding of small ad hoc ethnic minority projects, which may meet some aspect of community need. But they equally fail to tackle the underlying institutional structures that produce shortfalls in service and employment opportunities. Again central and local government have failed to develop a genuine partnership with national and local black agencies and organisations in the strategic use of these resources (Stewart, 1983). Radical black commentators meanwhile criticise this whole style of funding of self-help groups for diverting groups away from political action (John, 1978).

The ideological assumption that race is essentially a question of ethnicity/immigration or class/urban deprivation along with the organisation of Section 11 and Urban Programme resources, have encouraged the growth of marginal, cosmetic or token responses. However the permissive and ambiguous context within which such resources are made available means that some authorities have made little or no use of these methods to meet the needs of black communities, whilst others have used the resource for purposes other than race.

Equally, the *Race Relations Act of 1976,* whilst exhorting local authorities to promote equal opportunities and enabling them to take limited forms of positive action, provides no incentive for change and no sanctions against passivity. The enormous length of time, the cumbersome procedure, the legal limitations and the lack of serious penalties involved in conducting a formal investigation into a local authority constitute a weak pressure on local politicians and officials, and are of little more than moral or promotional value.

ANTI-RACIST AND BLACK POLITICAL STRATEGIES
IN BRITAIN TODAY

This discretionary context is compounded by the ideological and material 'new right' assault on 'positive discrimination' and multi-cultural or anti-racist education, and by the government's attack on local authority spending. In this context, pressure from black and anti-racist organisations can be significant in breaking down resistance and obstruction by arguing the case for change in local structures, policies and procedures which discriminate against black communities.

A number of different strategies are being followed by anti-racist and black organisations in Britain (Ben-Tovim *et al.,* 1982, 1986). For some, the main form of struggle consists of militant, including street level, opposition to the overt manifestations of racism, concentrating on the police, the immigration laws and deportations, and the activities and physical attacks of extreme far-right racist groups. Other community groups are involved in meeting needs that are not met by mainstream institutions – the provision of community centres, supplementary education, cultural and welfare facilities, advisory work, or training activities. Both forms of action, though indispensable, may fail to tackle the mainstream sources and structures of racial discrimination and disadvantage.

Some groups have adopted the approach described by Phillips (1982) as the 'penetration of mainstream political structures'. This was a key element of the strategy adopted by sections of the black community in Liverpool. For example, an alliance of local black and anti-racist organisations was established from below the city's equal opportunity policy and committee structure in 1980 and has since then attempted to use it to push for policy change. However this path has been temporarily cut off by the Labour Party's opposition to providing a place in the decision-making process for independent community representatives.

This hostility to power-sharing with black community organisations is by no means unique to Liverpool. The failure to genuinely consult with independent community organisations and to engage them in decision-making is endemic to local government structures and to local outposts of central government. They provide no space for the representation of group interests except through the conventional structure of the electoral system. This orthodox approach to local democracy unites all major parties, which share the view that the elected city councillors are the only legitimate decision-makers. This view has been challenged by both the movement for black rights and by feminists who have attempted to create black/ethnic minorities committees or women's committees as

legitimate new local council structures. But they have been opposed by
all sides of the political spectrum and have frequently been marginalised.
Conflicts over the issue of 'representativeness' and political sectarianism
and manoeuvring help keep these structures in line with orthodox party
positions (Ouseley, 1984; Goss, 1984).

This reliance on local politicians and officials to secure the representation of black interests in formal policy-making structures provides no
secure access to political power for minority organisations. As well as the
push for the democratisation of local politics, there has been a substantial
move by many black political activists to seek power through formal
party political channels, particularly the Labour Party which the black
population in Britain have consistently, and overwhelming, supported
(Fitzgerald, 1984; Anwar, 1986).

There are growing numbers of black councillors in many cities with
substantial black populations, and the black vote is increasingly being
recognised as influential in key marginal areas. There is however still
resistance to the nomination by party caucuses of black councillors. As a
consequence, they are severely under-represented in relation to their
proportion in the population as a whole. Some black organisations
entirely reject the Labour Party, and indeed other mainstream parties,
on the grounds that they are reformist, careerist or racist, and adopt a
more revolutionary, Pan-Africanist or independent perspective. In the
May 1986 elections in Liverpool for the first time an Independent Black
candidate stood on an anti-Labour platform.

RACE AND THE MAJOR POLITICAL PARTIES

The response of the major parties to the increasing political assertiveness
of the black community has varied. The Conservative Party has attempted to solidify its small black support amongst the entrepreneurial and
professional strata by establishing Anglo-Asian and Anglo-West Indian
Conservative Associations. The Conservatives have, however made few
concessions to the race relations lobby in policy terms, which remains
punitive on immigration, and passive and indifferent on race equality
issues, as Lord Scarman (1985) observed in his recent review of 'post-
Scarman' initiatives. The Social Democratic Party has given a high profile to its black race relations spokespersons, and has developed some
positive race equality commitments, which are shared by its Liberal
partners. The Alliance, however, has relatively limited black political
support, and their track-record on local councils, as in Liverpool, has
not been impressive, with little attempt made to implement paper com-

mitments.

The Labour Party is clearly the most significant arena of black party involvement, in terms of its support amongst black voters, black membership, and its virtual monopoly of black councillors, council leaders and prospective MPs. Over the last few years, black members of the Labour Party have developed a particularly high profile through the work of the Black Sections movement. This has spear-headed the development of black caucuses in the Labour Party, and has provided the organisational support and ideological coherence necessary to promote black councillor and potential parliamentary representation.

The Labour Party leadership has, however, handled the issue in an inept, if predictable, way. In response to the growing grass-roots black pressure, its National Executive Working Party on 'Positive Discrimination' was created in 1983. This recommended support for the demands of the Black Sections Committee for official recognition of Black Sections in the Party structure, as well as places on the National Executive for people elected through this constituency. These proposals were made to a federal party structure, which already recognises trade union, women and youth sections, a form of Jewish sections, and a wide range of socialist societies. However some of these 'sections' have limited though contested powers – for example, the women's 'representatives' on the National Executive are voted in, not by the Labour Party women's organisations, but by the trade union block votes.

But leading figures in the Labour Party (including its Leader, Deputy Leader, and shadow Home Secretary) fiercely opposed the Working Party recommendations as 'divisive' and a form of 'apartheid', 'racist', 'not acceptable to black members' and 'impractical'. With these arguments, plus the weight of the trade union block votes, they defeated the Black Sections Movement at the Party Congresses of 1984, 1985 and 1986. This has culminated in the highly divisive decision of the National Executive to set up their own Black and Asian Advisory Committee which is being boycotted by members of the Black Sections Committee on the grounds that it is a 'colonial imposition' set up to undermine the existing structure of autonomous black organisation.

On paper the Labour Party is now moving towards a progressive set of race policies, including greater pressure on employers to adopt equal opportunity policies, the use of contract compliance measures, improvement of the government's own employment record, opening up higher education to disadvantaged groups, the wider use of monitoring in fields like housing. However whether they will deliver on these commitments if they form a government (on their own, or in uneasy coalition with the

Alliance), will depend on the ability of the organised black lobby to exert pressure to prioritise the issue of racial inequality, and prevent its disappearing in the more generalist policy changes with which a new government will be primarily concerned.

These concerns, such as reducing unemployment, enhancing local authority resources, restoring cuts in the health service, attacking poverty, would of course be of enormous potential benefit to the black population in Britain. The general economic and social policies of the Conservative government have had a devastating effect on black employment prospects and life-chances. But unless some mechanism is built in to ensure a racial dimension on these policies, then, as in Liverpool, such general initiatives may be marginal to the black community, or even exacerbate inequalities, by disproportionately benefitting the white population. The utter failure of the Labour leadership to find space for an autonomous black voice – the mirror reflection of the resistance of Militant in Liverpool to the Black Caucus – indicates that the representation of black interests will be one of continuing struggle.

The record of Labour governments in the 1960s and 70s, though superior to the Conservative's in its efforts to develop Race Relations legislation, introduce inner-city initiatives and overhaul Section 11 funding, was still inadequate. It failed to set a lead as a major employer on race equality, to use its powers of influence on local authorities and employers, and to tackle racial inequalities in service delivery, let alone its more oppressive approaches in the field of immigration. Similarly, the record of many Labour local authorities gives little grounds for confidence in the commitment of a future Labour government to radical race initiatives.

CONCLUSION: TOWARDS RACIALLY EXPLICIT POLITICAL AND ECONOMIC CHANGE

Despite such circumstances, however, a pattern of 'good practice' is emerging, frequently from Labour authorities in London and it is spreading to some provincial cities. In some cities, there has been a substantial input of political will into the development of race equality programmes, including: the overhaul of recruitment practices to ensure more black employees by 'normal' procedures; the extensive use of positive action schemes to train and promote black workers; the development of monitoring and race equality targets for employment and service delivery; the use of contract compliance sections; race training; the appointment of black specialist advisory staff in race relations units; the involvement of black consultative committees; the setting up of specialist departments to support the growth of black businesses; the development of multi-cultural or anti-racist initiatives in education, social work, and housing departments.

But the development of this comprehensive package has often been opposed and subverted by politicians from all parties, council officials, trade unions, and the media. It may encourage cosmetic, rhetorical or token responses rather than fundamental changes in local council policy and practice. A great responsibility lies with black groups and race relations organisations to monitor and intervene in the local policy-making process, to prevent the diversion or dilution of these initiatives and enforce genuine consultation.

Where such explicit structural race mechanisms have been instituted, there is growing evidence that the number and location of black employees, support for black businesses and distribution of council services can be significantly improved (Ouseley, 1984; Greater London Council, 1986). If the expertise and commitment reflected in these developments could be reproduced within a post-Thatcher government, and enhanced by a more directive legislative framework, the prospects for progress towards race equality are substantial. If however, such a future government develops only generalist programmes of public sector led economic revival and redistribution, then entrenched racial inequalities will not be automatically ameliorated.

For example in Liverpool, a population of three or four generations of settlement in Britain has remained almost totally excluded from the economic resources of the local society, both in the 60s boom and the recession of the 70s and 80s. Liverpool's black population has experienced generations of chronic unemployment and marginalisation, whilst being subjected to the more punitive aspects of state attention. In fact the rest of Britain may well be developing a 'Liverpool pattern' of race relations. The massive problem of unemployment and alienation amongst the British born black population will be turned around only by radical and race-specific measures developed in the closest co-operation with the black community.

Whether such measures and such co-operation will emerge is an open question. The black community organisations and the race relations lobby will no doubt continue to put the issue of race on the agenda, through negotiation with government, the political parties, the voluntary sector network, the unions, the media, and doubtless through the streets. But the major controllers of the economy – the public and private sector employers, central and local government, and the financial institutions with a few exceptions have entirely failed to take on board the race dimension. Furthermore, the unions have been indifferent to the implementation of the equal opportunity policies which they formally support.

Finally there is great scope for the academic community to use its resources to work with black groups and anti-racist organisations, as well as statutory and voluntary agencies, in this task of working for practical change. Despite the proliferation of a large academic race relations industry, few of these resources are used in an interventionist political or policy-oriented direction. Research has a major role to play in documenting and analysing inequality, monitoring change, and helping devise and implement strategies for racial equality and justice. Perhaps this is where Britain has lessons to learn from America.

NOTES

1 The author has been heavily involved in local politics during the last decade, currently as Chairperson of Merseyside Community Relations Council and as a member of Liverpool Black Caucus, a body which comprises representatives of black organisations on the City Council's Race Relations Liaison Committee. Most of what has been learnt about race and local politics has been derived from a process of struggle in Liverpool in association with various local anti-racist and black community groups (Liverpool Black Caucus, 1986). The paper also draws on the related action-research project involving colleagues in Liverpool and Wolverhampton (Ben-Tovim et al., 1986).
2 It should be noted, however, that the riots were primarily a response to grievances over police harassment and malpractices.

REFERENCES

Anwar, M., (1986), Race and Politics, London, Tavistock.

Ben-Tovim, G. S. (ed.) (1983), *Equal Opportunities and the Employment of Black People and Ethnic Minorities on Merseyside,* Merseyside Association for Racial Equality in Employment/Merseyside Area Profile Group.

Ben-Tovim, G. S., Gabriel, J. G., Law, I., Stredder, K. (1982), 'The politics of race in Britain 1962-1979' and 'A political analysis of race in the 80s', in C. Husband (ed.), *Race in Britain, Continuity and Change,* London, Hutchinson.

Ben-Tovim, G. S., Gabriel, J. G., Law, I., Stredder, K. (1986), *The Local Politics of Race,* London, Macmillan.

Brown, C. (1984), *Black and White Britain – the Third PSI Survey*, London, Heinemann.

Central Office of Information (1981), *Social Welfare In Britain,* London, HMSO.

Commission for Racial Equality (1984), *Race and Housing in Liverpool – a research report,* London, CRE.

Commission for Racial Equality (1985), *Review of the Race Relations Act 1976,* London, CRE.

Department of the Environment (1977), *Policy for the Inner Cities,* London, HMSO.

Edwards, J. and Batley, R. (1978), *The Politics of Positive Discrimination,* London, Tavistock.

Fitzgerald, M. (1984), *Political Parties and Black People,* London, Runnymede Trust.

Glazer, N. and Young, K. (1983), *Ethnic Pluralism and Public Policy,* London, Heinemann.

Goss, S. (1984), 'Women's initiatives in local government', in Boddy, M. and Fudge, C. (eds.), *Local Socialism?,* London, Macmillan.

Greater London Council (1986), *Working for London – the final five years,* London, GLC.

House of Commons Environment Committee (1983), *The Problems of Management of Urban Renewal,* London, HMSO.

John, G (1978), 'Black people and social and community work in Britain', *Social Work, Community Work and Society,* Block 7, Open University.

Liverpool Black Caucus (1986), *The Racial Politics of Militant in Liverpool* – the black community's struggle for participation in local politics, 1980-1986, Runnymede Trust/Merseyside Area Profile Group.

Merseyside Area Profile Group (1980), 'Racial Disadvantage in Liverpool – an Area Profile', in Home Affairs Committee, *Racial Disadvantage,* 2; also published by Department of Sociology, University of Liverpool.

Merseyside Community Relations Council & Liverpool Black Caucus (1986), *Racial Discrimination and Disadvantage in Employment in Liverpool,* Evidence to Select Committee on Employment Merseyside Area Profile Group, Department of Sociology, University of Liverpool.

Newnham, A. (1986), *Employment, Unemployment and Black People,* London, Runnymede Trust.

Ouseley, H. (1984), 'Local Authority Race Initiatives', in Boddy, M. and Fudge, C. (eds.), *Local Socialism?,* London, Macmillan.

Ouseley, H. et al. (1982), *The System,* London, Runnymede Trust.

Parkinson, M. (1985), *Liverpool on the Brink,* Policy Journals.

Phillips, M. (1982), in Ohri et al., *Community Work & Racism,* London, Routledge.

Scarman, Lord (1985), 'Injustice in the Cities', *New Society,* 14, February 1986.

Stewart, M. et al. (1983), *Ethnic Minorities and the Urban Programme,* Bristol, University of Bristol.

11

The politics of planning New York as a world city

NORMAN I. FAINSTEIN
New School for Social Research, New York

SUSAN S. FAINSTEIN
Rutgers State University, New Jersey

Transformation of the world economy produces changes in the functions of cities. A sectoral shift towards service production in the US and other core nations has combined with new technologies and multinational corporate organisation to rearrange the urban hierarchies of the manufacturing period (Stanback, 1985). At the top of the emergent system of cities sits a handful of global control centres, characterised by headquarters locations, concentration of financial institutions, advanced corporate services, and industries aimed at fulfilling the consumption needs of corporate managers and wealthy tourists (Sassen-Koob, 1985, p. 238ff). New York and Los Angeles represent America in the network of global cities. In both places, economic restructuring and correlated flows of population create pressures for new land uses.

The actual character of land use change cannot, however, be deduced from global economic forces; rather it depends on previous usage and on the local political situation. The politics of land use involves cross-cutting bases of conflict among sectoral actors (e.g., manufacturers versus housing developers), as well as between sectorally and spatially defined interests (e.g., developers versus community residents). Local government plays an important role in affecting spatial and physical reconstruction, as it attempts to encourage economic growth, coordinate public and private decisions through a planning process, mediate conflicts, and serve essential needs for housing, public services and infrastructure. The particular outcome of conflicting actors and objectives inevitably reflects the unique history of a city, even while the forces at work may be generally similar from place to place.

In this paper, we examine how economic restructuring plays itself out in the politics of land use planning in New York. First, we identify recent economic trends and the pressures they create for new land uses. Next we describe several cases of land-use politics and planning in New York City. We then try to explain the relative weakness of planning revealed by the cases. In doing so we consider the behaviour of governmental actors and citizens within a historical context structured by the dominant idea of economic growth, by institutional arrangements which fragment planning capabilities, and by organisational resources which offer communities some defences against development pressures but little ability to implement alternative models of change. We conclude with a brief discussion of the consequences of the incapacity to plan, and of the conditions which might produce a revival of more comprehensive urban planning in New York.

ECONOMIC CHANGE AND PRESSURE ON LAND USE IN NEW YORK CITY

The reorganisation of the New York economy has been under way for three decades. More than 600,000 jobs in manufacturing were lost between 1950 and 1983, along with contraction in trade and transportation activities, as the city's economic activities shifted from the loft, the market and the port to the office building, the medical centre and the hotel. Thus, service employment increased by 460,000; finance, insurance, and real estate (FIRE) industries by another 160,000; and the government sector by 140,000 (NYCTCCF, 1976; Table 1; REBNY, 1985a; Table 56). As a result, the proportion of workers engaged in goods production declined by more than half (Ehrenhalt, 1985, p. 47). While the growth of service-producing industries sustained aggregate employment until 1969, during most of the seventies the city experienced a sharp economic recession which began earlier and lasted longer than the national contraction of 1973-75. Between 1969 and 1977, payroll employment fell by 16%, from 3.8 million to 3.2 million. The fiscal crisis in 1975 added to the gloom of economic prognosticators.

Yet the local economy turned around in 1977 and has since rebounded sharply. Real output increased about 2% annually and by 1984 surpassed the 1969 level (Drennan, 1985; Table 1.1). Although the aggregate net employment increase of 218,000 has been insufficient to erase the earlier decline, it nevertheless constitutes the strongest growth phase in the post-war period (Figure 11.1), and surpasses by far the economic performance of the next largest older cities (Ehrenhalt, 1985, p. 26). Employment expansion has been led by corporate and consumer services and the tourist industry (Ehrenhalt, 1985; p. 35; PANYNJ, 1985: p. 17).

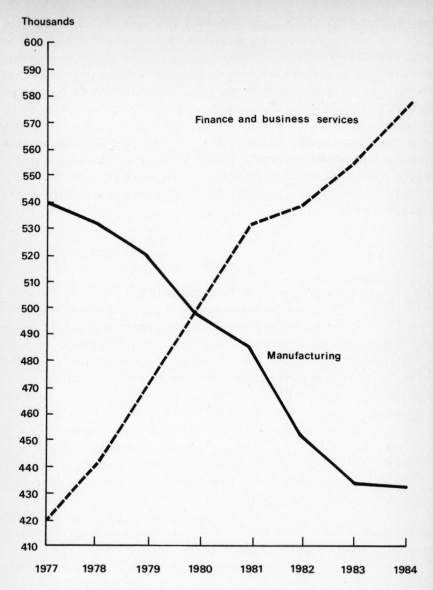

Thousands

FIGURE 11.1
PAYROLL EMPLOYMENT IN MANUFACTURING AND FINANCE
AND BUSINESS SERVICES, NEW YORK CITY, 1977-1984

Source: Samuel Ehrenhalt, 'Growth in the New York City economy – problems and promise', Proceedings of the eighteenth annual one-day institute sponsored by the New York City Council on Economic Education, p. 46.

The aggregate turnaround after 1977 has heightened pressure for conversion of land for use by growing industries.

New York must accommodate a new industry and employment mix within the built environment of the commercial and manufacturing city. Manhattan has been the site of the fiercest competition for land, both because it is already so densely built up, and because new employment has been mainly located here: the borough accounts for more than 85% of the net job increase citywide between 1977 and 1984 (Ehrenhalt, 1985; p. 30). The expansion of Manhattan's service industries has resulted in sharply expanded production of office space. Although investment in office construction has not reached the peak of the early seventies, its scale is nonetheless staggering. Between 1981 and 1984, more than 22m square feet of office space were completed (REBNY, 1985a; Table 157). Another 30 million will be built through 1987 (REBNY, 1985a; Table 156).[1] In addition, hotels, restaurants, and upscale retail establishments compete for prime Manhattan real estate.

The demand for office and recreational uses of land drives all but luxury housing out of the market in most of Manhattan south of 96th Street. Here there is also the greatest pressure on a dwindling stock of manufacturing loft space. Manufacturers in such industries as garments and printing argue that zoning protection must be maintained precisely because of the fragility of their economic position. In contrast, real estate interests point to the plummeting graph of manufacturing employment (Figure 11.2) as evidence that the sector has poor prospects in New York, and no place in Manhattan. They look askance at the tracts of Manhattan real estate still zoned for manufacturing, and conclude that 'the City is preserving an unnecessarily large number of obsolete buildings which are better suited for housing' (REBNY, 1985b; p.32). The demands for space of a growing and transforming economy along with a severe shortage of affordable housing would seem to call for active governmental interventions in the form of housing production and comprehensive planning.

THE POLITICS AND PLANNING OF LAND USE TRANSFORMATION

In fact, however, the city has failed to make construction of low-and moderate-income housing a priority, and it has virtually eschewed systematic land-use planning, much less any ambition for an integrated social and economic strategy. Nevertheless the city plays a central role in a contentious politics of urban development. Governmental action is sometimes limited to site plan approval of wholly private efforts; but in

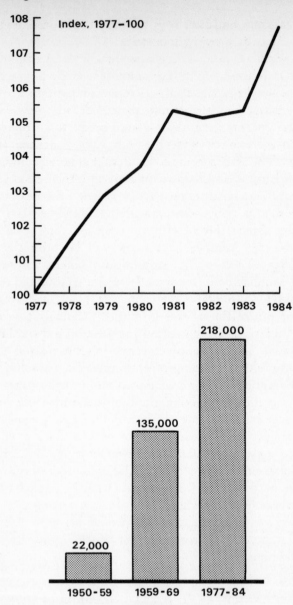

FIGURE 11.2
INDEXES OF PAYROLL EMPLOYMENT, NEW YORK CITY, 1977-84 [*above*]
PRIVATE SECTOR EMPLOYMENT GAINS IN NEW YORK CITY,
THREE GROWTH PERIODS [*below*]

Source: Samuel Ehrenhalt, 'Growth in the New York economy – problems and promise',
Proceedings of the eighteenth annual one-day institute sponsored by the New York City
Council on Economic Education, p. 19.

major projects greater public involvement is required to obtain large-scale investment. While not all projects provoke controversy, most evoke the widespread fear that their ripple effects will force up both commercial and residential rents in the surrounding territory. For this reason, where the city government tends to see almost any new private investment as enhancing the tax base and thereby good, community groups are equally likely to regard it as bad. Even projects built on vacant land can therefore elicit virulent resistance. The kinds of politics and planning that surround new land uses are illustrated through an examination of a group of actions aimed at commercial and residential development.

Commercial Development. Two very large projects, neither yet under construction, demonstrate the dominance of economic development objectives at the present time. One consists of the conversion of 42nd Street in Manhattan from low-level commercial and entertainment space to intense, first-class office uses. The other involves the creation on mainly vacant land of a mixed commercial and residential project in the Long Island City section of Queens. While neither project will cause direct residential displacement, both have mobilised opposition from adjacent residential neighborhoods that fear secondary displacement as a consequence of their making the area more attractive to upper-income people.

In the 42nd Street case the initiative for redevelopment came from residents and merchants in the area who wished to rid it of the high crime and sex-related businesses that dominated the street. When, after a number of years and an earlier abortive proposal, the mayor decided that Times Square (of which 42nd Street forms the southern boundary) was a key commercial site, he turned to the relatively autonomous New York State Urban Development Corporation (UDC) to act as lead agency in formulating a plan in conjunction with the city's Public Development Corporation (PDC). UDC provided a set of guidelines, then promulgated a request for proposals.

The ultimate plan came from a group of private developers. It will add four million square feet of office space to the Manhattan market, along with a 2.5 million square foot merchandise mart, and a hotel. The office buildings exceed the bulk permitted under the city's zoning by over 100%. Because of UDC's participation, however, the project is exempt from both the city's zoning regulations and the land-use review process which gives the city's community boards a significant advisory role. While public funds will not be directly provided to the project, it involves over $650 million of tax abatement and requires the use of eminent domain. Despite the vastness of the buildings, giving rise to criticisms that they would block out light and air, create extreme sidewalk and transit congestion, and destroy the vitality of the theatre district, the city's planners never made any serious effort to formulate an alternative plan comprising smaller-scale development (S. Fainstein, 1985, 1986).[2]

The proposal elicited vehement protests from the adjacent Clinton residential neighbourhood because of its potential gentrification effects and a chorus of opprobrium from civic groups because of its aesthetics. Efforts to block or modify it proceeded initially through the community board and the local city council members and state legislators. Objectors formed an organisation called the Clinton Coalition of Concern, which held rallies, lobbied representatives, vociferously made itself known at public hearings, and sent members to testify before public bodies. After the plan was unanimously approved by the Board of Estimate, further attempts at preventing its implementation were mounted in 22 lawsuits, brought by neighbourhood residents and property owners in the project area. Half of these are still pending as of this writing, and while none so far has halted the project, such an outcome is not inconceivable. Even though Clinton was unable to achieve any substantial modifications of the plan through the political process, it did manage to extract from the city and state a commitment of $25 million to be used for low-income housing and commercial rehabilitation (see S. Fainstein, 1985, 1986).

In the Hunters Point section of Long Island City, the Port Authority of New York and New Jersey (PA) is seeking to develop an equally large volume of first-class office space in line with its mission of job creation. Under bi-state legislation the PA is authorised to acquire and develop this and another site in Hoboken, New Jersey, for commercial uses. Although residential construction will also be involved, the PA is not allowed to develop for exclusively residential purposes and can only act as primary developer for the commercial section of the project. The rationale for expensive commercial construction here is to establish a Queens beachhead of businesses that formerly would either have chosen Manhattan or left the city altogether for a bucolic suburban setting. Yet, while there is a clear existing demand for residential units on the site, located immediately across the East River from midtown Manhattan, the prospects for office tenancy are murky. Acting jointly with the Queens division of the City Planning Department, the PA has hired a consultant to determine whether building the offices around a theme such as the entertainment or biomedical businesses would succeed in enticing Manhattan-based enterprise currently squeezed for space out to the borough. It is hoped that the site's spectacular views and its proximity to Manhattan will overcome reluctance to pay Manhattan-sized rents for a Queens location (NYCPC, 1984a; Gruzen Partnership/Beyer Blinder Belle, 1985).[3]

As in the instance of 42nd Street, a nearby low-income neighbourhood may find itself under pressure when workers in the office buildings seek convenient housing and the new residential development glamourises the area. Whereas Clinton encompassed a number of highly mobilised citizens who could form action groups based on a network of existing tenant advocacy organisations, Long Island City contains a much more passive community. The residents lack the tenant protections of Clinton, since most of the housing stock does not reach the six-unit minimum required for coverage by the rent-control and non-eviction statute. Long Island City is unlikely to mount a movement against the development and in fact may not possess the consciousness, some would say paranoia, that sees every development as threatening. The community board, rather than opposing the project, is seeking to receive a number of benefits from the Port Authority in return for its support, including senior citizen housing and improved services. The chairman of the community board sees little hope of altering the overall conception and thus is attempting, in emulation of the ultimate 42nd Street outcome, to gain concessions for the neighbourhood. The concessions being requested, however, would do nothing to mitigate the precarious housing situation of most residents.

The two projects resemble each other in the role of state agencies UDC and PA and their orientation towards providing space to accommodate service industries. The independence of these agencies makes them highly insulated from community input; while in both cases community leaders could recall meeting with project planners, they universally felt that these forms of consultation were used by state agencies to sell their plans rather than to elicit other viewpoints. Thus, there was much scepticism that neighbourhood interests would be incorporated in the analyses of agency planners; the leaders' only expectation of influence was through political channels.

Both projects arose in the context of generalised land use strategies of sorts. Times Square was part of an effort to shift development from the East to the West Side of Manhattan; Hunters Point reflects a concern with utilising the waterfront. But there is neither a comprehensive West Side plan nor one for the waterfront. Despite a glut of vacant office space in the metropolitan area and additional millions scheduled for construction, much without any public subsidy, public agencies are expending their resources to create even more. No planning agency concerns itself with setting targets for the amount of commercial development desirable in any one year. Rather, having identified the trend towards a service economy, the public planning agencies are emulating the boom and bust behaviour of the private sector by expanding commercial space on all fronts. Only the court-ordered demise of Westway inhibited the creation of a giant landfill site for even more development. The Battery Park City Authority, a UDC subsidiary, is anticipating 6 million square feet of office space for its waterfront site; another 1.5 million is projected for the Triborough Bridge and Tunnel Authority (TBTA) owned site at Columbus Circle, and PDC is sponsoring the development of more large sites downtown and in Brooklyn (Ponte, 1982: NYCPDC, n.d.; Wiseman, 1985). These will all be in competition with the millions more square feet intended for the New Jersey side of the Hudson.

The disjointed character of planning can also be seen in the development of two huge, tourist-oriented projects the construction of the Marriott Marquis Hotel in Times Square and of the convention centre on the riverside in the Thirties. The gigantic Marriott, out of scale with its surroundings and designed to internalise all its activities, was built over the vocal protests of theatre people, who condemned the demolition of three legitimate houses on the site. Sponsored by UDC and PDC, and making use of a federal Urban Development Action Grant (UDAG) plus tax abatement, the hotel was intended to foster the convention trade in the city (NYPDC, n.d.; McCain, 1985a). It was located, however, a considerable distance from the new convention centre (a joint project of UDC and the TBTA), which, while making use of unutilised land, is very poorly served by public transport. The convention centre's location was selected in a decision process which initially placed it on a site farther uptown. In order to assuage the federal Environmental Protection Agency, which wanted the city to restrict the number of cars entering Manhattan, the convention centre was designed without a public garage (NYCPC, 1984b).[4]

These tourist facility cases differ from the office schemes in that the public sector has unquestionably sponsored projects for which there is still pent-up demand. Given the very few sites available for the convention centre, its location, despite its drawbacks, may still be optimal. But it will open before any transportation plan or rezoning for the surrounding area (necessary for construction of a hotel) is in place, despite seven years' advance notice; and it will add its share to existing congestion and skyrocketing real-estate prices in the adjoining Chelsea and Clinton neighborhoods (Cecere, 1986; Trager, 1986).

Indeed the entire strategy of encouraging more intense West-Side development seems to have been devised mainly in reaction to over-development to the east. The West Side, however, while having more subway service, is swamped with cars and buses as a consequence of the Port Authority bus terminal, the entrance and exit to the Lincoln Tunnel, Lincoln Center, and the theatre district. This traffic congestion spills over into the residential communities, which, in their preoccupation with gentrification, complain but do not press very hard. So far such citywide civic associations as the Regional Plan Association, the Municipal Art Society, and the Landmarks Conservancy, which had strongly condemned the deleterious effects of development on the East Side, have had little to say, except in Times Square, about its impact on the West Side.

Residential development. Economic forces affect land use not only through the changing requirements of business, but also through their impact on the incomes and housing needs of the resident population. The shift to a service economy has been accompanied nationally by increasing income inequality among wage earners, families, and racial groups (Lawrence, 1984; USBC, 1985; N. Fainstein, 1985). The same trends have characterised New York (Sassen-Koob, 1984, p. 189; Tobier and Stafford, 1985, Table 2.5; Stegman, 1985, Table 2.28). Jobs in relatively glamorous service and FIRE industries tend to be bifurcated. Thus, growth and conversion in the city's economy have increased demand for managers and professionals, but also for low-wage service and clerical workers (Sassen-Koob, 1985, p. 257ff).

As can be predicted from the increasingly bimodal distribution of jobs and income, there has been heightened demand for both upper- and lower-income housing. At the upper end of the income distribution, managers, professionals, and doubled-up white collar personnel working in the Manhattan CBD are gentrifying almost all of Manhattan south of 96th Street, as well as some neighbourhoods in other boroughs. By one estimate, displacement caused by gentrification ranges from 10,000 to 40,000 people each year (Marcuse, 1985, p.12). At the other end of the distribution, New York City's foreign immigration has reached levels comparable to the early years of the century. The immigrant population, which may amount to perhaps 1.2 million excluding Puerto Ricans (Tobier, 1982, p.187), is adding to the demand and competition for low and moderate income housing.

Overall, the expansion of the low-income population and its reduced capacity to pay for housing have created a housing crisis. Between 1976 and 1982 the number of poor New Yorkers, as measured by the federal Census's threshhold level, increased by 37%, from 17.5 to 24% of the total population (Tobier, 1982, p. 36). This compares with a national increase over the same years of 27% (from 11.8 to 15%), indicating that the city's new prosperity is highly encapsulated. These increasingly impoverished families and individuals have had to compete for housing in a more and more restricted market. As a consequence, median rents since 1970 have grown from 20 to 29% of household income, and three of every ten tenants spend at least 40% of their incomes on rent (Stegman, 1985, pp. 140-1). For the first time in twenty-five years, measured levels of crowding increased between 1981 and 1984, with the worst conditions experienced by blacks and Hispanics (Stegman, 1985, pp. 169, 174). During the winter of 1984-85, more than 20,000 people a night were receiving lodging in city shelters; thousands more were being accommodated in single-room-occupancy hotels; and countless others were doubling up with family and friends (Marcuse, 1985).

Despite rising demand, housing supply has hardly expanded. The city's population grew by 78,000 between 1981 and 1984 (*New York Times,* 1985), yet the housing inventory expanded by only 11,000 units (Stegman, 1985, Table 9-1). New housing units constructed during 1981-84 totalled 25,000, 3,000 fewer than were built in the previous three-year period (Stegman, 1985, Table 9-1), and less than half the number entering the market during the single post-war peak year of 1962 (Sternlieb and Listokin, 1985, Table 12.2). Vacancy rates in 1984 were exceedingly small at all rent levels. Units in the most expensive census category (roughly the top quintile of rents) had a vacancy rate of less than 3%. The least expensive quintile of rental units had a vacancy level of about 0.5% (Stegman, 1985: Tables 3.9, 4.2). Since many of these units were uninhabitable, the actual availability of housing for the poorest New Yorkers was close to zero.

Nevertheless, adding to the housing supply is not a major preoccupation of the development agencies. Talk of establishing housing trust funds derived from a tax on development or real estate transfers, and examples of such funds in other cities, have so far failed to produce a serious proposal (see Pickman and Roberts, 1985). New York State has appropriated $24 million statewide for low-income housing, but regardless of the labeling of this appropriation as a housing trust fund, it does not have an earmarked source of revenue and is too miniscule to be meaningful (Sakano, 1985). The Department of Housing Preservation and Development, under the city's in rem programme for managing and rehabilitating tax foreclosed properties, operates 46,000 units either directly or under the alternative management programme (Stegman, 1985, p. 227). The operation is financed primarily out of federal Community Development Block Grant (CDBG) funds. While this is by far the city's largest active housing programme, it mainly preserves the exist-ing stock rather than adding to it. Given the method by which in rem units are acquired, it is obviously a wholly opportunistic programme rather than one of planned development.

Before the city's fiscal crisis, advocates of low-income housing pressed for its inclusion in all major housing developments. These days '[they] will take housing wherever and however they can get it' (quoted in Gottlieb, 1985b). Thus, all original plans for including subsidised low-income housing in the residential component of the Battery Park City project have been dropped. While the project's anticipated revenues for a housing programme, they would not be applied to the Battery Park site itself (Gottlieb, 1985b).

New housing development takes place almost wholly at private initia-tive.[5] Of the meagre 11,758 units built in 1983, almost half were con-structed in Manhattan, the great majority of which were luxury coopera-tives and condominiums, with an average cost of $340,000 for a four-and-one-half-room unit (REBNY, 1985a: Tables 130, 122, 125). Given this price structure, the impact of new construction on a neighbourhood is inevitably to raise average values. Thus, except on the already homogeneously wealthy Upper East Side, community leaders perceive new construction, even if theoretically it should lower prices by making more supply available, as endangering the income mix of the commun-ity. For example, some residents in the Union Square area of Manhattan opposed the development of high-rise apartment buildings on a site that had been occupied for many years by a derelict department store, despite the opportunity provided to rid the neighbourhood of an eyesore (Car-mody, 1984). East of Greenwich Village, community groups protested construction of dormitories by New York University, even though the student population would not be a wealthy one, on the grounds that the neighbourhood would become too attractive and the pace of gentrifica-tion would increase. A speaker at a rally held outside the building site was quoted as saying: 'Their [NYU's] success could lead to tremendous speculation in the area and that is why we have labeled them a Trojan horse' (Miller, 1985, p. 8).

Because there are few public funds for housing development, and private investors prefer the greater return realisable from commercial investments, conflicts over housing essentially revolve around main-tenance of the existing population in any neighbourhood. Neighbour-hood groups have succeeded in various locations in obtaining historic district designations and downzoning so as to prevent any major new development. The ironic consequence is that it becomes extraordinarily difficult to add to the housing stock, thereby making even more extreme the situation that causes every community to defend its status quo. Within this stalemate, planning for housing becomes unrealistic. Yet the priority given to economic development as opposed to housing by the city's leadership produces an outcome that jeopardizes the current prosperity:

> In essence, current housing policies fail to result in an adequate supply of housing. The city's new business functions, and hence its future economic vitality, increasingly depend on people who do not live within it. As a result, jobs are following residences at a loss to New York City (Sternlieb and Listokin, 1985: 392; see also RPA, 1985).

EXPLAINING THE WEAKNESS OF PLANNING

The political and social context within which urban restructuring occurs is as much a product of the past as the built environment itself. In order to explain the present state of planning in New York City, we must look to the historical context within which the mayor, planning agencies, and community groups function. Here we may usefully consider in turn the effect of (a) the present climate of ideas, and (b) the institutions and programmes which affect policy. In each instance, we will find that the legacies of radicalism in the sixties and of conservative reaction in the late seventies are both still apparent.

Prevailing ideas. While over time political leadership, social movements, and actual events transform the ideas in circulation, within the short run these ideas constrain available alternatives and alignments. In this way, they form the context for purposive action. At present, ideas about urban development are far more conservative than they were in the early 1970s, yet they establish a context very different from the fifties. Proponents of large-scale development projects whether the mayor, executives of public development agencies, or the New York Times – define the role of city government as facilitating economic growth. The principal aim of official planning is no longer 'rational' land use, much less comprehensive planning or a particular aesthetic vision, but job creation. The idea of social planning has disappeared almost altogether: equity is an 'unrealistic' planning objective. City officials act just the way that Paul Peterson (1981) and other public-choice theorists say they should, fending off fiscal crisis, combating their New Jersey rivals, asserting that the tide of economic prosperity will eventually raise all boats.

But unlike in the days of Robert Moses, no one claims that slum clearance actually helps slumdwellers, nor do people unquestioningly accept large-scale redevelopment as contributing to neighbourhood improvement. With official reports attesting to a vacancy rate of two per cent, it is nearly impossible to rationalise government-sponsored clearance of occupied neighbourhoods. Instead, disputes concerning residential impacts centre around the significance of the secondary displacement potentially caused by the ripple effects of new development. Moreover, there is a widely held view among neighbourhood activists that New York is run by a cabal of real estate developers and their paid politicians who should be challenged at every turn. As a consequence, project planners must constantly anticipate opposition and proceed more warily than might otherwise be the case.

Whereas in the early years of urban renewal the programme received the endorsement of 'progressive' elite groups, criticisms by Jane Jacobs, Lewis Mumford, and other opponents of the time have now been accepted by the city's civic establishment. Thus, influential citizens and lobbies regularly oppose development on the basis of aesthetic concerns, commitment to historic preservation, abhorrence of the automobile, or antagonism to chic consumption. Although property developers have mobilised support for tax breaks and other forms of municipal assistance, no widespread coalition supports a more interventionist role for government. Consequently, despite a seeming consensus around planning for economic development, reflected in the immense electoral popularity of the mayor, there are important constraints on the process. David Harvey's (1978) picture of planning as coordinating the interests of business accurately describes the activities of economic development planners. Nonetheless, it fails to explain why their scope is limited to facilitating specific projects rather than extended comprehensively to the relationships of projects to each other and to the housing and transit systems. This extremely circumscribed role must be seen as the consequence of institutional structure and community politics.

Institutional arrangements and programmatic resources. Conflicting viewpoints on growth are expressed through a variety of institutions that shape the development process. Predictably, development initiatives arise in executive agencies, and they are opposed by citizens' groups in the courts, Landmarks Commission, and community boards. The outcome is not, as some have claimed, the incapacity of the public sector to mount major projects (Gottlieb, 1985a; Roberts 1985), but rather, its inability (or unwillingness) to co-ordinate them, and its ineffectiveness in dealing with the housing crisis.

Public-Sector-Activity. Two chains of events, one national and the other local, have produced the current configuration of planning and development institutions in New York. Nationally, the switch from categorical to block grants embodied in the 1974 federal Housing and Community Development Act, the cutbacks in federal funding for urban programmes that commenced under the Carter administration and grew drastically under Reagan, the Reagan administration's de-emphasis of citizen participation requirements, and the federal thrust toward fostering economic development rather than directly assisting the needy, all resulted in a vastly changed context for local efforts. The shrinkage of the previously looming federal presence left New York to work out its own procedures for planning and community involvement and forced it, like all other cities, to rely heavily on the private sector for development funds. Having to respond to private-sector initiatives meant that development planning became increasingly reactive; if a firm threatened to leave the city or showed an interest in a site, the city would hustle to accommodate it, regardless of the long-run implications for overall development.

New York differs little from most cities in not imposing a development plan on the private sector. But it did enter the post-1974 period (an epoch we have elsewhere labelled conserving [Fainstein *et al.*, 1983]) with a much more unified planning and development apparatus than other places; both the creation and breakdown of this apparatus incorporate specifically local factors. For decades planning and development in New York City had proceeded in accordance with Robert Moses's set of priorities. When Moses's hegemony finally crumbled in the early 1960s, the reaction was to give primary responsibility for both commercial and residential planning to agencies under mayoral control: the Housing and Redevelopment Board (HRB) and the Department of City Planning. Later Mayor Lindsay merged HRB with other housing agencies to form a single 'superagency,' the Housing and Development Administration (HDA), with the object of creating a coherent programme that would integrate preservation and redevelopment efforts. Mayoral policy insisted that priority for neighbourhood and housing improvements be given to those areas that were the neediest (Fainstein and Fainstein, 1984). In its 1969 Master Plan, the City Planning Commission presented a general strategy of promoting incentives to office development in Manhattan and residential improvements in the boroughs (NYCPC, 1969).

During the depths of the fiscal crisis, capital spending in New York ground to a halt (Hartman, 1985). The institutional structure that emerged once the pace of development picked up again differed from its predecessor in composition but more importantly in the character of its lead agencies and their priorities. The Department of Housing Preservation and Development (HPD the remodelled HDA) now had few federal funds at its disposal; it exercised its reduced authority mainly in the realm of housing rehabilitation and no longer played an important role in guiding development. The Department of City Planning virtually gave up any pretence of overall land-use planning and devoted itself mainly to studies of specific zoning changes and project impacts. Although the chairmen of the CPC continued to play an influential role, they did so in their capacity as mayoral advisors rather than as spokespersons for any particular planning approach.

The PDC became the most important city agency affecting development. Formed in 1966 to facilitate industrial growth, it was transformed in 1979 into a 'real estate development and service organisation to promote all sectors of New York City's economy' (NYCPDC, n.d.: i). Although a public agency, its board of directors consists mainly of prominent businessmen. PDC is less a planning agency than a financial intermediary, putting together packages of land, improvements, tax abatements, and funding for specific development sites. It identifies potential locations for development, coordinates city efforts with state activities, responds to initiatives from private firms, and solicits developers. It does not concern itself with comprehensive land use planning, aesthetics, or housing needs, which it regards as the responsibility of other agencies. But other agencies are generally reluctant, once PDC strikes a deal, to jeopardise it in the name of adverse environmental impacts. Instead, they are put to work showing that the impacts are not quite as adverse as they might seem to the naked eye.

PDC in its larger projects works in tandem with the UDC and the Port Authority. These two entities have, corresponding to the tenor of the times, also redefined their missions. UDC, originally entrusted with developing housing for low and moderate income people, now is primarily concerned with commercial development. Its powers to override local regulations mean that, when it is operating in conjunction with city agencies, those agencies need not conform to the zoning code or to the city's citizen participation requirements. The PA has received a new legislative mandate to enlarge its role in the area's economy from simply providing infrastructure and developing industrial sites to acting as a developer of commercial property (the World Trade Center was as early harbinger of this new direction).

Community resources. Federal requirements for environmental impact statements (EIS) and citizen participation have been replicated in state statute and the City Charter. Consequently, even if federal funds are not involved, an EIS must be filed for all publicly sponsored projects. In addition, city-sponsored development must go through a review process which involves presentation of plans to community boards consisting of citizens appointed by the borough president. Even though the community board's decision is not binding, it is very influential with both the CPC and elected officials representing the district. The community board tends to be the principal forum for residential neighbourhoods fearing impacts of gentrification or congestion resulting from a project. Historic district and landmarks preservation statutes provide further access to those seeking to block development, usually citywide civic groups with substantial legal resources. Elected officials act as mediators between the central decisional bodies and their constituencies.

There tends to be a division between the Board of Estimate (the final decisional body consisting of the borough presidents, the president of the city council, the comptroller, and the mayor) and the district-based officials who sit on the city council and the two branches of the state legislature. The Board of Estimate almost always favours development; legislators and council members will usually adopt the neighbourhood's position. They are never bound by party discipline. Victories for neighbourhood groups generally occur when pressure is brought through both channels, the community boards and the political hierarchy even though the various legislators involved may themselves never vote on the issue at hand.

Because the development process does not take place within the framework of an overall plan for the city, contests between the forces favouring and opposing development occur project by project. The resulting outcomes do not necessarily represent the triumph of the economically powerful, as in the demise of the Westway highway and waterfront project. But inevitably, when community groups triumph, they do so through veto. Neither they nor any other political force seems capable at the moment of establishing a coherent strategic plan, much less of commanding the positive investment in housing so desperately needed in most city neighbourhoods.

THE UNPLANNED GLOBAL CITY: CONSEQUENCES AND POSSIBILITY

'The city has destroyed my investment,' says Gary Evans late one night in the kitchen of his co-op apartment at 66 Madison Avenue, near 28th Street. Evans is looking out his window and across a narrow courtyard to the back wall of the Prince George Hotel [which the city is using to house homeless families] (Pooley, 1986, p. 28).

At the Prince George, the city pays $1,590 per month for a family of four. Faced with explosive growth of its homeless population, most of whom are families on welfare, and virtually zero construction of low-income housing, the city has had to rent hotel rooms. Most of these have been in the Times Square area, with rates of more than $20,000 per year for a family of four. Responding to criticism that Times Square is no place to raise children, the Human Resources Administration (HRA) has sought out hotels elsewhere in the city. The neighbourhood immediately south of fashionable Murray Hill, site of both numerous hotels and expensive cooperatives, has therefore become a centre for the homeless. While the city administration pursues a logic of unplanned economic growth, social service agencies face the Hobson's choice of concentrating the homeless in sleazy Times Square a district the city is trying to redevelop or of placing them any place it can find a willing hotel owner, including some of the most attractive middle-class neighbourhoods in Manhattan.

The unplanned consequences of sheltering the homeless offer a dramatic example of the dysfunctions attendant on the de facto city planning policy: unbridled economic growth, with inattention to the housing needs of the expanding workforce or to the infrastructural requirements of ever more intensive development. Thus, planners are watching with bated breath to see what will happen at the convention centre, built as we noted without any parking facility whatsoever, and with no new public transit link to the midtown hotels or subway system. For years, there has been talk among business leaders and public officials of the need to modernise the city's decrepit subway system. But as in the case of housing, the city government has not taken a leadership role. Instead, functional agencies (like the Metropolitan Transportation Authority, the PDC, and HRA) pursue their own logics, utilising whatever resources they can command. The city has not fully exploited the opportunity presented by a significant influx of investment capital and a growing revenue base to rebuild its housing and infrastructure. Nor does it even attempt to develop a strategic plan.

The impact of the present mode of development planning is to make each project an *ad hoc* collection of bonding, tax expenditures, city loans, federal dollars, zoning concessions, and private financing. The resulting physical structures and ancillary amenities (to the extent that such can be wrung from the developers) are determined by the financial considerations internal to each project. Externalities beyond those specific to the immediate project area are no more included in the calculations of the public sector than was ever the case for purely private development. If any constraints are placed on development, they are the consequence of the set of institutions and resources that have given community groups access to the planning process.

The present weakness of planning in New York City does not mean that growth will be brought to a halt, or that an economic crisis will force the planners back onto centre stage. While planning offers the hope of rational and efficient development, it is also potentially costly to powerful economic interests. As we have argued elsewhere (Fainstein and Fainstein, 1985), planning forces development choices into a public arena where means and ends are openly identified and where private developers may lose control over their projects. Many vested interests therefore benefit from planning incapacity in particular the real estate developers so active in city politics. For this reason, we expect that any resurgence of planning will result not so much from a recognition of its functionality, as from a shift in the balance of political forces around city hall.

A possible scenario, the most appealing one perhaps, involves a coalition among some business elements, middle-class renters, and the poor. Service industries employing large clerical labour forces have long been aware of the city's infrastructural needs. They have been particularly concerned about how their workers will be housed and how they will travel to work. Some of their executives have spoken out in favor of responsible government intervention to rationalise market forces. A second constituency, with much electoral power, can be found among the middle-class renters who have long, and successfully, defended public regulation of rents. There seems little question that a housing effort like the old Mitchell-Lama programme, which provided tens of thousands of affordable apartments to the middle class during the last boom period in the sixties, would be extremely popular. If lower-income voters can be mobilised by a mayoral candidate who also appeals to some elements of big business and a large portion of the middle class, then we might well see a new regime in city hall. Such a scenario depends critically on the emergence of a political leader with a programme for directed growth and adequate housing for all. In that case, planning will not be the programme, but it will be the result.

NOTES

1 By way of comparison, the total office stock of Los Angeles is 28 million square feet and of San Francisco, 53 million; the Manhattan stock is 315 million (REBNY, 1985a, Table 164). The new office space which will be opened in Manhattan is greater than

the combined total of all projected office development in the remainder of the New York region itself an astonishing 25.7 million square feet (REBNY, 1985a, Table 165).

2 The discussion of 42nd Street redevelopment is based on interviews by Susan S. Fainstein with public officials and community leaders during 1984-85.

3 The discussion of the Hunters Point project is based on interviews by Susan S. Fainstein with public officials and community leaders during 1985.

4 The discussion of the convention centre is based on interviews by Susan S. Fainstein with public officials and a member of the convention centre board in 1984.

5 Tax abatement under the J-51 (conversion and rehabilitation) and 421 (new construction) programmes has been the major governmental inducement to housing production. In 1982, much of Manhattan south of 96th Street was excluded from the J-51 programme; a similar limitation goes into effect in November 1985 for new construction under 421. The J-51 restriction reflected the sentiment that such conversion and rehabilitation would proceed without assistance. The 421 restriction, which unlike the J-51 one applied to the West Side, represented an effort to limit the replacement of older, low-rent structures by new, luxury rentals (see REBNY, 1985a, Tables 142-50). The imminent restriction under 421 has precipitated a building boom in luxury highrises as developers race to take advantage of the tax benefits, causing the number of units under construction in 1985 to double the 1984 amount, and foreordaining a commensurately abrupt drop in the following year (McCain, 1985b).

REFERENCES

Carmody, Deirdre (1984), 'New day is celebrated for Union Square Park', *New York Times,* 20 April.

Cecere, Linda (1986), 'Transportation, parking woes snarl centre before its debut', *Crain's New York Business,* 2, 31 March, T6-T7.

Drennan, Matthew (1985), 'Local economy and local revenue', in Brecher, Charles and Horton, Raymond D. (eds.), *Setting Municipal Priorities,* 1986, New York, New York University Press, pp. 23-53.

Ehrenhalt, Samuel (1985), 'Growth in the New York City —economy problems and promise', in Proceedings of the eighteenth annual one-day institute sponsored by the New York City Council on Economic Education, pp. 11-64.

Fainstein, Norman I. (1985), 'The continuing significance of race in the economic situation of black Americans'. Paper presented at a conference sponsored by the Centre for Research in Ethnic Relations, University of Warwick, Coventry, England, September.

Fainstein, Norman I. and Susan S. Fainstein (1985), 'Is state planning necessary for capital?', *International Journal of Urban and Regional Research,* 9, 4, pp. 381-403.

Fainstein, Norman I. and Susan S. Fainstein (1984), 'The politics of urban development: New York City since 1945', *City Almanac,* 17 April, 1-26.

Fainstein, Susan S. (1985), 'The redevelopment of 42nd Street', *City Almanac,* 18.

Fainstein, Susan S. (1986), 'The politics of criteria: the case of Times Square redevelopment', in *Against neutrality: social values in policy analysis,* Beverly Hills, Sage.

Fainstein, Susan S. *et al.* (1983), *Restructuring the city,* New York, Longman.

Gottlieb, Martin (1985a), 'Public projects: are they viable in the city anymore?', *New York Times,* 4 August.

Gottlieb, Martin (1985b), 'Battery project reflects changing city priorities', *New York*

Times, 18 October.

Gruzen Partnership/Beyer Blinder Belle (1985), Hunters Point waterfront development, *Part I: Inventory and evaluation final report,* New York, Port Authority of New York and New Jersey, February.

Hartman, James M. (1985), 'Capital resources', in Brecher, Charles and Horton Raymond A. (eds.), *Setting municipal priorities,* 1986, New York, New York University Press, pp. 139-69.

Harvey, David (1978), 'Planning the ideology of planning', in Burchell, Robert and Sternlieb, George (eds.), *Planning theory in the 1980s',* New Brunswick, Rutgers University Center for Urban Policy Research, pp. 213-34.

Lawrence, Robert (1984), 'Sectoral shifts and the size of the middle class', *The Brookings Review,* Fall, pp. 3-11.

McCain, Mark (1985a), 'Architect champions Marquis in face of ongoing controversy', *Crain's New York Business,* 1, 21, 27 October.

McCain, Mark (1985b), 'Builders dash to beat city tax-break deadline', *Crain's New York Business,* 1, 21 October, pp. 1, 30.

Marcuse, Peter (1985), 'The state of the city's housing', *City Limits,* September, pp. 10-14.

Massey, Doreen (1984), *Spatial divisions of labour,* London, Macmillan.

Miller, Richard (1985), 'NYU flunks out', *City Limits,* 10, June-July, p. 8.

New York City Planning Commission (NYCPC) (1969), *Plan for New York City: critical issues,* 1.

New York City Planning Commission (NYCPC) (1984a), *Hunters Point: recommendations for a land use policy.*

New York City Planning Commission (NYCPC) (1984b), *The Convention Center area: recommendations for land use, zoning and development.*

New York City Public Development Corporation (NYCPDC) (n.d.), 1984/1985 development projects.

New York City Temporary Commission on City Finances (NYCTCCF) (1976), *The effects of taxation on manufacturing in New York City, New York Times* (1985), *19 February.*

Peterson, Paul (1981), *City limits,* Chicago, University of Chicago Press.

Pickman, James and Roberts, Benson F. (1985), 'Tapping real estate markets to address housing needs', *New York Affairs,* 9, 1, pp. 3-17.

Ponte, Robert (1982), 'Building Battery Park City', *Urban Design International,* 3, March/April, pp. 10-15.

Pooley, Eric (1986), 'To have and have not', New York, 31 March.

Port Authority of New York and New Jersey (PANYNJ) (1985), *The regional economy: 1984 review,* 1985 outlook for the New York-New Jersey metropolitan region.

Real Estate Board of New York (REBNY) (1985a), *Fact book 1985,* New York.

Real Estate Board of New York (REBNY) (1985b) 'Housing in crisis: 1985', *New York Regional Plan Association (RPA) 1985,* 'Prosperity projected for New Jersey-New York-Connecticut urban region, keeping up with U.S. growth by 1990 if housing is built for employees', *The Region's Agenda,* 15 August, pp. 1-4.

Roberts, Sam (1985), 'The legacy of Westway: lessons from its demise', *New York Times,* 7 October.

Sakano, Donald M. (1985), 'Albany's new housing fund', *City Limits,* 10, June-July, pp. 10-11.

Sassen-Koob, Saskia (1984), 'The new labour demand in global cities', in Smith,

Michael Peter (ed.), *Cities in transformation,* Beverly Hills, Sage, pp. 139-71.

Sassen-Koob, Saskia (1985), 'Capital mobility and labour migration: their expression in core cities', in Timberlake, Michael (ed.), *Urbanization in the world economy,* New York, Academic Press, pp. 231-65.

Stanback, Thomas (1985), 'The changing fortunes of metropolitan economies', in Castells, Manuel (ed.), *High technology, space, and society,* Beverly Hills, Sage, pp. 122-42.

Stegman, Michael (1985), *Housing in New York, study of a city,* 1984, New York, NYC Department of Housing Preservation and Development.

Sternlieb, George and Listokin, David (1985), 'Housing', in Brecher, Charles and Horton Raymond D.(eds.), *Setting municipal priorities,* 1986, New York, New York University Press, pp. 382-411.

Tobier, Emanuel (1982), 'Foreign immigration', in Brecher, Charles and Horton, Raymond D. (eds.), *Setting Municipal Priorities,* 1983, New York, New York University Press, pp. 154-201.

Tobier, Emanuel, with Walter B. Stafford (1985), 'People and income', in Brecher, Charles and Horton, Raymond D. (eds.), *Setting Municipal Priorities,* 1986, New York, New York University Press, pp. 54-83.

Trager, Cara (1986), 'City aims to polish up image of Clinton area', *Crain's New York Business,* 2, 31 March, T18-19.

United States Bureau of the Census (USBC) (1985), *Current Population Reports,* Series P-60, No. 146.

Wiseman, Carter (1985), 'Cashing in on the Coliseum', *New York,* 29 July, pp. 40-4.

Index

annexation 15-16

'black' economy 30
blacks *see* racial inequality
block grants, USA 19-21, 166
Boston, Massachusetts 99, 101-6, 108, 137
Bristol 7, 39-53
    economic change 40-5
    policy implications 49-52
    processes affecting employment 45-6
    uneven development 46-9, 52
business
    'good business climate' 15, 87, 93
    strategies to attract 7, 9-10, 23-4, 55-72
Byrne, Jane, Mayor of Chicago 131

California 15, 96-7, 99, 107-8, 137-8
capital, UK 32-3
Carter, Jimmy, administration 19, 22, 170
centralisation of authority, UK 33-4
Chicago 5, 128-40
    demographic trends 129-31
    linkage 97-9, 135-8
    politics and redistribution 139
    race 129-31, 139
    Washington plan 131-5
cities, USA and UK 1-8
    Bristol 39-53
    Chicago 128-40
    and federal system 9-24
    linked development policies 93-108
    Liverpool: fiscal crisis 110-26; racial inequality 141-54
    New York 156-75
    politics 3-5
    private sector regeneration 74-90
    size of 29
    social, political and economic trends 27-37
    Texas 55-72
Cleveland, Ohio 99

Community Development Block Grants (CDBG), USA 21, 166
competition, inter-state and inter-city 9-10, 23-4
Comprehensive Employment and Training Act, USA 19-20, 23
Conservative Party, UK
    centralisation 3, 33-4
    and Liverpool 110-14, 116-17
    public spending 4
    and racial inequality 142-5, 147-8, 150
    urban policy 1, 3, 7
corruption 131-2
Cucinich, Dennis, Mayor of Cleveland 99

Daley, Richard J., Mayor of Chicago 128, 131-3
decentralisation of authority 31-2
development
    and land use 16, 156-75
    linkage (*q.v.*) 5, 93-108, 135-8
    uneven: UK 46-9, 52, 85-8; USA 5-8, 23-4
Dillon, John, Judge 14

education 12-13
employment changes
    UK 40-5, 47-9
    USA 156-60
'enterprise zones' 16, 23
environment 15, 65-6, 171-2
exactions *see* linkage
exclusionary policies 11-12

federal system, USA 3, 9-24
    and inequality 23-4
    local urban policies 9-13
    national urban policies 17-24
    politics 21-3
    states 13-17
Flynn, Raymond, Mayor of Boston 103-5, 108
fragmentation, metropolitan 9-11

Georgia 15

Glasgow 80-8
  culture 84-5
  Glasgow Action 81-2
  Glasgow Eastern Area Renewal
    (GEAR) 78
  housing 75, 85
  promotion 82-3
  regeneration 82-5
  uneven development 85-8
Gramm, Phil, Senator 21
grants
  UK: central to local government
    113-14, 116, 118; Scotland 79-80
  USA 18-22, 166
Gruzen Partnership/Beyer Blinder Belle
  163

Hartford, Connecticut 97-9
Heseltine, Michael 125, 143-4
Hite, Richard 60
housing 5-6, 22, 30
  Glasgow 75, 85
  New York 159, 165-8, 170-4
  see also linkage
Houston, Texas 56-71
  Economic Development Council
    60-6, 66-70

Indianapolis, Indiana 12
industry, manufacturing
  decline of 28, 41-3, 47, 159
  high-technology 43, 48-9, 51-2
  see also service sector
inequality 11-13, 23-4, 165
  racial see racial inequality
  see also redistribution
inner cities 11, 13, 24
investment see business; development;
  planning; public–private partnerships

Job Training Partnership Act, USA 17
Johnson, Lyndon B., administration 17-18

Kennedy, John F. 17

Labour Party, UK
  Black Sections movement 142, 151
  and Liverpool 34, 111-12, 118-23,
    125, 145-7
  Militant Tendency 111, 115, 142,
    146

public spending 4
  and racial inequality 142-4, 145-7,
    150, 151-2
  urban policies 2-3
land use, planning and control of, USA
  16, 156-75
Liberal Party, UK 112, 150
Lindsay, Robert, Mayor of New York 170
linkage of development, USA 5, 93-108
  assessment of 105-8
  Boston 101-5
  Chicago 97-9, 135-8
  exactions 94-5
  reasons for 98-101
  varieties of 96-8
Liverpool, fiscal crisis 33-4, 110-26
  budgets and local politics 111-12
  and central government grants
    113-14, 116, 118
  culture of failure 124-5
  deficit budgets 118-23
  economic collapse 116-18
  future 123-6
  and government urban program-
    mes 115-16
  and the Labour Party 34, 111-12,
    114-15, 123
Liverpool, race 5, 141-54
  anti-racist and black strategies 149-
    50
  approaches to inequality 141-4
  City Council 145-6
  and class 146-7
  marginalisation 144, 147-8
  Merseyside Task Force 144-5
  and political parties 142-4, 150-2
Local Enterprise Grants for Urban Projects (LEG-UP) 79-80
local government 3-5
  UK 33-4, 113-14, 116, 118
  USA 9-17
Local Government Act, UK 147-8
London 32-3, 142, 153
Los Angeles 96-7, 156

market-mechanism approach to urban
  development 1, 7, 21, 31, 89, 124
Merseyside Development Corporation
  124, 126, 141
Merseyside Task Force 143-5
Mondale, Walter 22
multinational corporations 28, 32-3, 156

'new federalism' 17
New Mexico 15
New York 6, 156-75
    commercial development 161-5
    42nd Street project 159, 161-2,
    164-5, 167, 173
    Hunters Point project 162-3
    planning weaknesses 168-74
    pressure on land use 157-9
    residential development 165-8,
    170-1
    and state agencies 161-4, 171

Oakland, California 19
oil industry 55-6

parties, political 3
    UK, and racial inequality 142-4,
    150-2
    USA, social policy 18
Pennsylvania 14
planning
    economic *see* Chicago; linkage;
    Texas
    land use *see* New York
policies, urban
    UK: national 1-3; Scotland 75-80
    USA: linkage (*q.v.*) 93-108, 135-8;
    local 9-13, 23-4; national 1-2, 17-
    24, 169-70
politics
    city 3-5
    trends in 31-2
    see also parties
pollution 15, 65-6
population changes 29-30
private sector regeneration, Scotland
    (*q.v.*) 74-90 *see also* public–private
    partnerships
promotion campaigns 59-60, 64, 82-3
public-private partnerships 36
    Scotland 79-80
    USA 57, 66-8, 173-4
public sector 1, 3-4, 29

Race Relations Act, UK 143, 148
racial inequality 5
    Chicago 129-31, 139
    Liverpool (*q.v.*) 144-54
    UK approaches to 141-4, 147-52
Reagan, Ronald 16-17, 22-3, 31
    administration 21-4, 101, 170

redistribution policies 10-11
    Chicago 128-40
    and grants 18-20
    linkage (*q.v.*) 93-108, 135-8
regions, UK 33, 36, 50-1
revitalisation, urban 1-8

Sacramento 107-8
St Louis, Missouri 12
San Francisco 96-7, 99, 105, 137-8
Santa Monica 97, 99
Scarman, Lord 150
Scotland 74-90
    Glasgow 80-8
    policy, development of 75-80, 89-
    90
    public–private partnership 79-80
Scottish Development Agency (SDA)
    35, 74-80
    Glasgow 80-1, 84-5
Seattle, Washington 97
service sector 44-5, 156-8, 174
Social Democratic party, UK 150
'special districts', USA 12
states, USA 13-17 *see also* federal system;
    Texas
subsidisation of development 6-7
suburbs 10, 11, 24, 94-5

Tannahill, Heal 11
taxes, local 11, 34, 71, 98
Texas 6-7, 11, 15, 55-72
    economic crisis 55-6, 66-8, 71
    Governor's Division of Economic
    Development 57-9, 66-70
    Houston EDC 60-6, 66-70
    promotion 59, 60, 64
    public-private partnerships 57, 66-8
    Texas EDC 59-60, 66-70
    theories of the state 68-71
trends, social, political, economic 3, 27-37
    global 28-9
    impact on UK 32-7

unemployment 28-9, 42, 46-7, 117
uneven development
    UK 46-9, 52, 85-8
    USA 5-8, 23-4, 156-75
United Kingdom (UK) 1-8
    Bristol 39-53
    centralisation 33-4
    city politics 3-5

finance capital 32-3
Liverpool 110-26, 141-54
national urban policies 1-3
public and private sectors 36
regional differences 33, 36, 50-1
Scotland 74-90
trends, social, political, economic 27-37
welfare 1, 3-4
United States of America (USA) 1-8
Chicago 128-40
city politics 3-5
development 5-8
federal system 9-24
linkage 93-108, 135-8
national urban policies 1-2, 17-24
New York 156-75
Texas 55-72
welfare 3-4

Urban Programme, UK 49-51, 115-16, 148

Village of Euclid v. *Ambler Realty Co.* 16

Washington, Harold, Mayor of Chicago 128-36, 138-9
welfare, social 1, 3-4
White, Kevin, Mayor of Boston 102-3
White, Mark, Governor of Texas 57-8
Whitmire, Kathy, Mayor of Houston 56, 61
Wilson, Harold 142-3
Wisconsin 16

young people 46-7

zoning 16